LANGUAGE AND LANGU

Language Testing Sympos

LANGUAGE AND LANGUAGE LEARNING

General Editors: RONALD MACKIN *and* PETER STREVENS

Language Testing Symposium

A Psycholinguistic Approach

Edited by

ALAN DAVIES

London
OXFORD UNIVERSITY PRESS

Oxford University Press, Ely House, London W.1

GLASGOW   NEW YORK   TORONTO   MELBOURNE   WELLINGTON
CAPE TOWN   SALISBURY   IBADAN   NAIROBI   DAR ES SALAAM   LUSAKA   ADDIS ABABA
BOMBAY   CALCUTTA   MADRAS   KARACHI   LAHORE   DACCA
KUALA LUMPUR   SINGAPORE   HONG KONG   TOKYO

First published 1968
Second impression 1970

PRINTED IN GREAT BRITAIN BY HEADLEY BROTHERS LTD
109 KINGSWAY LONDON WC2 AND ASHFORD KENT

CONTENTS

ACKNOWLEDGEMENTS

Most of the contributions to this volume now appear in print for the first time. The Symposium was planned as a unity, as an approach to Language Testing from a number of related points of view. This plan involved commissioning papers from those with wide experience in the area. The Editor wishes to thank all those who have contributed. In addition the Editor would like to thank Mr R. Mackin and Dr A. E. G. Pilliner for advice and encouragement, Mr S. P. Corder for suggestions regarding the Introduction, the OUP for patience and Mrs Ethel Jack and Mrs Pat Bertram for help in typing.

The following have given permission for copyright material to be printed here: McGraw-Hill Book Company, New York, for material published in Chapter 11 of *Trends in Language Teaching* (edited by A. Valdman), by P. Pimsleur. Copyright © 1966 by McGraw-Hill, Inc.; the West African Examinations Council, for parts of the *Report on Oral English Testing in West Africa*, 1965, by A. Davies; the West African Examinations Council and the African Universities Press for Chapters 7, 13, and 16 of the *Report on English Language Examining*, 1963, by D. W. Grieve.

All references to books and articles throughout the text are indicated by author and date and will be found in the General References at the end of the book. In addition a Test List is given of Language Tests in print.

Spelling variants

No attempt has been made to make all contributions conform to one spelling convention. Where there are British and American differences these have been retained.

Hyphenization is even more arbitrary. Again individual uses have been retained.

CONTRIBUTORS

KEITH BROWN

taught for British Council in Uganda, lecturer in English, University College of Cape Coast, Ghana. At present lecturer in Linguistics, University of Edinburgh.

J. B. CARROLL

taught Psychology in universities; Professor of Educational Psychology at Harvard; now joined Educational Testing Service, Princeton, New Jersey, as Senior Research Psychologist. Author of *The Study of Language, Language and Thought, Language, Thought and Reality*, and with Sapon *Modern Language Aptitude Test*, etc.

ALAN DAVIES

taught English in secondary schools in England and East Africa. At present lecturer in Dept. of Applied Linguistics, University of Edinburgh.

D. W. GRIEVE

taught English in West Africa; assistant registrar of West African Examinations Council; now Senior Lecturer in English in the University of Ghana. Author of *English Language Examining* and many textbooks in English as a Second Language.

D. P. HARRIS

taught English Language in universities; worked on English Language Test construction at Michigan, Georgetown, and Educational Testing Service; first Director of the Program for the Testing of English as a Foreign Language (TOEFL); at present Director of the American Language Institute and Professor of Linguistics at Georgetown University, Washington, D.C. Author of several textbooks for students of English as a Foreign Language.

ELISABETH INGRAM is a psychologist. She has been a lecturer in the Dept. of Applied Linguistics, University of Edinburgh, since 1957; and has written articles on language learning and a Test of English Proficiency.

G. E. PERREN trained teachers of English at all levels in East Africa; formerly Director of English-Teaching Information Centre, British Council, London. Since 1966 first Director of Centre for Information on Language Teaching, London.

A. E. G. PILLINER taught Science and Maths. in secondary schools; since 1949 Lecturer, then Senior Lecturer in Education and Director, Godfrey Thompson Unit for Educational Research, University of Edinburgh. Author of articles in statistical and educational journals and part-author of Moray House tests.

PAUL PIMSLEUR taught Modern Languages in universities; Professor of Modern Languages and Education and Director of the Listening Center, Ohio State University, since 1961; author of articles on language learning, especially under-achievement, of Language Aptitude Battery and of Pimsleur Proficiency Tests in foreign languages.

ANDREW WILKINSON taught English in secondary schools in England; Lecturer, now Senior Lecturer, in Education, University of Birmingham. Director of current research project into Oracy. Author of *Spoken English*, articles on English teaching, etc. Editor, *Educational Review* and *English in Education*.

1

Introduction

I. LANGUAGE-LEARNING VIEWS AND THEIR INFLUENCE ON LANGUAGE
TESTING

Language Testing involves both linguistics and psychology because it is concerned with language and with learning. It is also experimental because it sets up learning tasks in order to study behaviour; and also evaluative because it makes use of statistical techniques in order to study that behaviour. There are, therefore, three strands in language testing: language, learning and evaluation.

It is not only in language testing that these three strands meet: the whole of Psycholinguistics is concerned with the relationship between language and learning and makes use of statistics like any other experimental science. It is difficult, therefore, to understand how language could be considered separate from learning. However, even today many do not regard language and learning as inseparable. Those who do not will probably take some account of learning but will be mainly interested in the language apart from the learner. By 'learner' here is meant not only the Foreign Language (LF) and Second Language (L2) learner, but the Mother tongue or First Language (L1) learner too. It is possible in considering the area of language teaching and testing in which linguistics, psychology and evaluation meet to disentangle three main positions that have been taken up over the last fifty years. The position taken up has two main effects on the teaching and the testing: on the content of the teaching, i.e. what is taught, and on the concern for the needs of the learner.

The first position is taken up by those we may call the *strict separatists*. They are not really interested in the learner at all. They see language as a *thing* in itself: for them 'real' language exists in texts; there is no spoken language; learning is a matter of gobbets like dates in history. Teaching is by the grammar-translation method and what the student is expected to do is to translate, if possible, in a 'stylistic' manner. The texts where the 'real' language is held to reside most truly are literary ones and so literature is emphasized in the teaching. No consideration is given to the needs of the learner because the point of it all is essentially one of mind-training, of transfer of training. Testing follows the teaching and is mostly concerned with setting translation tasks. Now it will be clear that the position caricatured here is the well-known classical language one which has carried over into both LF and Lı teaching. This is not to suggest that all present-day teaching of the classics follows this pattern. The associated linguistic theory is the traditionalist one, and since the learner is not taken into account, there is no theory of psychology involved.

The effect of these assumptions, held by those who take up this position, on the content of teaching material is that written texts from literature, narrowly conceived, are taken to be *the* language. The needs of the learner are not considered except that some attempt is made to sequence the teaching material so that the beginner starts with the easiest material and progresses to the more difficult as he becomes more fluent. The grounds on which such sequencing is done seem to be entirely subjective. Since the language is viewed as a whole there is equal stress on the past and on the present so that texts for teaching and for testing are historical as often as contemporary. In the early stages, of course, as well as the attempt to sequence material for the learner, there is also an attempt to *teach* him. But the language, for those who take up this position, is seen as a *thing* and so it is taught as if it were a series of facts. There is then, no connexion with Lı learning, but if there were, the assumption would be that the Lı learner of Latin starts off at about 18 months running through the *Mensa* paradigm and parsing *Balbus murum aedificavit*.

The second position is taken up by those we shall call the *separate but equal* supporters. They see language as a machine which acts as a stimulus-response mechanism. Learning for holders of this position in its extreme form, is always *shaped* and consists of conditioned responses to the environment. Language itself, as a machine, has no direct connexion with the environment; it is part of human behaviour. It may be regarded as a thing but it is still separate and complete in itself. Since language is separated from the environment in this way there is little recourse to meaning: there is little need felt to link language in any meaningful way with the world to which it refers. Linguistic analysis proceeds at least theoretically from sound to sentence (cf. Harris, 1951) with the unnecessary but frequently made conclusion that learning itself proceeds in the same way.

Teaching for those who hold this position must analyse language into its parts or, as is frequently said, *structures*. It is strange how often this term is used in isolation to refer to grammatical structures, ignoring the fact that the other language levels, e.g. phonology, semantics, have their structures too. Such an analysis into parts is sometimes known as an Immediate Constituent (IC) analysis, and such an approach taxo-nomic. Teaching thus begins with the smallest bits and deliberately works from sound to sentence, making use, in a laudable enough way, of all kinds of teaching aids and machinery. It may now be time to acknowledge that the hardware of the Audio-lingual, language laboratory, tape-recorder approach has given way to the software of Programmed Learning which actually underlay it all along. That is to say that the Audio-lingual approach at its best was essentially a Programmed Learning (PL) approach. Since the assumption of the classical PL approach has been of the Stimulus-Response kind the influence on the teaching has been to make the materials take the form of the exercise-drill type. This has been the effect on teaching content. Learning, it is assumed, takes place by generalization, by analogy on the basis of the learnt response. This position which we have labelled the separate but equal one is, in linguistic terms, structuralist, and in psychological terms, behaviourist. Testing inevitably follows on by providing drills for completion, gaps for filling and multiple choice answers for selection.

Those who take up the first position we considered set tests much as they set daily exercises; passages for translation may be regarded as a form of open-ended question.[1] There is for this point of view no real distinction between tests and exercises so that instead of saying, as we have just done, that tests are like daily exercises, we might equally well say that daily exercises are like tests; that all teaching is doing is testing. Those who have taken up the second position have mechanized their testing so that *after* construction a test becomes automatic. What is more, a test in this tradition will provide information as to learning in this tradition because trouble is taken to select suitable teaching material and sequence it (cf. Mackey, 1965); such a test will say whether a student has learnt by such a method, it will say nothing about whether the student knows the language at any level or can speak it in any real situation. Even this is a great advance on tests made by supporters of the first position because all their tests indicate is whether a student can do the test or not. There is no implication as to his general performance which is what the test is supposed to be an indication of. It is logically possible to learn a good deal about Latin grammar and prepare a number of average proses and yet not cope with a prose test. The reason for this is that the relation between one prose and another is not clear, that unless great pains are taken to limit the vocabulary and control the grammar such a test is just another exercise with no content and little predictive validity.[2]

Those who take up the third position we have spoken of hold a *united* view of language and language learning. They see language as creative and at the same time rule-based (Chomsky, 1965). Language

[1] See below, Chapter 2.
[2] See below, pp. 8-9.

and learning are inter-dependent because no one ever stops learning language, especially his own, because there is no such thing *in the world* as a state of language (cf. de Saussure, 1915) separate from people and therefore from learning. Attractive as this view of language learning is there are difficulties connected with it. No one ever really said, no linguist, traditional or structuralist, that language *in the world* is separate from people and learning. The language they describe is an abstraction and the language the transformational grammarians describe is also an abstraction which is as much divorced from learning in its formalization as any previous view or model.

It is really too early yet to see the influence those who take up this third position will have on teaching. However, three assumptions are already being made. The first of these is, as Carroll points out in Chapter 4, that it is competence that is being aimed at. Now since underlying all surface realizations is Deep Structure (cf. Chomsky, op. cit.) then what may well be important for the student to do is to learn the Deep Structure and the transformations that may be employed on it. The second assumption is that the L2 and LF learner will need to make the same kind of approach as the L1 learner. Now we still don't know which approach the L1 learner makes (cf. Lyons and Wales, 1966) but since the transformational generative approach is directed towards the way a native speaker learns his own language, its formalization will be in L1 terms and any teaching making use of it must also approach the L2 and LF learners in the same terms. The third assumption is linked to L1 learning too since it accepts the demands of *situation*, i.e. the environment in which language is used. Now this is not a necessary part of the theory but since its emphasis is on L1 language learning the situation must be taken into account in preparing teaching materials.

Here there is a close link with yet another view of language, that of the Firthians (cf. Robins, 1964). J. R. Firth's own approach to language description is probably to be reckoned as structuralist but he was greatly concerned with extra-linguistic features, with situation and its link with language which, after Malinowski, he termed context of situation. Now it may be, as Chomsky has argued, that situation cannot be categorized (Chomsky, 1966). But, as Firth maintained, in any community there is to be found a whole range of different languages, a network of sub-languages which interlock at different points so that any one speaker will control only some of these sub-languages or *varieties* and will certainly make use of different ones for different purposes and on different occasions. While the linguist may restrict his theoretical concerns to abstractions, to well-formed sentences and the like, the learner and the teacher will be as much concerned with the learning and with the situation. The linguist's real concern is with the state of the language, an abstraction divorced as much from the learning as from the situation. Firth's emphasis on situation, therefore, is no less important or relevant than Chomsky's on learning. While both may be difficult for the linguist to formalize, they provide valuable hints and starting points for the teacher and tester which they may follow up in their own work.

The influence on teaching of the view of language held by those who take up this united position is likely to emphasize tasks and problems rather than patterns and repetitions, strategy rather than memory. The argument runs thus: the L1 learner learns his language in some 'principled' cognitive way, not by storing every possible sentence type in his head, so the L2 learner needs to be taught in some way that simulates this procedure. And, so the argument continues, the L1 learner learns, again not by being fed lists but by meeting problems, making mistakes. So the L2 learner must be provided with problems for solving. The aim of the teaching is to provide *least assistance*, so to structure the problem that good learners need no assistance. Teaching and testing meet here since the measure of achievement depends on how much assistance is demanded (cf. Williams, 1961). And the argument concludes, since the L1 learner always learns in a situation so the L2 learner must be provided with meaningful, contextual exercises. L2 teaching attempts to simulate in a structured way the L1 environment. The reader will have noted the links implied in this paragraph between teaching and testing and programming. The potential strength of PL lies in its almost infinite use as a method of arranging and trying out hypotheses as to learning structures.

It should be clear by now that the good test is an obedient servant since it follows and apes the teaching; this is particularly true for the Achievement test (see below p. 7). There will be a great difference between our second and third positions in so far as they influence teaching. The difference as regards testing will not be so obvious. A third position test will be much more situational because the teaching is. It will be less concerned with 'pure' language features, e.g. segmentals, stress, because the teaching is less so concerned; it will be as much concerned with objectivity because it is also a good test. What it will do that is different from a second position test is to set 'problems' which are not all that different from the translation problems of the first position test but are directly related to the corpus which has been taught. It will set tasks such as comprehension which need resolution actually during the task and are not channelled through the stimulus-response funnel of question and answer *after* the passage. What is more it will probably attempt to tap the L2 learner's creativity which our third position teaching will have re-directed by allowing the learner to make use of the rules he has learnt in order to establish how far he has internalized them. This is very different from a multiple choice answer to a stimulus involving, say, intonation, because what is being demanded is use of the rules to produce a sentence or 'response' which is new. There is no reason why such a creative new sentence should not be incorporated within an objective multiple choice framework, thus:

Example 1 (teaching of the Imperative in English has been completed)
Jane and her brother, Tom, are waiting for the bus home after school. 'Let's go swimming,' says Jane. But Tom has another idea. What does he say?
1. Swimming?
2. Don't let's go swimming, let's . . .
3. Let's go swimming.
4. You go swimming.
5. Don't go swimming, go . . .

It may be objected that it is some kind of translation that is being tested here or, if not translation, that learners are being expected to think in terms of formal categories. This may be so. What is being claimed is that as well as relating test to rule, it also makes situation important. Such a test could well be drawn up in picture format which would cut out all need for explanation.

Compare this with a second position test.

Example 2
Tom does not want to go swimming with Jane but he does want to go somewhere else with her. What does he say to her?
1. Do let's not go swimming.
2. Let's go swimming.
3. Don't let's go swimming.
4. Don't go swimming.
5. You go swimming.

2. LANGUAGE TEST USES

There is some confusion in the use of terminology in Language Testing and it may be useful to discuss some of the conflicting terms. They occur especially in the area of test uses, so that the terms *achievement, attainment, proficiency, diagnosis* and *aptitude* are often confused. There seem to be three main usages, to two of which the readers of this volume are exposed. The first usage links Proficiency and Aptitude, Achievement and Attainment, and has, as all three usages have, Diagnosis separate. Thus we speak of Proficiency (Aptitude) *for* or *in* something to do something else; we speak of Achievement (Attainment) *in* something by itself; and we speak of Diagnosis *of* something. Thus in this usage Proficiency (Aptitude) tests the student's present ability for future learning. Achievement (Attainment) tests his present knowledge as indicative of past learning, and Diagnosis is the teacher's concern for what has gone wrong.

The second usage is the present writer's. It distinguishes four uses, combining Achievement and Attainment, in terms of time and of subject matter. Thus if we use an arrow of time going both ways and if X is the test, then we may symbolize as follows:

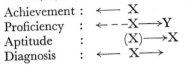

Achievement or Attainment tests are concerned with assessing what has been learnt of a known syllabus. This may be within a school or within a total educational system. The use of Achievement tests is to find out how much has been learnt. They are concerned, therefore, entirely with the past though they often are used for predictive purposes. That they should be used predictively, i.e. to make claims about future performance, is probably inevitable though it is not the function of an Achievement test to predict. All an Achievement test can do is to indicate how much of a syllabus of what has been taught has been learnt. It cannot make predictions of itself as to pupils' future performance unless the syllabus has been deliberately designed, as it should be, with the demands of teaching and learning in mind.

If Achievement tests are concerned entirely with the past, which explains the arrow only going one way, then Proficiency tests are concerned both with the past and with the future. But there is no syllabus control over the past, as with Achievement tests, and so the test constructor cannot draw on the syllabus for the content of his test. Instead he must make up his own syllabus. A good Proficiency test is, or implies, such a syllabus. This lack of a syllabus is indicated by the broken arrow. The Proficiency test also looks forward, i.e. it is used to predict skill in language for some extra-linguistic purpose, e.g. proficiency in English for something else. Hence the symbol Y.

An Aptitude test also looks forward, but to a *language* skill. Thus it is concerned with assessing skill in e.g. language for language. This assumes that skill for future language learning, proficiency, say, in acquiring a second or third language, should and can be measured in existing first language skill. The uncertainty here is indicated by the brackets round the first X at the side of Aptitude. Notice that Aptitude, unlike Proficiency, has no interest in the past.

Diagnosis does not fit readily into this scheme of uses because it relates entirely to the use made of the information and not at all to the presence of a skill in the learner. That is to say we can speak of a learner's Achievement, Proficiency and Aptitude but not, of course, of his Diagnosis. A Diagnostic test is for teacher consumption; it is a use made by a teacher of the information provided by one of these skills, Achievement, Proficiency and Aptitude. A Diagnostic test may be constructed for itself or it may be an additional use made of an Achievement or Proficiency test. If it is specially constructed it could be argued that the learner's absence of skill is being tested so that another name for a Diagnostic test might be a Non-Achievement test. There is the further argument that such a specially constructed test is concerned with establishing systematic errors and not at all with randomly occurring mistakes so that it is not absence of skill but difference of skill between L2 learners at different stages of learning which is being tested.

This discussion of terminology deals with *uses* of tests. Under use we have considered Achievement, Attainment, Proficiency, Aptitude and Diagnosis. *Kinds* of test would include such terms as Oral tests, Writing tests, Comprehension tests, L1 tests. All the uses considered here could be made of one *kind* of test. An oral test could be used for achievement, diagnostic or even aptitude purposes. It all depends on what the user of the test, i.e. the teacher actually making the particular use, is looking for.

The third usage is that of Ingram (in Chapter 5). What she does is to use Attainment as a major class of which Achievement and Proficiency are both members. Since, as we have seen, Achievement and Proficiency uses are closely related and since there is the special Proficiency case of Pre-Attainment in which a test samples the content of a course which students wish to enter (cf. Mialaret and Malandain, 1962; Davies, 1965a, p. 48), it may well be that such a classification is the most useful. Ingram uses Aptitude and Diagnosis as described above.

3. EVALUATION IN LANGUAGE TESTING

As well as concerning itself with *language* and with *learning* language testing is also very much concerned with *evaluation*. As part of Psycholinguistics it is experimental and therefore must make use of the appropriate statistical procedures. What these do (see Chapter 2) is to ensure the Reliability and Validity of the test. Full discussion of these ideas is given by Pilliner in Chapter 2. But it is worth emphasizing here the equal partnership in language testing of evaluation with linguistics and psychology.

Pilliner (Chapter 2) deals with the *meaning* of validity and its implications in evaluation. He discusses three kinds of validity: Predictive, Concurrent and Content. A fourth kind, Construct Validity, is sometimes invoked. The distinction he makes (p. 31), following

Wiseman, between the syllabus-content approach and the goal-oriented approach to a test is our distinction between Achievement and Proficiency tests. The Achievement test is syllabus-content based; the Proficiency test is related to the demands and aims of the learning process. This relatedness can be measured quantitatively, as Pilliner describes, drawing on Predictive or Concurrent Validity. It can also be assessed logically by Construct Validity. Where Pilliner uses Content Validity we would use both Content and Construct. In addition there is the fifth kind, Face Validity. This may appear trivial since it refers to acceptance by the layman. But in education it is often important to show as well as know that what is being done is relevant. Face Validity may therefore not be so trivial after all.

We now can produce the following scheme for validities:

Type	related to	Criterion
Face	⟶	Lay view of language
Content	⟶	Syllabus analysis
Construct	⟶	Theory of aims in Language Teaching
Predictive	⟶	Later test of language ability
Concurrent	⟶	Another test or measure (e.g. teacher's assessment) of language ability given at same time

TABLE I

Ingram points out (Chapter 5) that it is only after looking at the statistics that we know the worth of a test. However, there are degrees of knowingness and they differ for the different uses and for the different validities. There is a relationship of likelihood between test use and validity so that it is likely that for an Aptitude use the test constructor will be most concerned with a theory of language learning and therefore with Construct Validity; and at the other end of the scale, for a Proficiency use he will be most concerned with Concurrent or Predictive Validity. Now Predictive Validity is the most demanding statistically of all the validities since it seeks to establish the adequacy of a test by relating its scores to a criterion of future performance, the real 'pay-off' of any test. Concurrent Validity is also established statistically but does not expose the test's scores to such hard probing, confining its correlations to parallel or already existing tests. None of the other validities *demands* statistical procedures though they may use them. Hence the Scale below (Table 2) where we represent our over-simplified connexions between test uses and kinds of validity and suggest a linking scale of Statistical Revelation. What this implies is that there is a further relationship of likelihood between test use and type of validity such that some test uses demand more statistics than others.

Use	Validity		
		Less	
Aptitude	Construct	↑	
Achievement	Content		Statistical
Diagnosis	Content		Revelation
Proficiency	Concurrent		
Proficiency	Predictive	↓	
		More	

TABLE 2

All test uses will still need the run of the mill statistical analysis for item analysis, reliability and inter-test correlation. Measures of central tendency, means and standard deviations are necessary for comparative purposes and for assessing the comprehensiveness of the test. Even so, it is, as Pilliner and Ingram point out, validity that really matters. So much does it matter that it is possible to imagine a test with very low item discrimination because many heterogeneous abilities are being tested, poor reliability because the range is small; and yet such a test could have high validity, and this is what counts. It is the test constructor's assumptions in language learning that are really being analysed. A good test is a device for framing these assumptions and as much a learning device as a language laboratory or a programmed text.

4. LANGUAGE TEST ANALYSIS

Various kinds of Language Test analysis have been suggested. They all depend on the analyst's view of language. Both Carroll and Ingram (Chapters 4 and 5) provide schemes which involve such analyses. One scheme they do not discuss follows on from a discussion of language-performance by Corder (1966). This links a Piagetian developmental scheme with a language level plan. The balance is provided by the *channels* of production and reception though many items will need a combination of both channels. Thus we have the following table (Table 3) utilized for testing purposes, so that the items actually appearing in the cells are test techniques.

CHANNELS

	Productive ← — — — — | — — → Receptive		
Extra Linguistic Skills	Free Essay | | Interview		
Semantic Skills	Oral Composition Dictation Vocabulary Networks	| | Questions and Answers |	Listening Comprehension Reading Comprehension
Organizational Skills	Reading Speed	Reading Aloud | |	Intonation (minimal pairs) Grammatical Sensitivity
Motor Perceptive Skills	Phoneme Approximations Stress	| | | | | |	Phoneme Discrimination Stress

TABLE 3

A skill such as Reading which we may now designate an 'old-type' skill will appear in a number of different places in this Table. It will appear under Receptive as Reading Comprehension and under Productive as Reading Aloud. Or, if preferred, both Reading Comprehension and Reading Aloud could appear under the joint Receptive and Productive though for different reasons. Reading Aloud is an activity which *necessarily* involves both channels. Reading Comprehension necessarily involves only Comprehension. Production is introduced only in order to manifest to someone else that the comprehension has taken place. Reading is probably best regarded as numbers of skills, not as a single skill. Reading Comprehension may therefore be a technique for eliciting control over the 'old-type' skill of Reading. But Reading is now well recognized as a group of skills; is it any longer appropriate to regard it as a unitary skill? Reading itself, then, through Reading Comprehension and other techniques may be better regarded as a means of approaching a more basic skill such as Semantics or Language Organization.

Once more what is illustrated here is the influence on the tester of the approach he takes to language-learning. Of course it is possible to push this argument too far in that no scheme will permit the tester to abandon so basic a technique as Reading Comprehension. What this argues is the similarity of linguistic models and approaches to language learning and therefore schemes for analysis. Where the differences will appear is in areas such as collocation.

5. THE APPROACH OF R. LADO

Language tests in print are currently reviewed in Buros (1965) as Harris points out in Chapter 3. We do not intend to duplicate these reviews here, but it is important to look briefly at the work of Robert Lado and in particular the 'model' on which it is built. Lado represents both a whole testing movement and one branch of descriptive linguistics. Criticism of him then may be taken as criticism of the structural approach and of the assumption that test construction can be based on a contrastive analysis.

Lado's approach is well documented (Lado, 1961). His test theory may be stated: a learner has language learning problems; find the problems; test them. The problems to Lado are those of the major points of contrast between a learner's L1 and his target language. Both learning and language are involved. And, what is more, Lado stresses the importance of evaluation: 'final validation by correlating the scores obtained on the test with a criterion whose validity is well-established would be a necessary step in every case' (Lado, 1960). Lado's theory is thus linguistically based; it demands validation by an external criterion; and its technique is highly sophisticated. His major premise, that of the essential contrastive analysis to discover the 'problems' has been challenged both theoretically (Upshur, 1962) and practically (Strevens, 1961; Carroll, 1961; George, 1962; Mackenzie, 1961; Perren, 1967). If a test is constructed for a single group of students with identical language background and identical exposure to the target language then contrastive analysis is essential. But most students have varying lengths of exposure to English and varying abilities which affect comparable exposures. Contrastive analysis is not practicable when a teacher or institution is faced with a group of foreign students from a heterogeneous L1 background. As Upshur points out, contrastive analysis assumes an L1–L1 contrast; it does not embody a learning model at all.

The result is that Lado's own proficiency tests (e.g. Lado, 1951) do not follow his theory; as he said himself 'the task of preparing separate tests for all language backgrounds is so enormous that we may never hope to have such tests except for a limited few languages' (Lado, 1950). The structural approach could not bear the weight of an application which attempted to put its principles into practice. There is an awful warning here in that linguistic theory is pure not applied and not meant to be applied in any procedural way. Structuralism must be judged as a scientific theory by its parsimony and, possibly, its explanatory power. Whether the application of structuralism succeeds in teaching and testing and even writing descriptive grammars is neither here nor there. It is to be hoped that similar procedural mistakes will not be made with any application of transformational generative theory. It is nonsense for example to suggest that teaching of a language should start from abstract symbols and work through the transformations because the theory works in this way. Already some psycholinguistic experiments have rather naïvely assumed that performance can be measured as if it were competence, as Thorne 1966 pointed out. It is hoped that if application is to be made of TG linguistics it will be in terms of problems and situations rather than of patterns and drills.

6. SYMPOSIUM OVERVIEW

As has been mentioned above, the chapters that follow take up some of the issues and problems that have been outlined. Each takes a separate point of departure but inevitably there is overlap. This is desirable since each chapter is both part of the whole Symposium and also to be seen as a unity in itself. There are four main sections in this book: (1) the basic disciplines and their relevance to language testing, viz. evaluation, linguistics and psychology (Chapters 2, 3 and 4); (2) uses and types of test, viz. achievement, etc., aptitude, oral tests and mother-tongue tests (Chapters 5, 6, 7 and 8); (3) the influence of tests on education, tests as it were in use (Chapters 9, 10 and 11); (4) the item analysis needed (Appendix). We shall look now at the treatments given to these sections in turn.

6.1 *The basic disciplines*

Pilliner, in Chapter 2, deals with Evaluation. He distinguishes subjective and objective testing, item and essay, and points out that objectivity is essentially a matter of assessment: 'the distinction between a "subjective" and "objective" examination rests only on the manner in which the marks are to be assigned' (p. 21). In discussing the requirements of good examinations and tests he notes the lack of any absolute difference and takes for the purpose of his discussion, the usual one of 'subjective' equals examinations; and 'objective' equals tests. Pilliner outlines the demands of Reliability and Validity and offers the measured hope that language tests because of their 'relatively specific objectives' (may be) 'less unreliable than examining in other fields' (p. 29). The evaluation side of language testing is a necessary method of obtaining relevant evidence as to the value of a test. Pilliner shows the need for the kind of judgement which does not overvalue statistical nicety at the expense of linguistic sense. Harris (Chapter 3) shows the connexion between language theories and testing by giving the historical background. He comes to the realistic but sad conclusion that most current language tests lack any body of unified theory on which to draw. He gives three reasons for this situation: 'applied linguistics' is not a set of linguistic principles: 'the tests reflect the imperfect state of applied linguistics and our very incomplete understanding of the processes of second-language acquisition' (p. 44); linguists are not interested in testing except in the specialized field of Aptitude; not enough is known about learning at stages later than the first few years. Harris is describing the influence not of linguistics but of *language teaching* notions on language testing. While we share his regret that linguistics has had so little influence on testing there are links via language teaching such as those outlined in the first part of this chapter. Carroll in Chapter 4 shows the need for a psychology of language testing since: 'A test is an experiment in human behaviour' (p. 46). Whatever approach to language behaviour the tester makes is certain to influence his break-down of that behaviour into bits, rules, habits, competence and performance areas and individual skills. What is needed then is a series of breakdowns both of competence and performance, such as Carroll suggests, an itemization of language behaviour which is valid in itself and allows for tests to be constructed with exact relevance. He suggests that taxonomies such as his (e.g. Table 4, p. 63) may be adequate for any language testing task. The psychologist has then made his contribution and the onus is left with the tester to write appropriate items. Carroll's own favoured approach to language behaviour is apparent throughout his Chapter, and made specific when he says: 'The single most important problem confronted by the language tester is that he cannot test competence in any direct sense; he can measure it only through manifestations of it in performance' (p. 51).

6.2 Uses and types of test
Ingram's chapter (Chapter 5) moves into the more applied field of the uses of tests with her discussion of attainment (i.e. achievement

and proficiency) and diagnostic tests. Her firm emphasis on the need for much more work on the neglected *diagnostic* use is commendable: 'There is no satisfactory theory of language learning nor of failure of language learning. In my view there will be none until strictly controlled experimental teaching and careful diagnostic testing provide exact information of what is being learnt and not learnt by different kinds of learners under varying conditions of learning' (p. 73). Ingram then makes her approach to language behaviour and suggests various break-downs for language skill, levels and so on using the framework of a scale and category language theory (cf. Halliday, 1961). Her constant relaxed attitude to purity of tests and items is very comforting. She is at the same time ruthless about the *inefficiency* of items: they are judged by their statistics. However, since her sub-tests are constructed round her testing modes, skills and levels, her statistics are inevitably influenced by her linguistic assumptions. So once again, as with Pilliner, there is a judiciously combined linguistic-statistical approach. And Ingram is at pains to point out that everything in language cannot be tested: 'nor is there any point in pretending that what cannot be tested objectively cannot be real' (p. 97).

Pimsleur (Chapter 6) takes up the Aptitude use of testing in specific relation to the Language Aptitude Battery (LAB) constructed by him and others (Pimsleur, 1966a). As he points out there is both the practical value of such tests in their diagnosis of under-achievement; and there is the theoretical interest in their experimental investigations of the make-up of the language learning abilities. Pimsleur isolated three factors: verbal intelligence, motivation and auditory ability. A similar piece of experimental work (with adult students not high school children as with Pimsleur) was carried out by Carroll and Sapon in their construction of the Modern Language Aptitude Test (MLAT) (1959).[1] Carroll and Sapon made use of five tests specially constructed to predict success in second language learning. These tests were: number learning, phonetic script, spelling clues, words in sentences and paired associates. Experimental work with these tests indicated that four identifiable factors are present in measured language aptitude; these are: phonetic coding, grammatical sensitivity, rote memorization ability and inductive language learning ability. Carroll (1959) has reported satisfactory validity and produced tables of norms. Elsewhere (Carroll, 1963) he has pointed out that from his data foreign language aptitude is not specific to particular languages or particular groups of languages.

As well as uses for tests there are also limiting types of test which may be a use, e.g. proficiency, in a particular language area, e.g. the written language. Perren in Chapter 7 looks carefully at tests of

[1] A fuller description of the MLAT is given below (pp. 104-6).

the spoken language and underlines our need to know what the spoken language is before trying to test it. He makes various suggestions in both the receptive and the productive areas and points to the importance of linking language divisions with learning tasks, what he calls 'functional load' (p. 114). Perren has three urgent messages for his readers: language tests are essential for language teaching and may be the most important contribution to be made at present; something unteachable cannot be tested, however fancy—and true—it may be linguistically; and for a real test of the spoken language situation must be taken into account.

Perren notes the possible value of the term 'oracy', skill in the spoken language, both productive and receptive. This term was made well-known by Wilkinson who discusses tests of L1 Oracy in Chapter 8. Wilkinson deals first with Oral Expression and suggests two major categories of speech situation; reciprocal and formal, and then describes various test situations suitable to both categories. In this very practical chapter he goes on to kinds of scheme and methods of judging Oral Expression tests. Wilkinson gives a similar break-down of Listening Comprehension tests and then outlines a recent test battery in 'Oracy' for the Certificate of Secondary Education, a test in spoken English for native speakers of English.[1] His list of tests is wide ranging and the areas of language activity covered very impressive indeed. He makes 'washback' on schools the important criterion: 'The washback . . . will be in terms of speech activity . . . (and) increased awareness of the spoken language' (pp. 131-2).

6.3 Influence of tests on education

Wilkinson's emphasis on washback leads us into this third section, the influence of tests in education. All tests (and examinations) do have this effect and so it is probably necessary to ensure that they have a beneficial and not a constraining effect. All three chapters in this section deal with West Africa. Grieve's chapter (Chapter 9) shows how firmly a school system can be geared to an examination, even a very bad one, almost without the schools themselves being aware either of the link or of the badness. Grieve's chapter consists of excerpts from his Report to the West African Examinations Council (Grieve, 1963). These excerpts were chosen to indicate his approach to a traditional language examination, his discussion of its failings, particularly in the light of the school's own opinions, and his linking of English Language (and its testing) with the other subjects in the curriculum,

[1] This leaving examination was introduced into English secondary schools two or three years ago. Much emphasis has been placed on teacher control and practical curriculum.

all of which use English. Grieve underlines the need for a detailed syllabus as joint partner of a good test: 'an examination . . . should be a prescription of what the candidates are expected to know at the end of their course' (p. 142).

Davies's chapter (Chapter 10) is also part of a Report (1965b) to the WAEC. One of Grieve's recommendations was that a test of spoken English should be made compulsory at the School Certificate level. Davies examined this question and his chapter contains the body of his Report. This chapter is included in the present volume because, it is felt, it illustrates the way in which a testing orientation can be brought to bear on an educational situation. This is especially evident in the critique, both linguistic and statistical, of an existing examination (the McCallien Test) and in the discussion of the demands that any educational test must meet. Davies 'takes it as axiomatic that a test should have a firm educational purpose . . . The issue is therefore seen as an educational/social one rather than as administrative or even a linguistic one . . . This issue must be approached from three sides: that of aims, that of demands and that of constraints' (p. 168).

Brown in Chapter 11 again in reference to West Africa describes the use of tests from another angle. He shows how simply-made language tests based on some homogeneous view of the spoken language can be sensitively employed and analysed in order to test a theory, to question earlier findings and suggest new hypotheses. This is language testing in scientific experimentation and in his modest 'Intelligibility' discussion Brown illustrates the extreme edge of language testing where language testing becomes psycholinguistics proper, where such tests are tools of language learning to investigate language learning. His results, as he indicates, seem at variance with the earlier findings: 'It seems clear that . . . a reader from their own L1 is rather more comprehensible than anyone else . . . These results seem to us to be a truer reflection of the mutual intercomprehensibility of the accents tested than those suggested by Strevens (1954), and we would have been surprised if the results had been otherwise' (p. 188).

6.4 Item Analysis

The Appendix by Ingram on Item Analysis attempts to describe in considerable detail the main technique which a language teacher needs for test construction. No attempt is made to present sophisticated techniques, no mention of correlation, Factor Analysis or Analysis of Variance. Those who want such techniques can easily find them in the textbooks.

And so, from Evaluation in Chapter 2 we return in the Appendix to techniques of evaluation. But the stress throughout has been on the unity of the three components, language, learning and evaluation; a stress accentuated it is hoped by the common sense needed to make appropriate judgements.

2

Subjective and Objective Testing

A. E. G. Pilliner

1. 'SUBJECTIVE' AND 'OBJECTIVE'

The purpose of this chapter is to discuss two contrasting examination procedures. The first, or 'subjective' procedure, is that in which the examinee answers, in his own words, and at appropriate length, all or some of a relatively small number of questions. Typical key-words in the questions set in examinations of this kind are: 'Discuss', 'Compare', 'Contrast', 'Describe', and the answers they elicit may range from a single sentence to a dozen or more paragraphs. These answers are commonly called 'essays', the questions 'essay questions', and the whole examination is of the 'essay-type'. Assessment of the examinee's work is 'subjective' in the sense that its merit has to be evaluated or judged by the examiner.

Two examples of 'essay-type' questions requiring answers of very different length are:

(a) Discuss Shakespeare's Sonnets,
and

(b) Who said the following, and to what end? (Answer in not more than two sentences.)

> ' The quality of mercy is not strained;
> It droppeth as the gentle rain from Heaven
> Upon the place beneath.'

The second, or 'objective' procedure, is that in which the examinee responds to each of a large number of questions by selecting one or more of several alternative answers provided with the question; by supplying a single word; or by some other process (reflecting the ingenuity of the compiler of the examination) indicating his knowledge or lack of knowledge of the pre-determined correct answer. These answers are commonly called 'responses', the questions 'items', and the whole examination is of the 'objective' type. Assessment of the merit of the examinee's work is 'objective' in the sense that no evaluative judgement is needed on the part of the examiner. A marking key, previously prepared, is all that is required, and even this is redundant if the examination is compiled with machine marking or scoring in mind.

Reference is made to this chapter on pp. 8-9, 13-14 of the Introduction.

Two examples illustrating different types of 'objective' items are:
(a) Some words are missing in the following lines of poetry. Underline in the brackets the word that fits each space best.

Down on the hillside stood the trees,

1. Their song was soft and ———; (shrill/clear/sharp/low/sweet)
2. The blossoms in the gentle ——— (wind/breeze/trees/hands/
glows)
3. Were ——— like the snow. (falling/freezing/soft/white/not)
and

(b) In the sentences below underline the one word you would *stress*
to make clear (without actually saying) what is in the brackets.

1. Please close your desk lids gently now. (do not make a loud
noise)
2. Please close your desk lids gently now. (do it immediately)

The use of the terms 'subjective' and 'objective' to distinguish these
two contrasting types of examination needs further clarification.
Evading the philosophical issues involved, let us agree that by 'subjective' we shall simply mean 'requiring judgement' and by 'objective'
simply 'automatic'. Let us note also that three processes common to
examinations of all kinds are (a) the compilation or construction of
the questions; (b) the answering of these questions by the examinee;
and (c) the marking or scoring of the examinees' answers to these
questions.

Now it would be clearly absurd to describe the first (construction)
process as other than 'subjective' in the sense described above. The
domain to be examined is usually too extensive to be covered completely
in a single examination, so that some kind of selection must be made.
Different constructors are likely to choose different topics from among
the many available, their choices reflecting different priorities, different
emphases, different personal foibles. Even when they agree on the
topics to be examined, different constructors will frame their questions
differently. These differences of topic selection and of treatment of
topics selected are a major source of examination unreliability, a matter
that will be discussed later.

If the first (construction) process is inevitably 'subjective', the
second (answering) process is even more so. The examinee faced with
the question on Shakespeare's Sonnets must first decide on the line
to take, and plan accordingly. In writing his answer he must decide
how best to implement his plan, which illustrations to use, which
points are most telling, which phrase is happiest to use, and so on.
If, as often happens, he is allowed to choose his questions, he may
decide to avoid this one altogether.

The examinee answering the question on *The Merchant of Venice*
also exercises choices. He may know, or think he knows, or simply not

know, who said these words, and he can answer the first part of the question by naming any one of the characters in (perhaps not even in!) the play. It is irrelevant to the argument that only one answer is correct. In answering the second part, he must make decisions similar, though on a smaller scale, to those outlined for the previous more ambitious question.

Finally, answering the two 'objective' questions is no less a 'subjective' process. In each case the examinee chooses from among the several alternatives before him. Although the clues presented with the question are sufficient to enable him to answer correctly, he may choose to do otherwise.

It is not denied that a deeper level, different degrees, and even different kinds of 'subjectivity' are involved in answering these questions. This, however, is not the point, which is simply that in answering any kind of examination question the examinee must make choices, come to decisions, and express them in one way or another.

The third process in any examination is that of marking or scoring the examinees' answers. It is here, and only here, that the distinction exists between 'subjective' and 'objective' (as previously defined). If the examiner has to exercise judgement; if he has to decide whether the answer is adequate or inadequate; if he has to choose between awarding it a high or low mark; then the marking process is 'subjective'. If, on the other hand, he is precluded from making judgements; if he is forced to accept decisions made beforehand by someone else; if, in short, he is reduced, for the purpose of marking, to the status of a machine (and in some cases can even be replaced by a machine); then the marking process is 'objective'.

In summary, all examinations are 'subjectively' compiled and 'subjectively' answered. Only their assessment may be 'subjective' or 'objective'. The distinction between a 'subjective' and 'objective' examination rests only on the manner in which the marks are to be assigned.

2. 'EXAMINATIONS' AND 'TESTS'

One further point of nomenclature should be mentioned. A loose distinction is often made between 'examinations' and 'tests'. Since both give rise to measures of some attribute possessed by some individual, the distinction in terms of outcome is difficult to justify. Sometimes the distinction is made in terms of time allowed—a typical 'examination' lasts two, three, or more hours; a typical 'test' one half to one hour. Out of this has grown the custom of calling a group of 'tests', all administered to the same persons, an 'examination'. Or the distinction may be hierarchical. A university professor 'examines' his

Final Honours students in English Literature; a primary school teacher 'tests' her nine-year-olds in spelling. Finally, the distinction may depend on whether assessment is 'subjective' or 'objective'. In the first case, we have an 'examination'; in the second, a 'test'.

There is thus no single conventional distinction that is universally accepted. For the purpose of this chapter, that last mentioned will be adopted: 'subjective' examining instruments will be called 'examinations', and their 'objective' counterparts 'tests'.

Examinations have a long and occasionally disreputable history. At least as early as A.D. 400 and for the next 1,500 years entry to the Chinese Imperial Service was governed by an extraordinary series of eliminating heats in which essay-writing predominated. Morris (Wiseman, 1961, p. 3) concludes his account of this remarkable obstacle race with the words: 'It is a nice thought that the Supreme End-product of the most lengthy and gruelling chain of examinations in history was just another examiner.'

The tradition of examination by dissertation was maintained in Europe through medieval times and persisted until the beginning of the nineteenth century. Early in the century, first Oxford and then Cambridge established public examinations, followed in 1836 by London. The tradition has persisted, and examinations now play a dominating role at many points in the educational systems of the world.

Nor is the search for objectivity as recent a development as is commonly supposed. As early as 1827, Jeremy Bentham proposed a Civil Service examination in which the questions were to have one correct answer only, while a properly random selection of questions for a particular testee was to be ensured by means of a procedure involving a child too young to be suspected of fraud. However, it is more usual to ascribe the inception of objective tests to Binet in 1905, though in fact Ebbinghaus had devised earlier (1897) a Completion Test which, interestingly enough in the present context, contained items of the form:

One (   ) (   ) eagle (   ) with the (   ) birds (   ) see
(   ) could (   ) (   ) highest.

The necessity to select rapidly and *en masse* from American Army recruits during the 1914–18 War gave impetus to the testing movement which has continued ever since. In the Western World at least, the use of tests for a wide range of purposes continues to increase at an astonishing rate.

3. REQUIREMENTS OF GOOD EXAMINATION AND TEST PROCEDURES

As with other tools, the efficiency of an examination or test cannot be gauged in isolation from the procedure of which it is part, or the purpose to which it is put. A test useful in one situation may be useless in another. Thus a test which discriminates excellently among students from overseas in their control of English language may fail to do so among native English speakers. Again, in testing a person's pronunciation, it is a sensible procedure to engage him in conversation and listen. But if the topic is one unfamiliar to him the conversational situation becomes a test of vocabulary and grammar rather than one of pronunciation.

For this reason the following discussion will relate to examination and test *procedures*, it being understood that this is what is meant when reference is made to 'examinations' and 'tests'.

The conditions which must be satisfied if an examination or test is to be efficient may be stated in a single sentence:

An examination or test procedure, if it is to be efficient, must discriminate among the subjects examined or tested both reliably and validly.

However, the discussion arising from this brief sentence is necessarily lengthy.

3.1 Discrimination

The purpose of the instrument, whether examination or test, is to reflect differences in the attribute concerned which are presumed to exist among the subjects. In the field of language testing, the attribute may be the extent of vocabulary, ability to spell, power of comprehension, control of language in speech or writing, or any other attribute considered sufficiently important to merit testing. The extent to which a single subject manifests the attribute becomes meaningful only in relation to the corresponding manifestations by others. If we are told that someone can run 100 yards in nine seconds we are impressed because we already know that such a feat is beyond most of us. If we are told, however, that someone has scored 80 per cent in a comprehension test, we withhold judgement until we know how others have done in the same test.

If then, an examination is to tell us something about an individual, it must be capable of discriminating among the group of which he is a member.

3.2 Reliability

3.2.1 Basic principles

It is not enough that the examination or test should discriminate. For it to be efficient, it must be consistent in the discriminations it makes. Scores on it must be *reliable*. Ideally, this means that on repeating the procedure, (i) the scores should not be subject to fluctuations, and hence (ii) the persons obtaining these scores should maintain their standings relative to one another.

In the physical sciences, in which replication is a commonplace, it is usually possible to employ a direct method of determining the consistency of measurement. The same quantity of material can be weighed repeatedly and the observed weights recorded. Or analyses can be conducted on successive samples taken from the same batch of material. In general the observations will fluctuate somewhat from one weighing to another, or from one analysis to another. If there are enough replications, the observations will tend to distribute themselves symmetrically in a bell-shaped or 'normal' fashion about a central or average value. The departure from perfect consistency which this distribution of discrepant observations reflects may be expressed statistically as a variance, and is called the 'error variance of measurement'. Its square root is the 'standard error of measurement'.[1]

Unfortunately, this simple and direct method is rarely applicable outside the realm of the physical sciences. Elsewhere, the characteristic measured does not 'remain constant' over a series of repeated measurements. An alternative method must be brought into play whenever the attribute to be measured is itself subject to modification by the very process of measuring it.

This alternative procedure also makes use of many measurements, but their impact is different. Measurements are now conducted on each of a number of individuals, and the number on each is reduced to two. The correlation coefficient for the two sets of measurements furnishes an index of the consistency of the measurement procedure and is called the 'reliability coefficient'. From it can be inferred the error variance, and hence the standard error of measurement.[2]

It is clear that the second, indirect procedure is appropriate in assessing the consistency with which attributes relating to human behaviour are measured, including those attributes with which language testing is concerned.

3.2.2 Types of reliability

Each of the four types of reliability outlined below is based, directly or indirectly, on the concept of two examinations or tests administered to each of a number of subjects.

---

[1] If there are n observations $x_1, x_2, x_3 \ldots, x_n$, and their mean is $\bar{x}$, then the standard error of measurement is $\sqrt{[(x_1-\bar{x})^2+(x_2-\bar{x})^2 \ldots (x_n-\bar{x})^2]/(n-1)}$.

[2] If s_t^2 is the variance of test scores, and r_{tt} the reliability coefficient, then that proportion of the test variance due to differences among the individuals in the attribute tested is $s_t^2 \, r_{tt}$; that due to random errors, the error variance of measurement, is $s_t^2 \, (1-r_{tt})$; and the square root of the latter, the standard error of measurement, is $s_t\sqrt{(1-r_{tt})}$. It can be shown that the standard error of measurement thus estimated is equivalent to the average of the directly measured standard errors for the individuals in the group concerned.

(*1*) *The Coefficient of Stability*. This is the correlation between the scores obtained by the same subjects when the same test or examination is administered to them twice with a specified time interval between the administrations. It is an index of the constancy over a specified period of the abilities measured by a particular test or examination. It is frequently termed 'test re-test with the same test'.

The Coefficient of Stability can of course be determined directly.

(*2*) *The Coefficient of Equivalence*. This is the hypothetical correlation between subjects' scores on the test or examination in hand and scores that would have been obtained by the same subjects on an equivalent form of the test or examination that might have been substituted for it on the single occasion of testing. 'Equivalent' here means equivalent expressions of the constructor's theory and intentions. This coefficient is an index of the degree to which differences among the individuals tested would persist if, on the single occasion of testing, a different though equivalent testing procedure were substituted for that used.[1] It is an index of the accuracy with which a particular kind of test measures the abilities it does measure at the time when it measures them.

The Coefficient of Equivalence must be estimated indirectly from the internal relationships of the parts of the test.

(*3*) *The Coefficient of Internal Consistency*. This is an index of the homogeneity of the test or examination. A High Internal Consistency Coefficient indicates a high degree of inter-correlation among the parts of the test, which in turn is usually considered to point to similarity in the factors underlying the attributes which these several parts test. Conversely, a low Internal Consistency Coefficient indicates that the several parts of the test do not 'march together' in this way. An objective language test including such sections as vocabulary, syntactic structure, phonemic discrimination and stress is likely to show a low Internal Consistency Coefficient; a test of similar overall length consisting of items of only one of these types is more likely to show a high Internal Consistency Coefficient.

This form of coefficient is popular among test constructors because it can be estimated from the scores obtained on a single administration. The 'boosted split-half' coefficient derived from the correlation between scores on half-tests (such as the odd and even items) is

---

[1] An examination or test relating to a particular domain is one sample out of several equally acceptable samples that might have been chosen. Examinee A, who does well on the sample chosen, might have done less well on another, and conversely for Examinee B. The extent of the unreliability which results can only be revealed by *ad hoc* experiment.

one estimate of the Internal Consistency Coefficient.[1] Another and better estimate is that obtained by the use of the Kuder-Richardson Formula 20.[2]

This coefficient possesses a further useful property which is not generally known. It is a lower bound to the Coefficient of Equivalence of the test. Since the latter is relatively troublesome to estimate, the Internal Consistency Coefficient is frequently substituted for it.

(4) *The Coefficient of Equivalence and Stability.* This is the correlation between scores obtained by the same subjects when two 'parallel' forms of a test or examination are administered to them with a specified time interval between the administrations. It is an index of the constancy over a specified time period of the abilities measured in common by the two 'parallel' tests or examinations. Strictly speaking, 'parallel' here has the same connotation as that specified in the description of the Coefficient of Equivalence. However, a certain looseness of interpretation is not unusual. Thus the correlation between scores on two different essays is sometimes regarded as a Coefficient of Equivalence and Stability, even though it would be difficult to defend the thesis that the essays were 'parallel'.

This coefficient is frequently termed 'test re-test with "parallel" tests' and can of course be measured directly.

3.2.3 Discussion

The aim of the preceding discussion has been to show that there is no one reliability coefficient characterizing a test or examination. Depending on the procedure used, no less than four different coefficients can be derived from testing or examining one group of subjects. Moreover, the scatter of ability in the group itself also affects the outcome. A well-made objective test of English vocabulary designed for and administered to non-native speakers is likely to show a high reliability coefficient, no matter which procedure is used. The same test, adminstered to native speakers will probably show a lower coefficient. The constructors of a language test should therefore report (i) the

---

[1] If $r_{\frac{1}{2}\frac{1}{2}}$ is the observed correlation coefficient between scores on the two half-tests, then the estimated Coefficient of Internal Consistency r_{11} is

$$r_{11} = \frac{2\,r_{\frac{1}{2}\frac{1}{2}}}{1 + r_{\frac{1}{2}\frac{1}{2}}}$$

[2] One form of KR20 is as follows:

$$r_{11} = \frac{n}{n-1} \cdot \frac{s^2 - \Sigma\,p\,q}{s^2}$$

in which n = number of items in the test; s^2 = variance of test totals; p is the proportion of testees passing a particular item and $q = (1-p)$ is the proportion failing it. The summation sign indicates that the products $p\,q$ (one product for each item) are to be summed over all n items.

procedure used in estimating reliability, and (ii) the nature of the group used in its estimation.

The several sources of unreliability implied in the preceding discussion occur with all language tests or examinations whether objective (as with elements such as lexis or syntax) or subjective (as with skills such as speaking or writing). With subjective examinations, however, there is a further source of unreliability, that of inconsistency in assessment.

3.2.4 Unreliability of marking in subjective examinations

It is well known that the marks awarded by different markers, or even by the same marker on different occasions, are frequently inconsistent with each other when the process of assessment demands subjective judgement. As long ago as 1888 Edgeworth noted disagreements among examiners, and in 1913 Starch reported wide discrepancies in the marks awarded by Mathematics and English examiners. A major study in this field was that of Hartog and Rhodes, who published their findings in 1936. More recent studies are those of Wiseman (1949), Finlayson (1951), Pilliner (1952) and Vernon (1954).

From the statistical point of view, there are three main causes of disagreement among markers who independently mark the same set of scripts:

(1) The marks awarded may differ in average standard or level. One marker may be generally severe, another generally lenient.

(2) The marks may differ in their scatter or spread. One marker may employ the whole range of the available scale, another only part of it.

(3) The marks may order the examinees differently. Discrepancies among the markers in rank order are reflected in low intercorrelations among the arrays of marks they assign.[1]

Techniques are available for assessing the relative contributions o these three sources of error to the total. Their results point the direction in which efforts to reduce error variance may usefully be made. Beyond this, they make it possible for the test constructors to report, for the benefit of test users, the error attaching to a test score which is attributable to unreliability in marking.

[1] 'Marker reliabilities' are frequently reported as correlation coefficients. Since these coefficients depend mainly on the third source of variation, and are almost independent of the other two, the information they convey is incomplete. It is conceivable that for two examiners, A and B, the correlation r_{AB} is unity. But if A marks severely, and B leniently, or if A spreads his marks out more than B, their individual examinees will receive different marks, despite this perfect correlation.

3.2.5 Methods of reducing marker unreliability

Most of the attempts to improve the consistency of subjective judgements have been concerned with the marking of essays. There are
three main directions in which these attempts have been made.

(*1*) *Analytic Procedures*. Marking control is sought by the isolation
and separate assessment of different aspects of the material to be
marked. Each aspect is allotted a mark out of some maximum which
reflects a previously made judgement of its importance in relation to
the whole. Which particular aspects should be isolated obviously
depends on the purpose of the examination. One analytic scheme,[1]
suggested for marking an essay included in an examination of English
as a foreign language, is as follows:

Aspects to be isolated:

(1) Content.
(2) Formal structure of the essay as a whole.
(3) Language. (a) Sentence structure, (b) Morphology, (c) Spelling,
    (d) Punctuation, (e) Richness of vocabulary.
(4) Mis-interpretation of the subject.

Studies such as those of Cast (1939) strongly suggest that the assessment made by a single marker who uses a framework of this sort are
more reliable than 'global' impression assessments made by one person.

From the point of view of the language tester, analytic schemes such
as this have much to recommend them. This point will be returned to
in discussing validity.

(*2*) *Increasing the Number of Questions*. The principle here is to increase
the number of *units* to be marked while decreasing the *size* of these
units to a minimum consonant with the purpose of the examination.
For example, from the point of view of the language tester concerned
with skill in writing, it is better to set two short essays instead of a
single longer one.

(*3*) *Increasing the Number of Examiners*. Wiseman (1949) has shown
that the sum or average of ratings assigned by four independent
examiners marking rapidly 'by impression' has a mark re-mark
reliability coefficient of nearly 0·9. This is probably higher than the
mark re-mark reliability obtainable by a single marker who uses an
analytic procedure, and whose cost in marker-hours is greater.

Cox (1966) has recently criticized the Wiseman method of achieving
reliability on the ground that 'the improvement does not represent
greater agreement on the value of the essay, (but) is merely a device

[1] For this scheme I am indebted to Miss Ruth Aronson, of the Department of English
of the University of Tel-Aviv. It was proposed for use with the English Language
section of the Bagrut (Matriculation) Examination conducted by the Israel Ministry
of Education and Culture.

for getting the same marks every time' (p. 8). If the agreement among the markers is poor, and if at the same time each is self-consistent in repeat marking of the scripts, there is some substance to this criticism. In the extreme case when the marks from the different examiners bear no relationship to each other, and if the self-consistency of each examiner is high, the reliability of the total (or mean) over the whole set of markers will be both positive and substantial. But this reliability will be an expression of the consistency with which each marker repeats his own judgements, a reflection of markers' enduring personal idiosyncrasies, a measure of the strength of the agreement to disagree. It will be independent of the differences which may be presumed to exist in the merit of different scripts. On the other hand, if there is a fair measure of initial agreement among individual markers about the relative merits of the scripts, Cox's criticism is invalid. Under these conditions, the aggregated marks from a team of several examiners will be more reliable than the marks from one alone.

(*4*) *Discussion and Summary.* Cox is pessimistic about the possibility of achieving consistent and valid marking by the use of any marking scheme, analytic or otherwise. In the context of the university examinations which he is discussing, his pessimism may be justified. The outlook is probably more hopeful, however, in the context of language examining, where the objective is different. The literacy assumed in the university student and employed by him to other ends is precisely the skill the language examiner aims at assessing. In that assessment a break-down is possible which can simplify the examiner's task. It was suggested earlier (p. 27) that the elements, such as lexis and syntax, can usually be tested objectively, so that for these important pre-requisites of language control highly reliable marking is possible. The unreliability always associated with subjective judgement is therefore limited to the assessment of skills such as speaking or writing. Though still difficult, the examiner's task is easier if he makes proper diagnostic use of the information provided by a previous objective testing of the elements.

To sum up: for examinations in the marking of which subjective judgement is required, some degree of marker unreliability must be accepted. It is superimposed on that previously described, to which all examinations and tests, of whatever sort, are prone. This marker unreliability can be reduced (1) by an analytic procedure in which different aspects of the material to be assessed are marked separately; (2) by increasing the number and decreasing the size of the units to be marked; (3) under certain conditions, by replicating an 'impressionistic' marking procedure. It is probable that because of its relatively specific objectives, language examining is less unreliable than examining in other fields.

3.3 Validity

3.3.1 General

Although this discussion of validity follows that of discrimination and reliability, in order of importance it undoubtedly comes first. Over-riding all other considerations, a language test or examination should be valid.

The validity of any examination or test procedure may be broadly defined as the extent to which it does what it is intended to do. A comprehensive definition of this sort is necessary because of the several different connotations of the word.

At the outset, it must be stressed that if validity is to be achieved, discrimination and reliability are necessary conditions. But they are not sufficient. A test may discriminate well and performance on it may be capable of reliable assessment, but it is invalid if it fails to test what it should. Spearman (1936) puts it in this way: 'The inter-relations of reliability and validity are one-sided. Low reliability necessarily involves low validity, but the converse is not true. Whenever we find bad agreement between different measurements, then we can safely say that the examination is bad. But when the measurements agree we can*not* forthwith say that the examination is good.'

3.3.2 Predictive validity

It is interesting to trace the evolution of the concept of validity in the area of examining and testing. In much the same way that the word 'intelligence' was appropriated from common usage by the psychologists, or, similarly, the word 'affinity' by the chemists, so, too, the word 'validity' was first employed by the examination and test statisticians in a special and restricted sense. For the statistician it meant *predictive* validity, a numerical expression of the correspondence between performance on the examination used as a predictor and some criterion of later success. The predictive validity after four or five years of the completely objective English Attainment test used as part of 11+ allocation procedures in England is 0·8 or better when the criterion is secondary school success as measured by teachers' assessments or by O-level marks in the GCE examination. The Davies English Proficiency Test is designed to select for control of English among non-native English speakers who intend to study in Britain. Its predictive validity will be measured by its success in selecting those students whose proficiency in English is adequate for the courses they intend to take and the criterion will be the assessments of that proficiency made by their teachers in Britain.

In short, predictive validity is a quantitative concept.

3.3.3 Concurrent validity

The validation process for a new test is often shortened by correlating scores on it with scores obtained by the same testees on a test already existing and known to be predictively valid. The correlation between the two sets of scores is the *concurrent validity* of the new test, and a high concurrent validity suggests[1] that the new test is also predictively valid.

3.3.4 Content validity

But examinations and tests have another purpose besides prediction of later success. It is axiomatic that their content inevitably influences the teaching and learning which precede them. 'Question-spotting'; the pre-packaged essay contorted during its regurgitation into some semblance of relevance; coaching and practice aimed at the achievement of high marks in a specific examination with scant regard to educational considerations; all these undesirable concomitants of the examination process are only too well known.

However, the influence of the examination or test is not necessarily bad. Properly constructed, it can foster and reinforce good teaching and sound learning and discourage their opposites. To achieve these ends, the test constructor must start with a clear conception of the aims and purposes of the area of learning to which his test is relevant. If the content of his test directs the previous learning of potential testees towards the achievement of these aims and purposes; and if that content enables the test user to evaluate the extent to which the testees have achieved these aims; then the test possesses *content* validity.

To possess content validity, an examination or test must do more than furnish a record of achievement in covering the subject syllabus.

Were this the prime consideration, the conventional method of gearing the test to the syllabus would be enough. But this procedure has its dangers. As Wiseman (1961, p. 148) says: 'The syllabus-content approach tends to perpetuate ineffective educational practices; it is a reactionary instrument helping to encapsulate method within the shell of tradition and accepted practice.' He continues: 'The goal-orientated test is exactly the opposite: it evaluates learning—and teaching—in terms of the aims of the curriculum, and so fosters critical awareness, good method, and functional content.' If the aim of teaching English is specified as fluency in speech and literacy in reading and writing, then the English examination should be directed at testing this fluency and literacy. There is no need to include in the examination questions on the terminology of formal grammar, even

[1] A high concurrent validity suggests, but does not guarantee, a high predictive validity. If the concurrent validity for tests A and B is 0·90, and the predictive validity of test A is 0·80, then that of test B *could* be as low as 0·46.

though some teachers consider it a powerful tool in developing literacy in their pupils and hence include it in their syllabus. In short, the syllabus is a means to an end, and should be regarded as such.

The responsibility thus rests squarely on those compiling an examination or test of analysing and clarifying ultimate objectives. Moreover, it is essential that these aims be specified in concrete and not abstract terms. It is perhaps not entirely useless to specify as an aim 'the inculcation of aesthetic awareness', but for all practical purposes it is so until it is re-expressed in terms of abilities, skills or attitudes and then translated into elements of behaviour which are observable and which can be evaluated. The aesthetic aim is unlikely to trouble the language tester unduly, but even the aims mentioned earlier, 'fluency in speech' and 'literacy in reading and writing', which are very much his concern, stand in need of re-expression and translation into specific and testable elements of behaviour. It is suggested that 'command of fundamental processes' is an appropriate starting point— though only a starting point—for the language test constructor. Among linguists there is a fair measure of agreement in the specification of these 'processes', in the acts performed (in appropriate situations) by those having 'command' of them, and in those performed by those lacking such 'command'. Once the detailed specification is completed, it is the task of the language tester to provide situations in which these acts can be performed, and a workable scheme for both classifying and scoring these acts as successful or unsuccessful.

Content validity, then, is concerned with the relationship between test or examination content and detailed curricular aims. It therefore differs from predictive validity in that it cannot be quantitatively measured, but demands instead logical analysis and subjective judgement.

It is perhaps naïve to enquire which of the two is the more important. On the one hand, a language proficiency test, the purpose of which is to help overseas students to decide whether their command of English is sufficient to justify a lengthy and expensive course of study in Britain, is useless if it does not serve this purpose. On the other hand, a test which relates to insufficiently worked out objectives, or which is geared to a teaching syllabus open to objection, or which in some other way wrongly influences the educative process, is not only useless, but also positively undesirable. Language is crucial for all else, and the language tester must aim at both content and predictive validity. It may be speculated that in seeking the first he will find the second.

3.3.5 Summary

Discrimination and reliability are pre-requisite to validity, which is of overriding importance.

Predictive validity is a quantitative measure of the correspondence between scores on the test and scores on some subsequent criterion.

Concurrent validity measures the extent to which scores on the test 'predict' scores on a test already in existence and of acceptable predictive validity.

Content validity is a qualitative assessment of the extent to which the test probes ultimate objectives.

4. ITEMS FROM ENGLISH LANGUAGE TESTS

4.1 Grammatical structures[1]

In these items, which exemplify the multiple choice procedure, the testee has to choose and indicate the one correct structure.

(a)   1. would you like
            What 2. do you like   to do tomorrow?
                        3. could you like
(b)   1. went up
This new building 2. has been going up   since Christmas.
                        3. goes up

By this means, rapid coverage of a large number of structures is possible.

4.2 Listening test[1]

Each item consists of three spoken words A, B and C (tape recorded). The testee has to decide which, if any, of the three words are the same and to indicate his answer by circling one of the five groups of letters below (the symbol O stands for 'none the same'):

AB   BC   ABC   AC   O

4.3 Reading comprehension (i)[1]

These items exemplify the 'open-ended' procedure in which the testee supplies the missing letters. Scoring, however, is completely objective.

(a) ——— o——— these words a——— missing.
(b) I——— fact, women are being asked t——— play roles
        w——— are as yet, i——— our society, i——— conflict.

(b) is the first sentence in a nine-line passage containing in all 26 words to be completed.

4.4 Reading comprehension (ii)

This is another form of comprehension test in which the testee has to show his understanding of a passage he has read by the responses he chooses in the items which follow.

[1] These items are taken from the Davies English Proficiency Test.

Seven-a-Side Rugby[1]

The wide open spaces invite spectacular handling and running so that runaway tries are commonplace, the ball is frequently flipped from player to player in basketball fashion, the overall pace of movement is, at times, bewildering, and there is a particular sense of urgency abroad, for each tie, except the final, lasts for only fourteen minutes, and where the teams are level at the end it becomes a case of sudden death, first score decides.

The next questions are about what you have just read. Underline in the brackets the word or phrase which completes each sentence correctly.

1. This kind of writing is called
   (classical/journalese/historical/science-fiction/broadcasting)
2. 'spectacular handling' (in the first line) means that the players
   (wear spectacles/make spectacles of themselves/use spacious tactics/make remarkable and showy performances/run in rectangles).
3. The passage is all one sentence but the
   (grammar/spelling/vocabulary/description/punctuation) is sometimes quite incorrect.
4. The account is written in this way to give an impression of
   (speed and raciness/spaciousness/accuracy/importance/violence).
5. 'a case of sudden death' is
   (a descriptive exaggeration/a fact/an active possibility/an impossibility/a shock).
6. The sense of urgency is due to
   (the runaway tries/the open spaces/the likeness to basketball/the short time allowed for each team's first tie/flipping the ball).

4.5 Word order in a sentence[1]

(a) I've called for ———— ———— ———— ———— ————.
    (1) us (2) promised (3) you (4) books (5) the new
(b) Would you be so kind as ———— ———— ———— ———— ————.
    (1) this letter (2) the reason (3) explain (4) for (5) to

In these the testee has to select the best order for the words given and to write the identifying numbers in the appropriate spaces.

5. ESSAY SUBJECTS

For a fuller discussion of the issues involved in examining English composition, the reader is referred to Grieve, D. W. *Report of an Inquiry into English Language Examining* (West African Examinations Council, 1963).[2]

[1] These items are taken from Moray House English Attainment Tests.
[2] Chapters 7, 13 and 16 of this Report appear as chapter 9 of this Symposium, pp. 133–50.

Briefly, the points made by Grieve are as follows:

(1) The ability to write a language is manifested in the ability to use its lexis and structures in given situations.

(2) Creative ability, though important, is distinct from the ability to write a language, and, from the point of view of the language tester, irrelevant.

(3) Tests of composition are necessarily unreliable and of doubtful validity. Since, however, it is important that composition should be taught, and since, if not examined, it may *not* be taught, it should be included in a language examination.

(4) Whenever people write, in real life, they do so because they have
    (i) something to say;
    (ii) someone to say it to;
    (iii) a purpose in saying it.

The least the examiner selecting topics for composition can do is to have regard to these considerations. Taking into account points (1) and (2) above, it follows that much of the information necessary to the writing of the composition should be supplied to the examinee.

To illustrate these principles, Grieve suggests a number of essay topics, of which two are quoted below.

(a) Compose an advertisement for a post that you would like after you leave school and write a letter of application for that post. The advertisement should state the name of the firm or organization concerned, the title of the post, the nature of the duties, and the salary offered. In the letter of application you should outline your school career and qualifications, and make mention of your special interests.

(b) A local craftsman. (Where does the craftsman work? What does he do? What tools and material does he use? Describe one thing that he makes and how he makes it. What is his place in the community today? Is his livelihood threatened by competition from factory-made goods?)

This provision of ideas is likely to lead to greater marker reliability which, as pointed out on page 30, is pre-requisite to validity. What is more, validity is increased since the language tester can now concentrate on the examinee's ability to write the language required in a prescribed situation.

To Grieve's excellent suggestions, the present writer would add one more. Evidence exists that an individual's performance on a single essay may be misleading as an indicator of his ability to write. It is suggested that, instead of one long essay, two shorter ones, occupying the same overall time, should be set (see in this chapter, page 28).

3

The Linguistics of Language Testing

D. P. Harris

I. HISTORICAL BACKGROUND

Efforts to apply modern linguistic principles to the construction of foreign language tests may be said generally to date from the decade following World War II and to have proceeded from the application of linguistic science to the *teaching* of languages. Thus it is appropriate in any account of the development of modern language testing to refer to the recent history of foreign language instruction.[1]

In the decades prior to World War II, most language teaching in the United States, as in other countries, still followed the so-called grammar-translation method, with its comparative neglect of the speaking and listening skills.

One of its aims was to teach the 'grammar' of the language, by which was meant its inflectional paradigms . . . and certain rules for combining words into phrases and sentences. The teacher spent a large part of his time explaining the grammar; the students learned it by memorizing the paradigms and the rules; and they applied the grammar by translating English sentences into the foreign language. The second aim was to teach the student to read the foreign language. The teaching method employed was that of more or less word-for-word translation from the foreign language into English, accompanied sometimes by the memorizing of lists of words. (Moulton, 1961, p. 83.)

[1] It must be pointed out that three general limitations have been imposed on the following discussion. First, the treatment will deal very largely with language testing in the United States, the only area in which the writer has had much first-hand knowledge and experience. It is his strong impression, however, that most of what will be stated can be applied to language testing generally, and the absence of specific references to tests developed elsewhere is by no means intended to underrate the excellent work that has recently been done in other parts of the world. Second, the discussion will be concerned exclusively with foreign language achievement and proficiency testing, to the exclusion of any consideration of first-language testing or of measures of language aptitude, both of which will be treated elsewhere in this volume. Finally, the writer will consider only 'standard' foreign language tests, that is, tests published by established testing agencies for large-scale administrations. Thus no mention will be made of tests constructed by individual teachers for use in a local classroom situation.

Reference is made to this chapter on p. 14 of the Introduction.

Quite predictably, the grammar-translation method of instruction provided the basis for most tests of foreign language proficiency developed up to, and during, World War II. Thus, for example, of the 19 tests of modern foreign languages reviewed in Buros's *Third Mental Measurements Yearbook*, published in 1949 (Buros, 1949), only three tested auditory perception and/or comprehension, and none attempted to measure oral production. Of the 16 tests of grammar, vocabulary, and reading reviewed in the third *Yearbook*, apparently about three-fourths made use of English in some or all of the parts—that is, required translation from English into the foreign language or vice versa. Vocabulary items seem generally to have been tested in isolation, single words in the target language being matched with one-word equivalents in either the target language or English. In the reviews of the grammar tests, frequent comments are made about the stilted language of the contexts; the reviews of the vocabulary tests criticize the apparent lack of system in the choice and control of the lexical items and the failure to take account of obvious English cognates and borrowings—in other words, the reviewers criticize the lack of a sound linguistic basis for the tests. It should be added that other tests were listed in addition to those reviewed.

Most of the tests reviewed in the third *Yearbook* were, of course, several years old at the time; some dated back to the 1920's. It was during the War years of the early 1940's that the beginnings were laid for a dramatic change in the methods of teaching and, subsequently, of testing foreign languages. In the United States these changes originated with the work of the Intensive Language Program of the American Council of Learned Societies; yet it was the Armed Forces that must be credited with giving impetus to the new movement. Faced with the sudden need for young men and women possessing a practical knowledge of the spoken form of a multitude of foreign languages, both familiar and 'exotic', Washington set up a 'crash program' to develop new teaching methods and materials, and appealed for the help of the nation's linguists.

'It is safe to say that, before the Program was over, just about every trained linguist in the country, young or old, had become involved in it in one way or another . . . [And from their work] there emerged an outlook on language teaching which, even if we discount the special demands of the moment, was vastly different from that prevalent in the schools and colleges of the country.' (Moulton, 1961, pp. 85–6.)

With the return to peace, the 'new outlook' gradually began to win adherents among school and college language teachers throughout the country. And as more and more materials and instruction came to be based on the new methods, and as more and more educators came to acquire a new conception of what is meant—or ought to be meant—by 'knowing' a foreign language, it was only natural that the traditional methods of language testing should come under question, and the first attempts be made to incorporate new linguistic concepts into the measurement of language proficiency and achievement.

2. SOME BASIC LINGUISTIC PRINCIPLES AND THEIR APPLICATION TO TESTING

Of what, then, do these concepts consist; what applications do they have for language testing; and to what extent do current tests[1] actually make use of such applications? For the answer to the first of these questions, we turn again to the excellent little survey to which we have already referred above, William G. Moulton's *Linguistics and Language Teaching in the United States, 1940–1960*. Discussing the emergence of the new teaching methods during the war, Moulton quotes five fundamental linguistic principles 'in the forms which came to be the slogans of the day' (1961, p. 86). It would be safe to say that these five principles are still regarded as valid and basic by most 'applied linguists' today and may therefore provide a useful set of criteria against which to judge the extent of linguistic orientation of today's foreign language tests. Let us, therefore, repeat Moulton's 'slogans' (though in different order) and consider briefly their application to language testing.

(1) 'A language is a set of habits'

This principle has at least two very important implications for the writer of foreign language tests. First, inasmuch as a subject cannot truly be said to 'know a language' until he is able to respond *quickly and automatically* to natural language situations, the test writer must decide to what extent, if any, speed should be a factor in his test. Strictly speaking, a speed test is one in which the items are all so easy that, given enough time, all examinees could answer them correctly. In practice, of course, very few, if any, educational tests are pure tests of speed. Yet 'power' tests[2] can be timed so that only a certain proportion of examinees will be expected to reach the end before time is called, and the writer of language tests must decide whether some degree of speediness is required if his tests can really be said to measure the extent to which the subjects have mastered a 'set of habits'. One can perhaps generalize by saying that most present-day language tests are not highly speeded, but that the recognition of the importance

---

[1] A list of current tests is given at the back of this volume in List of Language Tests (p. 208).

[2] Power tests, in contrast to speed tests, are those in which the difficulty of the items is steeply graded, some items being too difficult for most—or any—of the subjects to answer correctly, though they will probably have time to reach them.

of automatic response has strongly influenced the types of items that are currently favoured in language testing. Thus, one of the great advantages of most objective item types over free-response types is that the responses can be made more quickly. A variety of experiments has even been conducted with the use of picture choices, rather than printed words or sentences as item alternatives. Yet few picture tests— at least beyond the elementary level—have proved entirely successful in the area of language testing, for pictures create their own special problems.[1]

The recognition that a language is a set of habits has had another very important implication for the writer both of language texts and language tests. Inasmuch as the learning of a second language involves the learning of a second set of language habits, one can and must anticipate interference from the first language as the student attempts to acquire the second. Thus arose the use of 'contrastive analysis'— the point-by-point comparison of background and target languages— as the basis for the selection and ordering (and, indeed, the method of presentation) of language materials in the modern foreign language text. In like manner when a foreign language test is being devised for subjects who share the same native language, it is efficient to use contrastive analysis to point up the new language patterns which, because of background language interference, are likely to pose the greatest problems for the learner. And the most effective distractors in a test item will be those which evoke first-language responses from those subjects who have not fully mastered the very different patterns of the target language. Thus, for example, the following structure problem from a test of English as a foreign language[2] would be expected to present particular difficulties for speakers of Spanish, a language in which modifiers of nouns are in inflectional agreement with the nouns:

'Is there anything you need for your room?'
'Yes. We need some ———.'
(A) desks lamps (B) desk lamps (C) desk lamp (D) desks lamp

It should here be noted, however, that in testing English as a foreign language, practical considerations generally prevent much reliance on contrastive analysis. Most of the important tests in this area must be designed for world-wide use; and inasmuch, therefore, as the test population will include subjects with the widest variety of background

[1] The greatest problem undoubtedly is depicting clearly and unambiguously the kind of oral or written stimuli that one would want to ask intermediate- and advanced-level learners of a foreign language to interpret. Moreover, pictures can easily become 'culture loaded', thereby reducing the validity of tests which seek to assess the language competence of subjects from another culture.

[2] All of the examples given in this discussion are taken directly from widely-used tests of English as a foreign language.

languages, the usual contrastive procedures are largely inapplicable. Instead, the test writer must find some means of sampling the full range of patterns that make up the English language and see that these patterns are represented in proportions that, insofar as possible, reflect actual use. That some test items will be easier for students of some language backgrounds than others is by no means a defect, for this situation accurately reflects the actual language-learning situation. Unfortunately, the linguists have been slow to provide full inventories of language patterns, ordered by frequency, for English or any other language. Therefore the test writer has had to rely in large part on intuition and 'intelligent guessing' in the preparation of 'universal' English as a foreign language test.

(2) 'Language is speech, not writing'

From this principle it naturally follows that, in tests of general language proficiency, measuring the aural/oral skills is fully as important as measuring the ability to read and write. Indeed, in the case of tests designed for beginning and low-intermediate students, the measurement of auditory comprehension and oral production ability becomes the prime objective.

Fortunately, excellent methods of testing auditory perception and general comprehension have been developed in recent years. These generally consist of presenting oral stimuli (isolated questions and statements, short conversations between two speakers, and, on the advanced levels, excerpts from radio broadcasts, university lectures, and the like) to which the subjects respond by selecting the appropriate printed response (a logical answer to a question, an accurate paraphrase, etc.).[1]

In contrast, as will be explained in detail elsewhere in this volume, efforts to devise reliable and easily administered tests of oral production have not yet proved entirely satisfactory. Yet the important point is that, although oral-production sections are still missing from most comprehensive foreign language tests, it is certainly not because of a general failure by the test writers to recognize the importance of such measures, but rather because the language and measurement specialists have so far failed to find methods of assessing oral proficiency which completely meet the criteria of reliability and practicality.

(3) 'A language is what its native speakers say, not what someone thinks they ought to say'

This principle has at least two important implications for the writer of both language texts and language tests. It means, first, that language

---

[1] As indicated earlier, some tests have used picture responses, though these have not proved completely satisfactory.

materials should be *descriptive*, not *prescriptive*. That is, they should be based directly on the *actual speech* (or, on some advanced levels, the *writing*) of informants who use widely acceptable social and regional varieties of the language. They should not attempt to impose an artificial, 'ideal' variety of the language which has no existence outside the classroom. And second, a clear distinction must always be maintained between forms and patterns characteristic of the spoken language and those confined to, or clearly more appropriate for, the more formal and 'grammatically conservative' written language.

In the 'pre-scientific' era of language testing, most tests required the subjects to make a series of decisions about grammatical 'correctness'. Very frequently the directions simply asked the examinees to choose or write the 'correct forms'. The level of usage was seldom explicitly identified, and the contexts of the items often ranged from the literary to the conversational, yet somehow the implication was conveyed that the 'correct forms' were always to be those of careful classroom composition. Fortunately, most students understood how they were meant to play the game. A single example, taken from a widely-used test of English for foreign students, will suffice.

Directions—Insert 'shall' or 'will' in the following.

Don't worry, I ——— have plenty of time.

In the best of today's tests of foreign languages, a careful distinction is made between problems involving the colloquial language and those calling for sensitivity to written style. Directions for the former often simply ask the examinee to select the alternative that sounds most like what a native speaker of the language would say. The contexts are written to reflect colloquial usage, including contractions, short answers (even 'sentence fragments', where these would be normal), and other phenomena of the spoken language, and the lexicon is that of everyday conversation.

'Did you tell the postman you didn't get the letter?'

'No, I don't know ——— he could do about it.'

(A) that (B) what (C) how (D) where

(4) 'Languages are different'

Modern linguistics may be said to have begun when scholars turned their attention away from the familiar European languages and attempted to describe those 'exotic' tongues with no grammatical relationship to Western languages, particularly Latin and Greek. Not only did they learn that the non-Indo-European languages could not be analyzed in terms of the traditional grammatical categories but—more importantly for the present discussion—they came to understand the futility of attempting word-for-word translations 'since it was realized that the full meaning of a word in one language can rarely be matched by a word in another language, and that therefore no translation is ever fully satisfactory'. (Moulton, 1961, p. 89.)

Once it came to be recognized that ability to translate elegantly is a special skill quite different from ability to speak, understand, read and write, translation lost favour as a teaching and a testing device save at a very advanced level. Thus it is that translation plays little or no part in the best of the modern language tests of general proficiency, where both problems and alternative solutions are kept in the target language.[1]

(5) 'Teach the language, not about the language'

This cardinal principle of applied linguistics simply means that in language instruction, grammar should be used as a means to an end, not as an end in itself. Teaching the student to make statements about the language is a wasteful activity that deprives him of precious time that he ought to spend learning to imitate the forms of the new language correctly and practising them until they become automatic. On the beginning level some simple grammatical explanation may occasionally be useful in facilitating understanding of new patterns. Thereafter, however, the student should be asked only to manipulate the patterns, not explain them.

As applied to language testing, the principle obviously is to *test the language, not about the language*. That is to say, language tests should be designed to evoke specimens of language or other direct responses to language, not to elicit discussion *about* language, such as by requiring the examinee to identify parts of speech or sentence types. Similarly, most linguistically oriented test writers avoid item types which ask the student to express his feelings about the meaning of a pattern. They would for that reason tend to reject the following kind of test problem:

> Directions to the Examiner—The sentence shall be read by the examiner in two ways: (a) with the normally stressed falling tune (the glide-down), and (b) with the emphatic tune, stressing the pronoun *he*. The examiner then asks the candidate [to explain] the difference in meaning.
> He 'thinks it's 'green. (Glide-down.)
> "He thinks it's green. (Emphatic stress on *he*.)

[1] Another reason why translation is generally avoided in modern language testing is directly related to Principle Number 1. Inasmuch as 'knowing' a foreign language involves automatic use of a new set of habits, it is appropriate that the test keep the examinee working with the new habits only, rather than forcing him to shift repeatedly from one set of habits to another, as by presenting lexical items or sentences in the target language and asking for their equivalents in the background language.

3. A LINGUISTIC VIEW OF THE CURRENT FOREIGN LANGUAGE TESTS

As one reviews the current standard tests of foreign languages from a linguistic point of view, one's feelings are apt to be very similar to those one has when examining modern foreign language textbooks in the aggregate: encouragement over the best of them, discouragement with most. For it is unquestionably true that the test writers as a whole have been slow in adopting the new principles. For example, an examination of the reviews in the latest edition of the *Mental Measurements Yearbook* (Buros, 1965) reveals that a large proportion of the most recent tests still emphasize grammar, vocabulary, and reading and make at least some use of translation in measuring these skills, even in objective items—shortcomings which, thankfully, the reviewers are quick to note.[1]

On the other hand, a few of the most carefully prepared of today's language tests do show that the writers were deeply conscious of the 'linguistic method' by their adherence to certain characteristic features of that method—the features pointed out in our previous section. That is, in these tests a distinction is maintained between the conversational and the formal-written varieties of the language; there are strong auditory comprehension components and sometimes even an attempt to measure oral production; test problems employ only the target language; and the problems in some cases have obviously been selected on the basis of contrastive analysis.

Application of such linguistic principles would surely seem to lead to improved language tests, especially when these tests are used as placement instruments or measures of achievement for language programs based on the new methods of instruction. Yet it must in all fairness be conceded that even when linguistics has been applied to testing, it has been applied unevenly: none of the current tests can, it is submitted, be said to reflect any sort of *unified theory* or to apply linguistic theory or practice with equal rigor throughout the test. (What panel of 'theoretical linguists' would, for instance, approve of the bases on which lexical and grammatical items are selected in the current language tests?) Moreover, although there is a considerable body of *psychometric* data on the language tests prepared by the most

---

[1] The following excerpts from the reviews are characteristic:

'It seems somewhat strange that a new test in this area fully follows traditional form and fails to reflect the language study approach based on modern linguistics. Oral-aural skills are not assessed by the tests, and no indication is given that any efforts to do so are being made in any supplementary tests.

'In the over-emphasis on meaning . . . we find the most disappointing aspect of the test, an aspect which reveals the strong influence of the popular fallacy that a language is its vocabulary.'

'In certain respects . . . the test [seems] to retain features of the traditional grammar-translation approach.'

responsible of the testing services, there has been relatively little *psycholinguistic* research into these measures. (What evidence do we really have, for example, to justify the neat division of most language tests into listening-speaking-reading-writing-grammar components as the most accurate and efficient means of evaluating language 'competence'?)

There appear to the writer to be three principal explanations for the current state of the linguistics of foreign language proficiency and achievement testing.

First, as pointed out earlier, the linguistic principles we apply in testing have derived very largely from our methods of teaching languages, and thus the tests reflect the imperfect state of applied linguistics and our very incomplete understanding of the processes of second-language acquisition.

Second, it is unfortunately the case that relatively few linguists have chosen to involve themselves deeply and directly in the problems of language testing. And in the instances where linguists trained in educational measurement *have* interested themselves in language testing, very often that interest has focused upon the measurement of language aptitude rather than general proficiency or achievement, though to be sure the knowledge gained from research into the former may in time make very substantial contributions to the latter.

Third, for very practical reasons most of the standard foreign language tests developed in recent years have been designed for inter-mediate- or advance-level learners, not for beginners, and many of the abilities that apparently must be measured at the more advanced stages of learning—e.g. ability to comprehend and produce extended stretches of speech and writing, sensitivity to oral and written style[1]— have not yet been subjected to much systematic linguistic analysis. Worth mentioning, in this connexion, is the very recent development of great interest, at least in the United States, in tests to measure children's command of English as a second language or dialect. The development of such tests—on the elementary level and necessarily designed for subjects at a pre-reading stage—would appear to offer the perfect opportunity for the systematic application of linguistics, and from the instruments so developed might very well come know-ledge and techniques of the greatest value for other kinds of language testing.

---

[1] Thus, for example, 'At the advanced level [of reading a foreign language] are the contextual abstraction of partial meanings and extended meanings of lexical items in their full vigor, the stylistic variations that are readily understood by native readers, the full range of sequence signals and organization, and the handling of longer paragraphs and series of paragraphs into lexically unified selections.' (Lado, 1961, p. 232.)

4. SUMMARY AND CONCLUSIONS

Despite the obvious shortcomings of today's language tests, the writer does not mean to end this brief discussion on a negative note. We have seen how a small number of the recent foreign language tests do utilize linguistic principles to about the fullest extent that the current state of the science will allow. That these tests represent only a minority of the total number now in circulation should not disturb us unduly; it would doubtless be safe to say that in *any* field of educational testing the percentage of really first-rate instruments available at any time is never large. Moreover, the history of linguistically oriented testing is, after all, still a relatively brief one. The important point is that in language testing, as in language teaching, the critical turn in the road has already been reached, and the leaders have set off—with varying degrees of skill and confidence—in a new direction. The importance of linguistic principles to language measurement is now sufficiently well established that henceforth all language tests will inevitably be judged in large part by their linguistic soundness. And as linguists provide us with more complete analyses of languages and with deeper insights into the nature of second-language acquisition, we may anticipate that these findings will surely be incorporated into our measures of foreign language competence.

4

The Psychology of Language Testing

J. B. Carroll

A psychological or educational test is a procedure designed to elicit certain behavior from which one can make inferences about certain characteristics of an individual. The procedure may be very informal, as when it consists of a question that has suddenly come to the mind of an examiner, or it may be very formal, as when it consists of a series of thoroughly edited and validated 'test items' printed in an examination booklet and administered to the examinees under carefully controlled conditions, including a specified time limit for the performance. It may be very brief, as when it consists of the measurement of a single reaction time, let us say, or it may be very extensive, as when it consists of a three-hour oral examination administered by a panel of examiners. The characteristics that it is designed to test may vary from inherited capacities or predispositions (as when one attempts to measure 'native intelligence' as much as possible unaffected by learning experiences) to acquire knowledges or skills (as in the case of the usual educational examinations). But throughout all these variations, the essential purpose remains the same. In a sense, a test is an experiment in human behavior. It is therefore not without justification that this book on language testing should include a consideration of its psychology— that is, the psychological principles underlying the elicitation of language behavior and the interpretation of that behavior.

I. LANGUAGE BEHAVIOR

Ideally, a complete psychology of language testing would entail a satisfactory theory of language behavior. The relatively undeveloped state of the theory of language behavior will limit us, however, to tentative hypotheses and speculations. For conciseness, I will list and discuss a series of propositions about language behavior that need to be taken into account in language testing.

(1) A 'language' can be described in terms of a system of 'rules' for generating utterances (or written representations thereof) that will be accepted by the members

Reference is made to this chapter on p. 14 of the Introduction.

of a given speech community as 'correct' or 'grammatical' and understood by them as having a possible semantic interpretation.

Let us look at this proposition more closely. It states that a language *can be described in terms of a system of rules.* Such description is the task of the linguist. But the linguist is concerned only with the formal analysis of a language; one hesitates to *equate* a language to a system of rules, because the language resides somehow in the collective competence of the speakers of the language—speakers who learn and use the language without necessarily becoming aware of the 'rules' by which the language can be described in its phonological-orthographic, syntactical, and semantic components. This is true, at least, if we take a 'rule' to be a description of some invariant property of a language system that can be stated and communicated so that a person who does not know the rule can henceforth 'know' it and follow it.

Proposition (1) states also that the rules by which a language can be described will generate utterances that will be accepted by the members of a speech community as 'correct' or 'grammatical'. But speakers of a language can do this only by virtue, again, of some 'competence' they have acquired and internalized. We must therefore make a psychological interpretation of what 'language competence' is; see proposition (2).

Finally, proposition (1) refers to the fact that members of a speech community will understand grammatical utterances as 'having a possible semantic interpretation'. This implies that members of the speech community have a competence such that even if an utterance contains terms with unknown semantic reference, or is logically false, or is ambiguous, or is so complex that it cannot be immediately comprehended, they will nevertheless recognize it as an utterance which is properly within the scope of utterances possible in the language and which could be understood if it were explicated by further utterances, by appropriate situational contexts, or by detailed study. Again, however, we need to make a psychological analysis of the competence that permits this.

(2) *'Competence' in a language consists of a series of interrelated habits (acquired stimulus-response mechanisms) which can be described in terms of stated 'rules'.*

'Habit' is a somewhat old-fashioned term that can easily be misinterpreted, but there is no better one, in psychology, to refer to an acquired (learned) disposition of an individual to respond in a certain way (or class of ways) when an appropriate stimulus configuration gets presented either externally (i.e. through sensory receptors located in the body) or internally (i.e. through usually covert mental mechanisms

that can be presumed to take place solely in the individual's central
nervous system), or with some combination of external and internal
stimulation. A large part of the subject matter of psychology is concerned with the nature of habits and with how they are learned and
forgotten.

We say that competence in a language consists of a series of *interrelated* habits because (1) the fact that a certain set of habits pertains
to a given language system, e.g. English, French, or Swahili, or even
to a subsystem like 'educated formal English in the dialect of Mississippi'
or 'colloquial Iraqi Arabic', means that they are in some measure
segregated in the behavior of the individual—not only from other
language systems that he may possess, but also from non-linguistic
systems of habits, such as, for instance, the ability to play the piano—
and (2) any language system itself involves an interrelatedness of the
corresponding habits. Expanding on this latter point, we must note,
for example, that even the utterance of a single word in a language
entails phonological habits that are at least partially similar to those
involved in the utterance of many other words in the language.
Further, when a given word is uttered in a sentence, a considerable
assembly of grammatical habits similar to those involved in the
utterance of other sentences is also called upon. Current linguistic
theory has shown that the rules by which certain grammatical phenomena can be described can be arranged in an ordered manner; e.g.
that in generating sentences according to transformational rules, a
passive transformation rule must be applied before a question-forming
transformation. There is evidence (Miller, 1962) that the ordering of
these rules is in some way represented in behavior, and if this should
prove to be the case after the further investigations that are now being
conducted in many psychological laboratories, it would add weight to
the notion that language habits are interrelated.

When we speak of 'habit', we mean to imply no narrow interpretation that would suggest that language users draw on tight connexions
between stimulus and response such that one and only one 'response'
can be made in a given situation. The habits of language users only
rarely concern highly routinized sequences of 'memorized' utterances
or parts of utterances (e.g. set phrases like 'in point of fact', or mottos
like *honi soit qui mal y pense*). In principle, they refer to relations between
broad classes of stimuli and broad classes of responses. For example,
the construction of sentences from 'noun phrases' and 'verb phrases'
can be said to represent a habit. Likewise the construction of sentences
in which the number of the noun phrase agrees with that of the verb
phrase may be thought of as depending upon a habit.

The stimulus-response mechanisms represented by language habits
must in fact be enormously complicated. If we are restricted to the

task of trying to elicit language behavior only through the presentation of external stimulation, there are many language habits that are extremely difficult to call forth except in trivial, uninteresting ways. For example, suppose we have the task of determining whether an individual has a habit corresponding to the 'nominative absolute' construction in English (as underlies the first clause of the sentence 'My car being in the garage for repairs, I had to take the subway'). We could, of course, ask the subject to repeat this sentence, and he would probably be able to do so, but he could equally well repeat a sentence with a garbled nominative absolute construction like 'For repairs being my car at the garage' and we would still have no evidence that he possessed a habit corresponding to the nominative absolute conconstruction.[1] We might ask him to talk freely for five minutes, but it is relatively unlikely that he would use the nominative absolute construction in such a free discourse, even if he possessed this construction, simply because it is not a very common form. Nevertheless, there must be *some* conditions (i.e. *some* stimulus configuration) which elicit the nominative absolute construction whenever anybody knowing this construction actually uses it spontaneously. The difficulty of eliciting such habits presents an acute problem for the language tester, for he would like to arrange a test containing precisely those conditions so that they will call forth the nominative absolute construction in anybody who possesses the requisite habit structure, and *not* call forth that construction in anybody who happens *not* to have that habit structure. In the present state of knowledge, we simply do not know enough about the stimulus configuration that elicits the nominative absolute construction in spontaneous language behavior; in making tests, we will have to use various expedients to create artificial conditions for the elicitation of such a construction, e.g. presentation of a fill-in item such as 'My car ———— at the garage for repairs, I had to take the subway'.

There are, of course, many language habits whose elicitation is not so difficult. If we want to find out whether a child can pronounce a certain sound properly, we might ask him to repeat or to read aloud a sentence containing that sound. If we want to know whether a person knows the meaning of the word 'anonymous' we might ask him to select the one sentence, from an array, in which the word is used properly and meaningfully. In general, phonological, orthographic, and lexical habits seem to be easier to elicit than grammatical habits. But we will say more about this later.

---

[1] Repetition tasks have sometimes been used to test the possession of certain grammatical habits in very young children, or in mental retardates (Lenneberg, Nichols, and Rosenberger, 1964). A child who does not possess the requisite grammatical habit will, it appears, not be able to repeat the sentence properly.

(*3*) *The actual manifestation of linguistic competence (considered as the posses-sion of a certain set of interrelated habits) in behavior may be called linguistic performance, and is affected by a large number of non-linguistic variables.*
In the extreme case, a person might possess a perfectly adequate set of language habits—'the ability to speak and understand English', say—and yet not be able or willing to speak on a given occasion. Perhaps he is a schizophrenic, out of touch with reality, or an aphasic, with a brain lesion affecting his speech centres, or a person whose articulatory mechanism is paralyzed. But even in the case of the normal person, linguistic competence must be regarded as something quite different from linguistic performance. The person may have a temporary block whereby he forgets a certain word (the 'tip-of-the-tongue phenomenon' recently studied by Brown and McNeill, 1966). Or the person to whom he is speaking may embarrass him to the extent that he stumbles and stutters in his speech. When there are no such interfering conditions, there will still inevitably be variation in the degree to which the speaker's utterances conform, in a strict sense, to his underlying competence: he may start a sentence and cut it off in midstream, produce a chance inaccurate pronunciation, or through inattention say a word he did not intend to say. Likewise, in hearing or reading language material, the individual's actual degree of comprehension on a particular occasion may not measure up to what he is capable of.

The language tester must bear this distinction between competence and performance very carefully in mind, for he must decide whether he is interested in testing competence, performance, or some combina-tion thereof. If he is testing ability in a foreign language, it is most likely that he is interested in competence: he wants to find out to what degree the examinee has acquired the set of habits that corresponds to the competence of a native speaker of the language in question. If he is testing the attainments of a person in his native language, he may be interested not so much in competence, but rather in performance—e.g. in the ability to give a public speech or the ability to use a wide variety of styles in writing. There may be some situations in which the language tester is interested *solely* in performance apart from compe-tence—e.g. in a test of fluency of association in which the concern is with how rapidly the individual can give the opposites of a list of adjectives. Indeed, from a psychological point of view there is some difficulty in distinguishing between competence and performance. If 'competence' is a matter of whether a habit is present in the indivi-dual, 'performance' is partly a matter of the 'strength' of the habit—that is, the inferred degree to which the habit can be elicited, the rapidity of responses based upon it, and the extent to which it resists interference from other habits.

The single most important problem confronted by the language tester is that he cannot test competence in any direct sense; he can measure it only through manifestations of it in performance. Inevitably, therefore, there is the danger that non-linguistic variables in performance will mask the manifestations of competence. Accurate measurements of competence are only an ideal to be approached by various means—experimental and statistical—of controlling the sources of variation in performance that are independent of competence.

(4) There are individual differences, both in competence and performance variables, that may be a function of either constitutional or experiential variables.

Fundamentally, the language tester is interested in measuring competence and performance variables in individuals, either for themselves or with reference to certain standards that may have been established. The child's competence and performance with his native language are a function of age, heredity, and maturation to the extent that his neurological and psychomotor constitution is ready to permit progress at any point, and they are a function of age and environment to the extent that he has been exposed to learning experiences that permit him to acquire competence and performance facility. The relative extent to which acquired competence is a function of constitutional or of experiential variables is a matter that has been a concern of psychologists for many years; it would appear that both kinds of variables have substantial weight in the determination of the individual's competence and ability in performance. But the language tester *qua* language tester need not be concerned with the degree to which his measurements reflect hereditary differences; his first task is to develop procedures that will validly measure the degree of competence possessed by an individual, regardless of how he acquired it.

Neither in competence nor in performance variables are individual difference variables 'unitary'. That is to say, neither language competence nor language performance varies along a single dimension. It is not the case, for example, that an individual who has a degree of competence in one part of the vocabulary of a language will necessarily have a corresponding competence in another part of the vocabulary, nor will he necessarily have a comparable degree of competence in the syntax or the phonology of the language. Ultimately, the individual's competence in a language must be assessed by considering each particular habit belonging to that language, for it is possible that any particular habit may have been acquired (or not acquired) independently of any other habit. As a practical matter, however, it would be impossible to attempt the assessment of each particular habit in a language; we can only sample from the array of possible habits.

Empirically, it is found that many language competencies tend to occur together in individuals who have learned a certain language. For example, if we consider native speakers of English of, say, age 10 or above and with at least 'normal' intelligence, we would find that if a speaker has competence in any given grammatical feature of English, he would also have competence in a large number of other grammatical features, simply because they are all high-frequency phenomena in English learned by nearly every native speaker. Similarly such a population would almost uniformly have competence in the phonological features of English as well as in most of the morphophonemic and semantic aspects of some thousands of high-frequency English words. But even so, some variations in competence could be observed in this population. Some highly educated people would have 'vocabularies' of more than 100,000 words, while the vocabularies of other less privileged individuals might be restricted to something like 10,000 words or less.[1] There might also be some variations in phonological and grammatical competences, associated partly with dialect variations and partly with differences in level of education, native capacity, and other factors. Actually, except for the case of vocabulary development, we have little research available to indicate how much variation in language competence occurs in the population defined as above. Lacking such research, the language tester would do well to sample different areas—phonological, syntactical, and lexical—in order to obtain a satisfactory profile of an individual's competence in his native language.

The problem of different areas of competence becomes much more acute in dealing with a second or foreign language, where the experiences of learners are likely not to be as homogeneous as those of native language learners, and where various well-known difficulties interpose themselves in learning—the interference of the native language, the slow progress due to the student's lack of time or motivation for study, etc. Furthermore, since learning a second language often makes much more use of written material than does learning a native language (where reading is rarely started until the spoken language is fairly well mastered), competence in spoken and written aspects may develop somewhat independently, and these competences must be separately assessed. It is also much more important to observe the distinction between productive and receptive skills because progress in these two aspects may not proceed *pari passu* as it ordinarily does in the native language. It is quite possible for a competence to relate specifically to production and not to reception, or vice versa.

[1] Measuring vocabulary size is a complicated problem that must take account of the nature of the word units to be counted, the kind of competence tested, etc. On this point, see Lorge and Chall (1963).

For example, cases are reported in which a learner cannot discriminate two foreign language phonemes spoken by others and yet is able to produce them in a distinctive fashion; the reverse case is even more frequent. Thus, productive and receptive skills must be separately tested because they are less likely to be highly correlated than in the case of native language competences.

Whether one is testing competence in a native language or in a foreign language, it is useful to start from a classification of different areas of language competence in which individual differences are to be sought and measured. Such a classification is presented in Table 1. Thus it becomes possible to pinpoint different kinds of language competences and specify them in detail. For example, under 'lexicon' it would be useful to have an explicit list of the some thousands of forms for which one might wish to test competence. An unabridged dictionary might constitute a good starting point for this enterprise, together with word frequency counts, spelling lists, and such other reference works that would help in the construction of tests. Under 'grammar', the desideratum would be a complete list of the grammatical features of the language; we know, however, that thus far linguists have been able to produce only approximations to such lists.

One of the 'factors' of individual differences that has appeared most clearly and consistently in factor-analytic studies of psychological tests is the V or 'verbal knowledge' factor (Carroll, 1941; French, 1951), or, as it is called in British studies, the 'verbal-educational factor' (Vernon, 1950). To a large extent, this probably represents general linguistic competence, in that it measures the extent to which the individual has acquired the lexicon and the more sophisticated grammatical features of his native language.

It is not as easy to make a systematic chart of linguistic performance variables, because psychologists have not yet devised an adequate taxonomy of behavior. If we look at the evidence from factor-analytic studies again, however, we find the suggestion that linguistic performance varies with respect to the following dimensions:

(1) Speed of response—how rapidly can a given response or series of responses be made?

(2) Diversity of response—given a cue, how many different responses appropriate to the cue can the subject give?

(3) Complexity of information processing—at what level of complexity can the individual process linguistically-coded information?

(4) Awareness—to what extent is the individual aware of the features underlying his linguistic competence?

It would appear that these dimensions can apply differentially to various aspects of linguistic competence—phonology, lexicon, and grammar.

		Phonology and Orthography	Lexicon		Grammar	
			Morphemes, Words, Idioms	Semantic and Grammatical Components of Lexicon	Morphology and Syntax	Semantic Components
Spoken Language	Receptive Skills (Listening)	Phoneme recognition and discrimination; ability to discriminate words or phrases differing in one phoneme or distinctive feature [List phoneme pairs to be discriminated]	Recognition of lexical elements as belonging to the language [List lexicon]	Recognition of semantic and grammatical meanings (i.e. word class assignments) of lexical elements	Recognition	Understanding — of morphological and syntactical features and associated phonology [List]
	Productive Skills (Speaking)	Phoneme production; ability to produce phonemes or allophonic variants in word forms or phrases, with accuracy at either phonemic or phonetic level [List phonemes of language with variants]	Ability to produce lexical elements fitting semantic and grammatical specifications		Ability to produce	In appropriate contexts — Morphological and syntactical features with appropriate phonology

Written Language			
Receptive Skills (Reading)	Recognition of the graphemic symbols of the language, with (as appropriate) ability to name them and give their sounds [List graphemes]	Above, plus recognition of meanings and pronunciation of written forms (including special graphemic symbols, abbreviations, etc.) [List]	Above, plus recognition of special grammar-related conventions of the written language, such as punctuation, capitalization, certain spelling changes, etc. [List such conventions]
Productive Skills (Writing)	Ability to write (by hand or other method) the graphemes of the language, state their customary ordering [List any details not covered above]	Spelling	As for receptive skills, plus ability to produce written conventions in appropriate contexts

TABLE 1. Chart of linguistic competences to be filled out for a language system

But since the use of language in ordinary situations calls upon all these aspects, we must further recognize that linguistic performance also involves the individual's capability of mobilizing his linguistic competences and performance abilities in an integrated way, i.e. in the understanding, speaking, reading, or writing of connected discourse.

Table 2 is a tentative schematization of these linguistic performance abilities, based largely on factor-analytic investigations (French, 1951; French, Ekstrom, and Price, 1963; Carroll, 1941, 1962). As in the case of Table 1, the suggestion is that a complete profile of the individual's linguistic performance abilities in any language, whether native or acquired, must take account of all these possibly separate dimensions. It must, of course, be recognized that linguistic performances depend crucially upon underlying competences; performance cannot be expected when the underlying competence is absent. Nevertheless, there appear to be individual differences in language performances even among individuals of approximately equal linguistic competence. At the present time we have very little scientific information about the etiology of these individual differences, and even the evidence for their existence is sparse.

While the emphasis of the preceding few pages has been on the desirability of measuring separate aspects of linguistic competence and performance in order to obtain a complete assessment of the individual's knowledge and skill in a language, from a practical point of view it may often suffice to construct tests that measure only integrated performance based on competence. For example, a general test of proficiency in a foreign language is often found to yield just as good validity when its items are complex, each drawing upon a wide sample of linguistic competences, as when each item has been contrived to tap competence in one and only one specific feature of the foreign language. Psychologists in the U.S. Army constructed two pictorial auditory comprehension tests, each measuring the examinee's ability to identify, in a multiple-choice format, pictures described by spoken sentences. One test had items designed to test the examinee's ability to discriminate sentences on the basis of carefully prescribed linguistic elements known to be difficult for English-speaking learners of the foreign language in question (similar to those recommended by Lado, 1961, p. 212); the other simply presented a more or less random assortment of pictures and sentences that appeared to be intuitively good test items but that had no specific linguistic rationale other than that they incorporated fairly complex sentences requiring considerable lexical and grammatical knowledge for their understanding. The latter test proved to have validity at least equal to, if not superior to, that of the former test. Apparently the extent to which a language test should attempt to measure specific aspects of competence depends upon

	Phonology	Lexicon	Morphology and Syntax	Integrated language performance
Speed of response	Articulation ability (Speed and accuracy of speech sound production)	Naming facility (Speed of responding with the names of things when presented in rapid succession)	Expressional fluency (Ability to compose rapidly sentences fitting given grammatical requirements)	Oral speaking fluency
Diversity of response	'Word fluency' (Ability to recall words with given phonetic-orthographic characteristics)	Ideational fluency (Ability to call up names or ideas fitting given semantic characteristics)		Listening comprehension
Complexity of Information Processing	Auditory memory for speech sounds or sequences of sounds	Abstract reasoning ability (Ability to process complex linguistically coded information)		Reading comprehension (and speed)
Awareness of Linguistic Competence	(No pertinent evidence)	Awareness of the structure of the lexicon; facility in giving opposites, superordinates, etc.	Grammatical sensitivity (Ability to find analogous grammatical elements in sentences)	Writing ability

TABLE 2. Suggested chart of linguistic performance abilities (all based on underlying competences)

3

its purpose—that is, the extent to which there is need for diagnosis of specific skills as opposed to a generalized, overall assessment of proficiency.

At the same time, it would be possible for the test maker to deceive himself as to the scope of the skills measured by a test. A frequent error made in foreign language proficiency test construction is to develop tasks or items that, instead of measuring general competence, depend very largely upon vocabulary knowledge, such that a person who can recognize word meanings but who knows little about the grammar can reason out the meanings of sentences from words alone (helped, sometimes, by lexical cues in the distractors) and thus make 'correct' responses. One can verify that this has happened by seeing whether a native speaker of the target language can answer the items correctly even when grammatical cues such as inflectional endings and word arrangements have been eliminated.

2. THE TAXONOMY OF LANGUAGE TEST TASKS

For the purpose of gaining a clear notion of the possible diversity of language testing tasks and of examining what kinds of competences and performances they can measure, it is helpful to develop a taxonomy or classification scheme. This is done here in such a way as to embrace both tasks designed to measure native language proficiency and tasks designed to measure proficiency or achievement in a foreign language.

This taxonomy is intended to apply to tasks at the level of the single question or 'item'. Such an item presents instructions and relevant stimuli that are expected to elicit behavior, on the part of the examinee, that can be 'scored' or otherwise evaluated. (Actually, of course, each task can be broken down into subtasks such as 'listen to the stimulus', 'mark an X', etc., but the intention here is to consider integrated task units. A test may consist of a substantial number of task units or items; it is often the case that a series of items have the same structure and therefore are controlled by a common set of instructions.)

Upon analysis, language testing tasks can be classified into four major categories:

I. *Tasks specified solely by instructions requiring language production.*

Any testing task requires instructions as to what the examinee is to do; this remark applies equally to all four categories of tasks, except that certain tasks in Categories II, III, and IV may have an internal structure such that many examinees will induce the nature of the instructions. But it is not safe to assume that the examinee will infer the instructions from the test items themselves; in fact, the examinee may make the wrong inference and thus perform (even 'correctly') not the task that the examiner intended him to perform, but some other task. Not only is it always important to give clear instructions as to the nature of the task; it is usually desirable to give easy examples of the tasks to be presented in the test, and sometimes to give examinees extensive practice in performing such tasks so that they will have a clear idea of what is wanted when they get to the test proper. This is particularly important in the case of examinees who have had little previous experience with tests.

Language tasks in Category I are those which are specified solely by general instructions to produce certain kinds of language performances. The specifications need to include:

A. The language in which the performance is to be made: the native language or a foreign language, and where appropriate, the particular variety of the language (e.g. standard *v.* dialect forms, educated *v.* informal and colloquial language).

B. The modality: spoken or written. If written, further specification as to the orthographic standard to be followed, the quality of handwriting, etc., may be needed.

C. The class of linguistic responses desired:

(1) *Phonological level:* 'Speak a series of syllables illustrating all the sounds of the language'; 'Create nonsense syllables or nonsense words that would be acceptable in the language'.

(2) *Orthographic level:* 'Say (or write) the alphabet of the language.'

(3) *Word level:* 'Say all the different words you can think of in the language in the time allowed'; 'Give words that start with the letter *R* and end in the letter *P*'; 'Say words that begin with the sound k.'

(4) *Sentence level:* 'Give examples of sentences containing *if* clauses'; 'Give examples of sentences that might be used to express astonishment.'

(5) *Connected discourse level:* 'Give a five-minute talk on a topic of your own choosing'; 'Write an essay on the advantages of schooling.'

II. *'Single-stimulus' tasks not requiring language production.*

A chart of the possible variations of tasks in Category II is presented in Table 3. In this and similar tables to follow, the reader must consider the various types of test items that can be constructed by suitable combinations of stimuli and tasks.

By a 'single stimulus' we mean a stimulus which in some sense is to be regarded as a unity for the purposes of the task; i.e. the examinee is to respond to the whole of the stimulus. The meaning

Stimulus (in language to be tested)		Task
Modality	Complexity	
Spoken Written	(a) Single phoneme, letter or character (b) Morpheme or pseudo-morpheme (c) Word (d) Phrase or clause (e) Sentence (f) Longer discourse	1. Evaluate: (a) Is it an element of the language? (Or, in the case of 'pictorial stimuli', is it coded in the language?) (b) Frequency, either in general, or in specified contexts (c) Acceptability in terms of (1) phonological rules (2) syntactical rules (3) orthography (d) Intelligibility: can it have a semantic interpretation? (e) Truth (by contextual fit with general knowledge, logic, etc.)
Pictorial: (Any presentation of non-linguistic experience)		2. Classify with respect to: (a) grammatical function (form class, gender, etc.) (b) semantic classes 3. Act upon the stimulus: (a) Follow directions contained in the stimulus, by some form of physical action (drawing, manipulating objects, moving in a certain way, etc.) (b) Physiological indicators (e.g. galvanic skin reflex)

TABLE 3. A taxonomy of language test tasks:
single stimulus tasks not requiring language production

of the term becomes clear in contrast to 'multiple-stimulus tasks'
(Category IV, see below) in which the examinee has to compare
two or more separate stimuli that are taken as unities for the purpose
of the test.

We classify as 'not requiring language production' any task where the examinee does not have to produce an actual sample of language performance containing one or more linguistic elements. Instead, his response can be made 'non-linguistically'—that is, by some sort of indication or action whose nature will reveal his linguistic competence or performance characteristics. This indication may be a choice among alternatives that are presented, a voluntary physical action, or even an involuntary response that can be observed only by special instrumental techniques (e.g. the psychogalvanic reflex). (When an involuntary response is to be elicited, the need for task instructions may decrease.)

Usually, the stimulus in Category II tasks is linguistic—either spoken or written. It can, however, be non-linguistic, requiring no language production, and yet the task can depend in some way on language competence. For example, the examinee could be asked to indicate the gender of the commonest name, in French, of a pictured object. (It is of course true that a covert kind of language production, whereby the examinee thinks silently of the word in question, may be involved here, but we are concerned only with the external structure of the task in terms of what is presented and what is actually evaluated.)

As indicated in Table 3, the complexity of the stimulus, if it is linguistic, may range from a single sound or letter up to long connected discourse. This will be true also of the stimuli in Category III and IV tasks.

The instructions for Category II tasks must specify whether the examinee is to perform some sort of cognitive, evaluative task, or some action that is dictated by the stimulus itself. In any case he must be told when he may expect to hear the stimulus, how long it will last, and when he is to make his response; or, if it is a written or pictorial stimulus, he must be told where he may find the stimulus, and when and/or where he is to make his response. In many cases the instructions must specify what parts of the stimulus he is to give particular attention to.

Generally, the outcome of the performance is evaluated in terms of some known standards that have been arrived at by linguistic or psycholinguistic analysis. One 'scores' performance by noting whether the choices, evaluations, or actions made by the examinee are 'correct' with reference to these standards. In some cases, 'correctness' is a matter of degree; for example, in asking the examinee to judge the frequency with which some linguistic stimulus occurs in specified contexts, we would evaluate the judgement in terms of its discrepancy from pre-established norms.

Performance in some types of tasks is evaluated with reference to the rate at which the examinee is able to 'learn' to give a correct performance. If, for instance, the stimulus is a complicated set of written directions to be followed, performance could be evaluated in terms of how rapidly the subject can complete it, or how rapidly he could achieve correct performance after successive presentations ('trials') of the stimulus material.

III. 'Single-stimulus' tasks requiring language production.

A chart of the possible variations of tasks in Category III is presented in Table 4. The stimuli can be either auditory (spoken), written, or pictorial. The term 'pictorial' is used for convenience to refer to any non-linguistic stimulus that presents some sort of experience, or representation of experience, to the examinee. A 'picture' may be a still picture or a motion picture; it may be presented for a very short period of time (tachistoscopically) or for as long as the examinee will attend to it; it may be black-and-white or in colour; it may actually consist of any auditory, visual, tactual, kinesthetic, or even gustatory or olfactory stimulus that is non-linguistic and that is to be responded to linguistically by the examinee.

Since we are here concerned with the production of language, the instructions must (as in the case of Category I tasks) specify the language in which the response is to be produced, its modality (auditory or written), and its general characteristics (complexity, type, etc.). It may also be necessary to specify something about the stimulus— what language it is to be in, its modality, and its general characteristics, so that the examinee knows what to expect and what set to adopt in attending to it.

Again, the examinee's performance is to be evaluated in terms of the degree to which his language responses conform to certain pre-determined standards of correctness. Sometimes these evaluations may be made with perfect objectivity—as where the scorer (who may not even know the target language) merely has to compare the examinee's response with a 'key' and can make immediate and highly reliable binary judgements as to whether the response conforms to the key or not. Most often, however, the evaluation of language productions depends to a large extent upon the scorer's own discriminative capacities and upon his knowledge of the target language. In such cases, proper specification of procedures for scoring, and adequate selection and training of scorers, are essential. One must determine the reliability of scoring by comparing the evaluations of the scorers on independent occasions or by comparing the evaluations of independent scorers. When reliability is found to be low, the procedures for evaluation, or the basis on which the scorers are selected, or both, may have to be revised.

Stimulus			Response		Task
Language	Modality	Complexity	Language	Modality	

N (Native)	A (Auditory)	a. Single phoneme, letter or character	N (Native)	A (Auditory, spoken)	1. Reproduce stimulus
					2. Reproduce a learned response or answer
					3. Produce equivalent response
					   a. Synonym or other restatement
					   b. Translation equivalent
					   c. Paraphrase, summary, restatement
					4. Produce association
					   a. Free
					   b. Controlled (opposite, superordinate, linguistic transform, etc.)
					5. Produce grammatical transform of a specified type
					6. Produce name or other determinate label
					7. Produce a more extended free response (description, imaginative story, etc.)

		b. Morpheme or pseudo-morpheme			
F (Foreign)	W (Written)	c. Word	F (Foreign)	W (Written)	
		d. Phrase or clause			
		e. Sentence			
		f. Longer discourse			
P (Pictorial) (or any other representation of experience)					

TABLE 4. A taxonomy of language test tasks: single-stimulus tasks requiring language production

IV. '*Multiple-stimulus*' *tasks requiring comparative judgements rather than language production.* (See Table 5.)

The meaning of 'single stimulus' and 'multiple stimulus' will now, doubtless, become clearer to the reader. When a task involves multiple stimuli, it is one in which the examinee has to compare two or more stimuli (or the responses based on them) in order to draw some conclusion as to their relationship. When the stimuli are contrived so that the examinee's conclusion depends in some critical way upon his linguistic competence, such a task can be a powerful means of determining linguistic competence.

In many tasks, the several stimuli may be 'pre-classified', that is, they occur in two or more sets (but usually only two) between which the examinee is directed to make a particular comparison. The usual multiple-choice item exemplifies such a task. It presents a 'primary' stimulus ('lead' or 'stem'), and then several alternative 'secondary' stimuli; the examinee must determine which of the several alternative 'secondary' stimuli shows a specified relationship to the primary stimulus. This kind of item can be called a 'matching-to-sample' task when the relationship of identity or similarity is called for.

There are also tasks, however, where the stimuli are not 'pre-classified'—that is, no one of the stimuli is designated as the 'sample' or primary stimulus. The minimum number of such stimuli is three. The examinee is to find two or more stimuli that are the same, or one stimulus that is different, in some respect. Generalizing, we may say that the task is to classify the stimuli in some consistent manner. For example, it would be possible to present a task with five stimuli, which we may represent by the sequence A C B A B, such that the subject is expected to classify them as A, A; B, B; C.

Both the primary and the secondary stimuli, in tasks with two pre-classified sets, may be either auditory, written, or pictorial (in the generalized sense defined above); the combination pictorial-pictorial would not very likely be found in a language test, however. Likewise, language stimuli may be either in the native or a target language. For a test of ability in the native language, the following combinations are thus possible:

Primary Stimulus	Secondary Stimulus Set
Spoken, native language	Spoken, native language
Spoken, native language	Written, native language
Spoken, native language	Pictorial
Written, native language	Spoken, native language
Written, native language	Written, native language
Written, native language	Pictorial
Pictorial	Spoken, native language
Pictorial	Written, native language

Primary Stimulus (S_1)			Secondary Stimuli (S_2)				Task
Language	Modality	Complexity	Language	Modality	Complexity	Number	
N (Native)	A (Auditory spoken)	(As in Table 4)	N (Native)	A (Auditory spoken)	(As in Table 4)	1	Judge whether S_2 is same, different, higher or lower in terms of some ordering principle, as compared to S_1.
F (Foreign)	W (Written)		F (Foreign)	W (Written)		2 or more	Find S_2 which is the same, different, or in some other specified relationship to S_1.
	P (Pictorial)			P (Pictorial)			

Three or more stimuli, undifferentiated as to which is sample. Usually all would be in the same language and the same modality.

Find 2 or more stimuli that are the same.
Find the stimulus which is different as contrasted with the others.
Classify stimuli into groups.

TABLE 5. A taxonomy of language test tasks: multiple-stimulus tasks involving comparative judgement

For a 'pure' test of ability in a foreign language (i.e. one that uses no native language stimuli), the following combinations are possible:

Primary Stimulus	Secondary Stimulus Set
Spoken, foreign language	Spoken, foreign language
Spoken, foreign language	Written, foreign language
Spoken, foreign language	Pictorial
Written, foreign language	Spoken, foreign language
Written, foreign language	Written, foreign language
Written, foreign language	Pictorial
Pictorial	Spoken, foreign language
Pictorial	Written, foreign language

If one is willing to mix native and foreign language stimuli for a 'mixed' foreign language test, the following combinations are also available:

Primary Stimulus	Secondary Stimulus Set
Spoken, native language	Spoken, foreign language
Spoken, native language	Written, foreign language
Spoken, foreign language	Spoken, native language
Spoken, foreign language	Written, native language
Written, native language	Spoken, foreign language
Written, native language	Written, foreign language
Written, foreign language	Spoken, native language
Written, foreign language	Written, native language

Many language testers believe that 'mixed' tests should not be used in testing foreign language achievement or proficiency—at least not in the early stages of language instruction. The claim is that if good foreign language instruction is done chiefly in that foreign language, students are unprepared to perform mixed language tasks and cannot be judged fairly by their performance on them. I know of no research evidence to support this claim directly. Indirect evidence that would tend to deny the claim comes from a study by Lambert, Havelka, and Crosby (1958), who found that individuals who had learned French and English in 'separated' environments were not significantly different from individuals who had learned French and English in 'fused' environments in ability to make rapid translations from one language to the other. But of course these subjects were not at elementary stages of language learning. In any case, one argument against the 'pure' foreign language test that has both sets of stimuli in the foreign language is that this may put the examinee under 'double jeopardy'. This can be explained best by a simple example. Suppose we are interested in whether a subject knows the meaning of German *Gespräch*, and we ask him to tell which of the words *Zunge*, *Gestrüpp*, *Verachtung*, *Pfad*, and *Unterhaltung* is closest in meaning. Obviously he has to know the meanings of both *Gespräch* and *Unterhaltung* to accomplish this. If one believes that 'mixed' foreign language tests are undesirable, the problem of double jeopardy can often be avoided for multiple-stimulus tasks by providing that one of the stimulus sets be 'pictorial', the other of course, being in the foreign language.

3. INTERACTIONS OF TASK, COMPETENCE, AND PERFORMANCE

It is difficult to specify in advance, except possibly on an intuitive basis, what competences and performance abilities will be brought into action by a given task set on a language test or examination. When the task is non-specific, as it is when the instructions are so general as 'write a theme', 'give a speech', or 'summarize this essay', one may be assured that a great variety of competences and performance abilities can be involved even when the performance is crude and of relatively low quality. At the same time, such a task does not necessarily sample the whole range of competences and performance abilities set forth in Tables 1 and 2. With ingenuity, the examinee can easily avoid disclosing the gaps in his knowledge by using only those words and grammatical patterns that he thinks he knows, betraying, perhaps, only his poor spelling or pronunciation. The examinee may even be able to impress his examiners with the reproduction of some previously memorized passage, without really having mastered the words and patterns of the language underlying the passage.

If a language test is to measure particular kinds of underlying competence, its items must call upon language skills and knowledges in a critical way; each task must operate in such a way that performance cannot occur unless there is a particular element of underlying competence that can be specified in advance. The extent to which this can be true is a function of the nature of the task and the specificity of its elements. Consider the various categories set forth in this chapter.

I. *Tasks specified solely by instruction requiring language production.* This type of task cannot be critical in the sense defined above unless the instructions call for highly specific performances such as naming the letters of the alphabet. It is true that a finely written and grammatically correct free composition would reveal much of an inferential nature about an individual's language competence, but it would reveal only those elements that happen to be present in the production.

II. *Single-stimulus tasks not requiring language production.* This type affords much greater possibilities of assessing particular competences, especially those of a receptive nature, but this is true mainly when the stimuli are relatively simple—single morphs or letters, words, idiomatic phrases, and the like. When the stimuli are complex, as in lengthy sentences or connected discourse, one cannot pinpoint the nature of the difficulty when there is a failure in response. For example, in a task requiring the following of spoken directions, the examinee may know all the requisite vocabulary and grammar except for one critical element, and yet it may be difficult to infer from his performance exactly which element is critical for him. On the other hand, when the stimulus is simple, if all the examinee has to do is to make a binary choice (yes/no, or true/false), the inference as to underlying competence may be unreliable because his response may have resulted from 'guessing' rather than knowledge. Sometimes the problem of unreliability can be solved by repeated testing on different occasions, or by presentation of a sufficiently large number of similar tasks based on the same underlying element so that guessing effects will cancel out.

III. *Single-stimulus tasks requiring language production.* Because the task usually requires the examinee to produce a response that matches or transforms the original stimulus in some rather determinable way, it is usually possible to use this type of task to pinpoint presence or absence of particular competences, except when the production required is relatively free and lengthy—a description, an imaginative story based on a picture, and the like. But the subject's failure in the task may be due either to his failure to comprehend the stimulus or to his lack of ability to produce the desired response, or both. In foreign language testing, this type of task thus runs into the 'double jeopardy' problem when the stimulus is in the foreign language and a foreign language response is required. Performance will inevitably depend also on a number of non-linguistic factors (lapses of memory and the like); to control such factors in a testing situation, the garnering of repeated samples of behavior is a partial expedient.

IV. *Multiple-stimulus tasks involving comparative judgement.* The great advantage of this type of task is that by careful preparation of the several stimuli, it is possible to arrange matters so that the judgement that is required of the examinee *must* depend (aside from guessing factors) upon the presence or absence of a single specifiable competence. For example, in a task in which the subject must find which one of four alternatives is a synonym of the stimulus, or contains the same phoneme as the stimulus, a failure would surely betoken absence of the requisite knowledge, and repeated success not plausibly explained by guessing would surely indicate presence of the requisite competence. But all is not clear sailing. When the stimuli are complex, consisting of numerous words and expressions, the task can demand complex judgements depending on numerous different competences. Such tasks are suitable for tests of general proficiency, but they may be unsatisfactory for tests which attempt to provide diagnostic evidence as to the examinee's achievements or weaknesses.

4. CARRYING THE PSYCHOLOGY OF LANGUAGE TESTING INTO PRACTICE

What this chapter has tentatively offered is a groundwork for language testing, at least in broad outline. It is hoped that the point has been made that successful test construction depends upon a careful analysis of the nature of linguistic competence and performance in terms of what one wishes to test for and in terms of the stimulus conditions and task instructions under which one may elicit relevant and interpretable behavior. From the taxonomic tables presented here, one can derive a very large number of types of language testing tasks. In fact, my intention has been to present a taxonomy that is complete enough to include any language testing task whatsoever. Because of limitations of space, I have not been able to demonstrate this, and I have been unable to add the very large number of details that might have to be considered for any given item type. Perhaps, however, the skilful language tester will be able to work out these details for himself.

5

Attainment and Diagnostic Testing

Elisabeth Ingram

We shall first consider tests and their characteristics and, second, go on to discuss language and its implications for testing.

I. TEST CHARACTERISTICS

All tests are for a purpose. A test that is made up without a clear idea of what it is for, is no good. Tests have no intrinsic value in themselves. Tests are only worth having if they measure accurately (reliably) what you want them to measure (validity).

What we want to measure are people. Not their physical characteristics like height and weight, but how they compare with each other in some aspect of their behaviour, for instance, their ability to learn and use a foreign language.

The tests themselves are tested, to discover how closely they achieve their purpose—how reliable and valid they are. The objective format of tests, the layout, the item-answer techniques are imposed on test constructors because otherwise we could not test the tests.

The basic difference between tests and traditional examinations is that the latter may be reliable and valid, but they cannot easily be shown to be.

The shape of tests then is in the first place determined by the need to assess their reliability and validity (see Chapter 2).

Further, all tests are either predictive tests or attainment tests which may, themselves, be further subdivided. There are, in addition, diagnostic tests. The purpose of predictive tests is to predict future attainment, for instance, to predict that a child will probably be able to pass his O-level examination three years from now, or to pick out from a fourth-form class those who will be able to understand and perform the mathematical operations in the sixth-form syllabus, from those who probably will not be able to. Predictive tests assess learning ability, i.e. ability to learn school subjects. Intelligence tests or verbal reasoning tests assess general learning ability. Aptitude tests assess ability to learn a particular subject, for instance, mathematics or foreign languages. There are at least two published language learning aptitude tests,

Reference is made to this chapter on pp. 14–15 of the Introduction.

The Modern Language Aptitude Test (MLAT) by Carroll and Sapon, and the Language Aptitude Battery by Pimsleur (see chapter 6).

In this chapter we are concerned with attainment tests. These estimate the present achievement of the learner, what he knows and can do *now* irrespective of how he learnt it or what his learning ability is. Attainment tests compare people with each other on the basis of their knowledge or skill in a given subject. There are attainment tests in arithmetic, in English as a mother tongue, in modern languages, in English as a foreign language, and so on.

The content of an attainment test is given by the field which is tested. An attainment test in arithmetic is used to find out how good a child is in arithmetic, compared to other children of the same age and stage. The content of the test is given by the arithmetic syllabus; the operations and problems contained in the test are examples of the operations prescribed by the syllabus. But one cannot include everything. The content of a test is a *selection* from the whole field. The field may be the whole of the subject, e.g. arithmetic in general, or the English language in general or it may be some specified part of it, already selected and defined in a textbook or syllabus. In all cases the content of the test can only be a selection from the field. The test maker hopes to select good and representative items, so that the work done by an individual during the testing closely reflects the work he is capable of doing in that subject in general. The test should be a concentrated work sample; the behaviour required in the testing should be a slice of the behaviour required by the subject in general. It is the behaviour of the learner which is sampled. The content of the test is important, but only in so far as it allows the learners to display their skills fairly. 'Fairly' here means that the level of attainment reached during the testing is closely comparable with the level of attainment that the individual displays in general.

Testing, like teaching, must be planned backwards. Teachers must first have the answer to the question: 'What is it we want the learners to be able to do?' before they can plan a course of instruction. Similarly testers must be quite clear about the kind of behaviour they are trying to test. Very often the answer is: the classroom behaviour. This is specified by the textbook and the syllabus, and by the prevailing teaching practices and techniques. Tests for this purpose are often called achievement tests. Achievement tests measure what has actually been learned in relation to what is supposed to have been learned.

The relevance of such tests for conditions outside the school situation depends entirely on the relevance of the course to anything outside the school situation.

The behaviour the tester is asked to assess may be specified in terms of competence to do a job. The question may be: what are the mathematical skills that an engineer needs to build a bridge, or how much English does a student need to follow an English-medium course in textile engineering. Tests which set out to answer these questions are sometimes called proficiency tests. Proficiency tests must be based on a job-analysis to determine the required behaviour. Only when one has a fairly clear idea of the required behaviour can one hope to sample it adequately.

Some attainment tests are achievement tests, some are proficiency tests and some are a bit of both. The names of the tests do not help much since the labels are applied rather loosely.

The English Language Institute, Ann Arbor, Michigan, construct fairly pure achievement tests for their own internal purposes: to assess the standing and progress of the foreign students who are taught at the Institute. They also construct and run the Michigan Proficiency Test of English as a Foreign Language. This is a proficiency test which is used to answer questions such as: Does this individual command enough English to enter on his studies at the University of Michigan (or other universities) without doing additional courses in English? If not, how much teaching should he have first? The Test of English as a Foreign Language (TOEFL), a more recently instituted text published by the Educational Testing Service, is also a pure proficiency test, used to answer the question: how much of what he needs to know (for this or that purpose) does the candidate actually know.

The Davies Test administered by the British Council and the English Language Battery Test (ELBA: OUP) are also proficiency tests, designed to assess whether a candidate's command of English is adequate for higher education against a British background.

The tests of modern foreign languages constructed and run by the College Entrance Education Board (CEEB), of the U.S.A., for high-school leavers, are partly achievement and partly proficiency. The tests are based on what is common to a number of courses in a number of schools, and are used as entrance qualification by certain colleges.

Language achievement tests and language proficiency tests are not very different to look at, or even to take. The difference is mainly in the preliminary work undertaken by the test constructor. In achievement testing the field is given, the terminal behaviour is specified implicitly or explicitly, for the tester. In proficiency testing the tester usually has to do the job specification, the analysis of the desired behaviour, himself. Achievement testing is easier, proficiency testing more interesting. But in the end two achievement tests may be no more like each other than an achievement and a proficiency test.

There is a second variety of non-predictive tests—diagnostic tests. The diagnostic tests for reading are probably the best known of this kind of test (e.g. the Schonell, the Burt, the Yates). Achievement and proficiency tests usually give an over-all quantitative estimate, a numerical score which is higher or lower than the average or near it. Diagnostic tests also give quantitative assessments, for instance, a reading age, but they also give a more detailed picture of precisely what the learner is good or bad at. A backward reader may be poor at phonic analysis, or he may reverse letters or syllables, and the test will detect this because the reader will score low in the sections designed to bring out the various types of faults.

In language testing, a listening comprehension test will give a part score, which can be used to contribute to the total score indicating the over-all proficiency of a student. If the listening test is also to be used diagnostically, it must be designed to give information on specific points, for instance, sound discrimination: a sentence is spoken on the tape, and the student asked to distinguish certain sounds. The listener by matching the sentence with a written sentence or an appropriate picture will show whether he has heard the sentence:

The boy is watching the car.
The boy is washing the car.

If a student fails this or similar items, it can be inferred that he does not discriminate between the ʃ and the tʃ sounds. This inference may be of help diagnostically. (One item testing the contrast is not enough; one failure may be due to anything, even a moment's inattention.)

So diagnostic tests give qualitative as well as quantitative information. Achievement and proficiency tests answer the question *how much* does the learner know. Diagnostic tests answer the question *what* does he know. Apart from answering the *what* question, a diagnostic test should also be able to answer the *why* question. If the learner can't handle fricative sound contrasts, or the use of *do* in questions and negatives, or the correct choice of the continuous present, why can't he? But so far diagnostic language testing has not received much attention. There is one honourable exception, the diagnostic grammar test of English as a foreign language first developed in 1957 by A. L. Davis of the American University, Washington, and since revised by D. P. Harris. Some work is being done in the Department of Applied Linguistics at the University of Edinburgh and doubtless in other places as well, but so far nothing else has been published, to my knowledge.

It is perhaps unfair to ask the tester to provide the answer to the *why* question. This would amount to an explanation of error in language learning. There is no satisfactory theory of language learning, nor of failure of language learning. In my view there will be none until strictly controlled experimental teaching and careful diagnostic testing provide exact information of what is being learnt and not learnt by different kinds of learners under varying conditions of learning.

I said earlier that the sampling provided by a test should be a sampling of the relevant behaviour. The content of a test is chosen not so much to be representative of the content of a course or a whole field, but so as to allow the standard of skill shown by the learner during the testing to be representative of the standard of skill of his total relevant behaviour.

In diagnostic testing the concept of relevant behaviour must be broken down in more detail than in achievement and proficiency testing. The purpose of diagnostic testing is nearly always to get information for remedial teaching. It does not help the teacher who plans the remedial teaching to be told that the learner came at the 70th percentile for his year and group. The teacher wants to know as directly as possible what specific things or areas the learners need additional training in: is it vocabulary work that is needed, or practice in listening, or attention to modals, or drill on gender and agreement, or spelling, or pronunciation, or what?

For attainment testing it may be sufficient to know that all aspects of language usage are highly correlated with each other. For remedial teaching, or work supporting theories about language learning, the field has to be broken down in detail, and each part of it tested separately. So in diagnostic testing content sampling becomes very much more important.

To summarize so far: there are three characteristics which will influence the shape of a language test. Firstly, the shape of all tests, whether predictive or non-predictive, language or non-language, is primarily determined by the need to test the tests for reliability and validity. This is why, for instance, the multiple choice technique of answering is so common. In language testing it means that we usually draw upon the skills of reading and listening.

Secondly, the shape of a test is determined by the purpose for which one is testing. Do we wish to predict future behaviour, measure comparative achievement in terms of a narrower or wider field, or do we wish to diagnose strength and weakness for remedial teaching or research?

Thirdly, the shape of tests is determined by the field which is being tested, more precisely by the kind of behaviour we wish to sample, whether it is language behaviour or mathematical behaviour or construction skill or typing skill.

2. LANGUAGE BEHAVIOUR

There is no satisfactory theory of language learning, nor is there any satisfactory theory of language behaviour. But there are some statements about language behaviour that one can make which most people would agree to:

(1) The purpose of language is communication. The so-called language skills describe different modes of communication. Speaking, listening, reading and writing are not intrinsically separate, they describe communication in terms of sending and receiving, in spoken and written language. This is often set out in boxes:

	SPOKEN	WRITTEN
RECEPTIVE	Listening	Reading
PRODUCTIVE	Speaking	Writing

Each of these modes is associated with a special sensory-motor, or perceptual-motor skill, involving co-ordination between eye and hand and ear and speech organs, paired accordingly. In discussions about language behaviour these perceptual-motor skills are not always clearly distinguished from the modes they are associated with. One may say, very roughly, that communication in any mode presupposes the relevant motor-perceptual skill, plus comprehension. ('Skill' and 'comprehension' as used here are merely *ad hoc* labels. I do not wish to imply that they are properly defined terms; in any case, the activities they cover interact massively.)

(2) Another commonly accepted point is that any effective action concerning language behaviour must be based on a coherent view of language, i.e. a linguistic theory, from which can be derived a description of the relevant language or languages. This holds both for teaching and for testing. A linguistic theory is not the same as a theory of language behaviour, though some of the statements made by transformationalist grammarians have not been helpful in keeping the distinction unblurred.

Nevertheless, a linguistic theory and a linguistic description of language is a necessary part of any theory of language behaviour and must underlie any effective sampling of language behaviour. There are competing models available. There is the traditional 'schoolbook' grammar. There are the various modern schools, agreeing in acknowledging their debt to de Saussure but fiercely debating their differences. Of these, Bloomfieldian or structural linguists have had a tremendous influence on language teaching in the last few decades. The fairly recent Chomsky school of linguists provide generative and transformational grammars, and they are already influencing the views of language teachers. There are linguists in many countries working in a broad post-Saussurian tradition, less extreme than either the Bloomfieldians or the Chomskyites. The basic approach adopted here is an

English variety of this, which is sometimes called (neo-)Firthian linguistics.

Language has to be analysed at more than one level. The central level is that of *form*, which deals with grammar and lexis. Grammar, as expected, is concerned with the regularly recurring patterns and systems of language. Lexis is concerned not with the meaning of words, but with the company that words keep, which words go with which. Meaning, or the contextual meaning of language, is dealt with at the level of *context*. The level of phonology is concerned with the significant sound patterns of a language. (Graphology is the corresponding term for written language, but this has received scant analytical attention.)

There are then three main levels of linguistic analysis:

(1) phonology (the corresponding skills are pronunciation and auditory discrimination);

(2) form (which includes grammar); and

(3) context (to account for the meaning of grammatical and phonological patterns as well as of words).

At this stage of generalization, levels correspond loosely to Chomsky's components:

LEVELS	COMPONENTS
phonology	phonology
form (grammar)	syntactic
context	semantic

The modes of communication, with their associated skills and the linguistic levels of analysis provide a crude but useful checklist of language behaviour. Such a checklist is not a proper description but it is the nearest we have and for the tester it provides a framework for sampling. The test constructor examines the checklist (this or some other) in the light of:

(1) the test's technical requirements imposed by the need to test for reliability and validity; and

(2) the particular purpose of the test, i.e. predictive, attainment (achievement and proficiency) or diagnostic.

In the following I shall concentrate on attainment testing, with occasional references to diagnostic testing.

3. SAMPLING MODES

Testing at whatever linguistic level for whatever purpose must be conducted in some mode or other. Few, if any, tests employ all four modes. Most tests use one of the receptive modes, i.e. listening or reading, some use both. Such tests do not require the learner to do any writing or speaking; he responds in terms of choosing between answers which he reads, or listens to. Speaking or writing by the learner is virtually ruled out by the test's technical requirements; it is too difficult to show whether methods of testing spoken and written communication are reliable and valid.

The assumption behind testing in only one or two modes is that the ability of the learner to handle the language in these modes corresponds closely to his ability to handle all modes, if all modes are required. This assumption may not always be justified, of course, but some available test correlations indicate that it sometimes is. I obtained a correlation of ·93 between Parts I and II of the English Language Battery, Part I using the mode of listening (and some reading), Part II using the mode of reading, for 320 overseas students. Lado reported a correlation of ·89 between his aural discrimination test and the first Michigan Proficiency Test (Lado, 1951).

Both these correlations are so high that they cannot be explained solely on the basis of the reading component in the listening tests.

Further, it is well known that in vocabulary testing of native speakers, multiple choice formats give results which correlate very highly with open-ended formats. In multiple choice testing the child chooses between alternatives which he reads on the answer sheet, in open-ended testing the child writes his own synonym or definition. In other words, testing in the reading mode gives results which are highly similar to the results one gets by requiring the child to write out his responses.

We know very little about the correlation between the mode of speaking and the other modes. There is simply no evidence, whatever people may feel in their bones about it. Oral interviews, however important they are in their feed-back effect on teaching, have been shown to be highly unreliable. Their results depend on so many things over and above the candidate's command of spoken language. Examiners know this, and as a result they are very cautious, and usually very lenient in their judgements. M. R. Campbell, the head of a highly-regarded language school which regularly trains candidates for the Proficiency Examination of English as a Foreign Language, found one year that the Oral interviews conducted by very experienced examiners did not make any difference to the placing of any of the 50-odd candidates that year; none who passed the written exams failed the oral, and those who failed the oral failed in at least one of the written exams. This could be taken to indicate close correspondence between ability to communicate in speaking and in writing, but since the examiners only have to make the simple decision of pass or fail, and since they play very safe, this conclusion is hardly justified.

To my knowledge there are no good techniques, traditional or test-influenced, for assessing command of spoken language. There has been a certain amount of not very fruitful discussion in recent years about 'fluency' both from the teaching and the testing points of view. This is not surprising, for 'fluency' is not a defined term, it is just a label, giving a misleading impression of simplicity to that very complex thing, command of spoken language.

4. TESTING MODES

Speaking and writing are not suitable for use as modes of communication in testing. However, one is often required to assess specifically and directly the learner's ability to communicate in speaking and writing and there are ways of improving traditional techniques of doing this which I shall discuss later.

The techniques of testing listening and reading comprehension are well developed and well known. Comprehension tests used during teaching are usually open-ended—the learners have to compose their own answers. Comprehension passages for testing purposes are always multiple choice—the learners choose from the alternative answers provided. There are a few suggestions one can make about what not to do when choosing or writing passages for comprehension.

(1) The content should not be common knowledge. It is useless to compose a passage about London: 'London is the capital of Great Britain. It is famous for . . .' It should not be possible to answer the questions without having understood the passage. Questions therefore often begin: 'According to the passage . . .' or 'In the opinion of the author . . .'.

(2) Ability to answer should not hinge on obscure items of vocabulary or very specialized technical terms.

A. 'Disraeli's manner and dress were egregious in the eyes of a large number of Victorians . . .'

a ( ) Many Victorians admired Disraeli's appearance.
b ( ) Many Victorians thought Disraeli's appearance outlandish.
c ( ) Queen Victoria was very fond of Disraeli because he was well dressed and charming.

The only two real alternatives here are a and b. The third alternative is the sort one throws in to catch people who only get a word or two but perhaps may know vaguely some history. But the choice between a and b depends solely on knowing the meaning of 'egregious'. If one wants to try out this word as a test item, it can be done much more economically in a vocabulary sub-test than in a comprehension passage.

(3) Comprehension passages should not be too long. It is wasteful to have to read through a very long passage in order to answer just a few

questions. Most passages seem to vary from 6–8 to 15–16 lines, with perhaps 4 to 6 questions on each. If the passage is very long, one might be able to get more questions on it, but it is better then to have two shorter passages, because it is rather difficult to find the right sort of passages and the right sort of questions, and one has to be prepared to throw out or rewrite passages and questions many times in order to get decent item discrimination figures. And the longer the passage, the more is lost by having to discard it.

For listening comprehension in particular, the passage or dialogue should be quite short, because otherwise there is too great a memory load. Some tests, ELBA, TOEFL, use very short items with only one question on each. The CEEB Listening test in Modern Foreign Languages use these; they play the passage first, then the candidates look at the questions and then it is played again. A statement is spoken on tape, the candidate chooses between written paraphrases:

B.   'John and Mary are married.' (Spoken)
  a ( ) John is Mary's wife.
  b ( ) Mary is John's wife.
  c ( ) John and Mary have five children.
  d ( ) John is a batchelor.

Or the candidates may have to choose answers to a question:

C.   'What shall we do tonight?' (Spoken)
  a ( ) I'm too tired to work after supper.
  b ( ) Let's watch the spy-story on television.
  c ( ) I never get to bed early enough.
  d ( ) That was a good party last night.

There may be incomplete sentences:

D.   'Unless I'd seen it with my own eyes . . .' (Spoken)
  a ( ) I wouldn't have seen it.
  b ( ) you wouldn't have known about it.
  c ( ) I wouldn't have believed it.
  d ( ) it wouldn't have been true.

These very short spoken items may be designed to test a particular expression or structure, but this is not what they are for, in my opinion. They are simply very short bits of communication, and if the item discrimination figures are good, the item is good and it doesn't matter whether one knows why in linguistic terms. I prefer these shorties, again because if one doesn't work only one item is lost.

The other extreme in listening comprehension is to have extracts of a lecture, lasting perhaps 8–10 minutes (TOEFL). This is an example of the job-sample idea and can be very useful in estimating prospective students. But the students should be told to take notes, and it can be difficult to find or write a suitable section in a subject that is about equally familiar or, better, unfamiliar to all comers. Comprehension sub-tests are usually a valuable part of any language test. It can be difficult to find good passages and questions and alternatives, but once you get them to show good discrimination figures, they usually correlate very highly with the total test, and they are usually among those sub-tests which show the highest correlation with the criterion:

ELBA (English Language Battery) 1966	$N = 320$
Total Score/Listening Comprehension	$r = \cdot 88$
Total Score/Reading Comprehension	$r = \cdot 79$

(The lower correlation of the reading comprehension together with the item discrimination indicate that the RC hasn't yet been made as good as it should be.)

Comprehension sub-tests have little diagnostic value; one never knows exactly what they test or why they work, but when they work they work well. They are, therefore, especially suitable for proficiency testing but I would advocate including them in achievement tests too, because they have the content validity of being job-samples, slices of fairly real behaviour, which the more diagnostic items, testing artificially isolated points of phonology or grammar or vocabulary, do not have. Whether to include them in diagnostic testing depends on one's point of view. If you like job-samples, you put them in, but they do take up a lot of time per item, so you may decide to improve your test by putting in three times the number of quick diagnostic items instead.

At elementary stages of language learning, comprehension testing and diagnostic testing merge into each other. Listening comprehension items for children who are taught by modern audio-visual methods tend to consist of one spoken sentence, embodying a simple phonological contrast or grammatical point, and the children respond by choosing one of four or five alternative pictures. P. J. Rulon, who taught languages for the U.S. Army at Harvard during the Second World War, probably pioneered the technique; R. Lado developed it. It is now being used by, among others, the CREDIF centre in France and by the National Foundation for Educational Research.

5. TESTING SKILLS

The perceptual and motor skills of language behaviour are necessary for communication and they may be considered separately from the modes they are associated with. Employing any mode tests both the motor-perceptual skill and the comprehension component of that mode. Modes, given the usual all-round teaching, correlate highly with each other (though we don't really know about speaking). But the learner's control of one skill need not necessarily correspond to his control over another. Pre-school children and illiterates totally lack the reading and writing skill; highly educated adults may be very good at reading and writing a foreign language, and rather poor at listening and speaking.

The difficulty of learning the skills of a new language varies not only with the differences between the first and second language, but also with what the learner can do already. There are two major variants: (1) The learner has already acquired control over the spoken language, or over a particular dialect of it, but is not literate in any language. If one wants to distinguish between 'second' and 'foreign' language learning, this is the not unusual 'second' language situation.

(2) The learner has already learnt to read and write his own language, he now has to learn the specific skills of reading and writing in the new language. But he is also expected to extend his knowledge of that language through reading. This is the typical 'foreign' language situation.

It is obvious that the learning loads, and therefore the teaching and testing orientations, are very different in the two situations. (One point of similarity may be overlooked: where the spoken dialect is not considered suitable for the written page, the students in the 'second' language learning situation are expected to learn the acceptable dialect at the same time as they are learning to be literate.)

5.1 Reading

Purely as a skill, reading consists of what teachers sometimes call 'barking at print'. Learning to read at all, the first time, represents a major intellectual advance, requiring usually a great deal of effort and all the help one can get. This is why methods of teaching reading to children receive a great deal of attention, and why nobody should be asked to learn to read and to learn the language (or dialect) simultaneously. There is no need to construct attainment and diagnostic tests, at least for English, for pure reading skill; excellent tests exist for native speakers, i.e. tests assuming command of the spoken language. Learning to read a foreign language after having learnt to read and write one's own is a comparatively minor affair. It is largely a matter of learning and practising a new set of sound-symbol equivalences. The sounds are always more or less different, the written symbols may or may not be.

Even if the symbols are different, it only takes that much more practice. (Different writing systems, however, are more difficult.)

In European contexts, where learners are literate and the written symbols are the same, pure reading skill is not really a problem. Since reading is used as a means of learning more of the language, comprehension reading tests are better samples of the relevant behaviour than, for instance, reading aloud, which in any case is difficult to test objectively. Reading aloud, however, is very useful for semi-objective assessment of pronunciation. (See below, p. 95.)

Reading speed can be tested objectively. Irrelevant words are inserted into a passage, and students are asked to underline as many of the intruding words as they can manage in a given time. This is one of the sub-tests in the Davies/BC test. This is not a pure test of reading speed, since it obviously involves comprehension, but that is probably what makes it useful. The one disadvantage is that though the marking is objective it is not mechanical; the marker has to scan the passage and count the underlinings, which takes time.

5.2 Writing

Since writing skill presupposes reading skill, the discussion of reading is also relevant to writing. Learning to be literate is the most difficult job. Next comes learning to use a new writing system, for instance, getting used to using a syllable-symbol system, or word-root/character system, when one has been taught the usual European sound-symbol convention. Merely learning to draw new symbols so that they are acceptable can be quite difficult. In general scripts and script forms obviously have a systemic graphological aspect as well as the more general communicative aspect of legibility, but graphology as a level has received far less attention than phonology, and even less is known about legibility than about intelligibility, and I have nothing useful to suggest about the testing of it.

The one thing that lends itself to objective testing is spelling. Learners can be asked to choose between correct and incorrect forms, or a word in a sentence is written out with the crucial letters missing, to be completed by the learner. But it is my impression that spelling is not in fact much of a problem in second language learning; certainly adolescents and adults learning English do not seem to have nearly the same kind of trouble with spelling that English-speaking children have.

It is also possible to construct objective-looking formats for testing punctuation. But personally I doubt the general validity of many of the commonly taught 'rules' of punctuation, and the few absolutely safe rules (indirect speech, questions) hardly seem worth bothering about, for testing purposes. The only tests involving spelling I find interesting are the various sound-symbol tests developed by Lado which are discussed under listening.

5.3 Pronunciation

In many language learning contexts, writing presents no problem, pronunciation always does. For a start, it is difficult to specify the desired terminal behaviour. It is easy to say perfection, i.e. completely faithful phonetic imitation of native behaviour, but one never gets it.

It is equally simple to state that one aims at intelligibility, but it is more difficult to say what intelligibility is. Intelligibility is a speaker-hearer concept, depending as much upon the hearer as on the speaker. Intelligibility is not simply a matter of pronunciation; familiar and expected statements are much easier for the hearer to understand than unpredictable and strange utterances. (See Chapter 11.) Intelligibility testing is still very much at the experimental stage; it is nowhere near being useful in practical testing.

Pronunciation is a productive skill and therefore difficult to test objectively, but Strevens, McCallien and Taylor worked out an interesting semi-objective solution (Strevens, 1954). There is as yet no practical solution to the testing of intelligibility, i.e. the communicative aspect of speaking skill. Objective testing of the skilled aspect of spoken language therefore deals with listening, and the underlying analysis is phonological.

5.4 Listening: Auditory recognition and discrimination

The difficulty in testing the perceptual skill of auditory discrimination and recognition is the lack of common terminology between tester and student. If all students knew some system of phonetic notation, e.g. that of the International Phonetic Association, one could test any sound by speaking appropriate words on tape and asking the student to choose the corresponding phonetic symbols. But this is not open to us. Two devices are usual in testing phonemes.

(1) One word is said on tape, three words are written down in ordinary spelling, the student chooses the written word which corresponds to the spoken word:

E. (Spoken) 'cat'
   (Written) a ( ) cat b ( ) cut c ( ) cot

   (Spoken) 'pest'
   (Written) a ( ) test b ( ) best c ( ) pest

(There are three alternatives, not four. It is impossible to find enough sets of four minimally contrasting words; to find three is difficult enough.)

The device can only be used when it is reasonable to assume that students are easily literate. The words chosen must be fairly common, and the discriminations must be possible for native speakers listening to taped reproduction. For English, this unfortunately rules out most unvoiced θ/ s and θ/ f contrasts, and voiced ð/ d and ð/ v ones. When all candidates share a native language, as often happens in achievement and diagnostic testing, the items can be chosen by contrastive analysis. In proficiency testing one usually has to take on

all comers, and then it is probably safest to base the items on a phonemic analysis of the language. When testing consonants one chooses
triplets so that each word differs from the two others by only one
feature: in terms of place of articulation, manner or articulation,
voicing, etc. For vowels the words in one item should embody vowels
next to each other on the vowel chart. Depending on the language,
this will probably yield 200 to 400 triplets (a guess based on common
European languages). Probably not more than half of these will work
out in the item analysis; you eliminate according to how many items
you can afford to lose. The item analysis discrimination index in
phoneme testing is always bad. In the ELBA I was horrified by the
figures I got; later I discovered that other people didn't do any better.
In the present version in the vowel section, items are retained if they
get an index of $+\cdot20$ or better, for the consonants the lower limit is
$+\cdot10$.

It may be possible to get better figures when testing at less advanced
stages, but the reliability of spoken items, in particular of non-
contextualized spoken items, is bound to be low.

Nevertheless, I believe that a phoneme discrimination test is worth
having in any test involving listening, provided there are enough items
to make up for the inherent unreliability. This format is very quick,
one can test 100 items in about 10 minutes. The correlation between
the 100-item phoneme sub-test in ELBA and the Listening part score
and the total score is as follows:

ELBA 1967   N = 320

Phoneme Discrimination/Listening Sub-total   r = $\cdot93$
Phoneme Discrimination/Test Total   r = $\cdot85$

The importance of having enough items is shown by the correlations
obtained on a sample test, constructed for demonstration purposes for
45 Belgian teachers of English, with only 20 items in the phoneme
sub-test:

Sample Test 1966   N = 45

Phoneme Discrimination/Sample Test Total   r = $\cdot26$

(2) The other device for testing sound discrimination, perhaps the more
favoured, is to pronounce three words on tape, and ask the candidates
to say which of them are the same, if any. Phoneticians have often
used the X, A, B format, where the question is: is it the second word A
which is like the first word, or is it the third word B which is like the
first word? This has the disadvantage of all 50–50 chance questions.
Lado devised the more complicated 1, 2, 3 format where the candidate
has to choose between five possibilities and mark one of five boxes:

( )   ( )   ( )   ( )   ( )
12   13   23   123   0

If the first and second words are the same, the extreme left-hand box is ticked, and so on.

Many people prefer this over the written triplet device, because it gives five against three choices, and because it is 'pure'; it doesn't involve any reading. I don't see the point in striving for purity, except possibly in diagnostic testing for research purposes, because in general the more impure the test, the better it works. In any case, this format takes much more time per item, so it is less economical, and some people make book-keeping mistakes on it. They hear all right, but forget the order of the words, or muddle up the boxes.

All phoneme tests are vulnerable to pronunciation standards. It is very important to have American voices for students who are taught American English, English voices for those who are taught English English, etc. Native Americans have made up to 10 per cent mistakes on the ELBA phoneme sub-test read by an English RP speaker. (Native English speakers (N = 30) made an average of 2 per cent mistakes.)

The phonological features of stress and intonation are very inconvenient to test without common terminology. If everybody knew, for instance, the Trager Smith notation, or the Halliday system of feet, tonic and tones, one could simply ask the candidates to choose the correct label for what they heard on the tape. However, other devices are necessary.

Word stress can be tested by asking the candidate to mark the syllable with the main stress:

F.   (Spoken)   'pronunciation'   'referee'
    (Written)   pro-nun-ci-a-tion   re-fe-ree
                 ( ) ( ) ( ) (x) ( )   ( ) ( ) (x)

(This may also be done purely as a pencil-and-paper test.) In my experience it is not worth doing with advanced students of English. It is much too easy for most of them, and one doesn't need a test to discover those who find stress difficult, e.g. French speakers and people from the sub-continent of India. (This is not inborn wickedness, it is caused by systemic differences between languages; stress in French is syllable-based, English stress is time-based, and most languages in India do not have significant stress at all.)

Testing sentence stress (Halliday: tonic) is more useful than testing word stress. A sentence is spoken on tape, it is also written down and the learner indicates the syllable which carries the main stress of the whole structure:

G.   (Spoken)   'Let me show you'   'Is something the matter?'
    (Written)   Let me show you   Is some-thing the mat-ter?
                 ( ) ( ) (x) ( )   () ( ) ( ) ( ) (x) ( )

In English this discriminates well between advanced students, even for Germans and Scandinavians whose own stress systems are very similar to the English. I don't know why it should; perhaps since sentence stress is not usually systematically taught it takes people with a good ear for language to hear it. This is a good sub-test for any listening test, whether attainment or diagnostic. It is not vulnerable to different pronunciation standards; Americans and Australians make the same judgements as Englishmen on sentence stress.

It is impossible to test intonation directly, in the absence of common notation. Intonation must be tested via meaning, which makes intonation tests a special sort of comprehension test. In ELBA Form 1 and 2 there was originally a 'direct' test of intonation; sentences were spoken on tape and listeners had to judge whether the intonation went up or down at the end. The inter-correlations between this sub-test and the other sub-tests and with the total gradually reduced itself to zero. The reason was simple: it was a test of judgement of pitch, which is a very different matter from linguistically meaningful intonation-patterns.

In English, as in other languages, it is possible to turn a statement into a question by changing intonation:

'he is clever'

said with a moderate falling intonation is a statement, said with a moderate rise it becomes a question, and with a marked fall-rise it becomes an exclamation of surprise. This can be turned into a test item:

H. (Spoken) 'He is clever'
   (Written) He is clever a ( ) the speaker is making a straight-
                               forward statement
                           b ( ) the speaker is asking a question
                           c ( ) the speaker is extremely surprised

This is a very impure test. Items either work very well or not at all. One danger lies in inventing meanings which other native speakers don't recognize, so a lot of pre-testing is needed. And there is no point in choosing sentences whose meaning is not easily changed by changes in intonation: 'I hate you' is not very convincing as a question, and 'What a beautiful girl' and 'I'm sick and tired of excuses' are difficult to turn into anything other than expressions of admiration and disgust respectively.

When testing the meaning of phonological patterns it is tempting to go for irony, for instance, turning a grammatically positive statement into a negative by the appropriate intonation and stress:

'I . . . 'like . . . 'that

Such utterances are clear enough in real life, where the meaning is heavily clued by the context. In a testing situation the context is deliberately neutral or removed, so the item remains ambiguous; and even natives cannot decide whether the utterance is meant as a very emphatic affirmation, or just the opposite.

The disadvantage of this format is in time; up to 20 seconds is needed per item, to allow students to read and choose from the alternative meanings. But with only 10 items the ELBA inter-test correlations are encouraging:

ELBA 1967   N = 320
Intonation (meaning)/Listening sub-total   r = ·73
Intonation (meaning)/Test Total   r = ·71

When intonation has to be tested via comprehension, there is probably not much point in doing it much below advanced levels. The reason why it is difficult seems to lie at least partly in the vocabulary which is needed to describe the meaning associated with different intonation contours. One or two skilled phoneticians who tried the test and whose English is not very good were able to reproduce the intonation contours, but were unable to choose the associated meaning, either because they didn't know, or because they didn't understand the words. At advanced levels, however, it is a useful test both for diagnostic and attainment purposes.

When intonation has been taught specifically and systematically, and students can indicate recognition of intonation contours by choosing the correct label, e.g. Tone 1 or 3 2 1 or level-fall and so on, there seems no reason why testing cannot be done almost at beginner stages.

Lado, in his book *Language Testing*, describes a large number of ways of testing listening discrimination and listening comprehension, using spoken stimuli, answers being given in terms of same/different or by choosing between written answers.

6. TESTING LEVELS

Adequate sampling of language behaviour presupposes adequate description of language. Syllabus-makers, textbook writers and teachers need to know about the language they profess, and so do testers. The knowledge that teachers have about the languages they teach is usually very extensive, but not always formulated and explicit. Testers do not usually have this knowledge derived from experience, and need to check their sampling against a formal linguistic account.

6.1 Phonology

Testing at the level of phonology has already been discussed under listening. Phonological/graphological relations, or sound-symbol operations can be tested without involving the spoken modes. Lado developed a number of formats for testing knowledge of sound-symbol equivalences. (Though he called them paper-and-pencil tests of pronunciation.) The basis of most of these is the old device of asking for rhymes. One of the most useful and interesting variants is his missing-letters/same-sound format, where items are matched if the sounds corresponding to the missing letters are the same:

I.   1. Please shut the wind....
      2. I don't care h.... you do it.
      3. When do you g.. to London?

         ( )   ( )   ( )   ( )   ( )
          12   13   23   123   0

This is not a test of pronunciation, but it does test one of the necessary elements of the skill of reading aloud and there is no doubt that ability to handle sound-symbol operations is important in language learning. Both the predictive language tests for English speakers (MLAT and Pimsleur) include sound-symbol sub-tests, because they have been found to contribute significantly to the prediction of language learning.

If I had no tape-recorder and wanted to have some check on the phonological level, I would use:

(1) Paper-and-pencil word stress. The words are written and students are asked to mark the syllable with the main stress. This is too easy for many advanced students, but one can use long words and the vocabulary testing aspect helps to keep the discrimination index respectable; and

(2) Missing-letter/same-sound. Both of these are Lado's; neither tests pronunciation but they are means of sampling the phonological level without facilities for sound recording.

6.2 Grammar

Testing at the level of grammar does not mean asking for grammatical rules (though one could fairly easily devise a test for that). Testing at the grammatical level means sampling the student's ability to choose correct grammatical forms and constructions. The sampling of the grammatical forms and constructions depends on the grammatical description one works with, the purpose of the testing and the chosen mode.

The reading mode is by far the most suitable, but one *could* use spoken stimuli, e.g. speaking two versions of the same sentence and asking the listener to choose the correct one:

J.   (Spoken)   a. I am better than you at swimming.
                  b. I am best than you at swimming.

      (On the answer-sheet): a (x) b ( )

This is quite useful if one wants to test points of structure where there are only two plausible alternatives anyway, but the method is very time-consuming.

It is also possible to introduce elements of writing, using write-in formats. The clueing may be done more or less as in drills:

K.   (Will): I wish you . . . . go home!

where the candidate inserts the right form of the word given in brackets. I see no point in this myself. It takes more time and it is much slower to correct than the equivalent multiple choice format.

One may use longer passages with gaps, relying on context and internal sentence structure for clueing:

L.   . . . . people prefer . . . . notes when they listen . . . .
     lecture, others are afraid . . . . they . . . . miss important points
     . . . . they are writing, ... prefer to rely on . . . . memories.

This is an interesting format, partly because it can test some aspects of sentence construction which are difficult to test in a multiple choice format. Such passages are difficult to construct, so that they are neither too easy nor too much of a puzzle, and they are, of course, extremely impure. When they work they work very well indeed. The only drawback is that they cannot be marked automatically.

In general then reading is by far the most convenient mode for the testing of specific structural points of grammar.

The difficulty level is important. At elementary levels one may usefully test for correct forms:

M. I . . . . the letter yesterday.   N. The typist has . . . .
   a (   ) writted   a (   ) of stamps a lot
   b (   ) writed   b (   ) many of stamps
   c (   ) wrote   c (   ) of stamps many
   d (   ) written   d (   ) a lot of stamps

Here the distractors are incorrect in themselves; they could not be used under any circumstances. There is usually not much point in proficiency testing at this level, because it is too elementary to have much relevance to any real-life situation. But items like these can be useful in diagnostic and achievement testing. Items like M. are often constructed on the 'irregularities' within a language; gender, formation of strong verbs, cases governed by prepositions, word order or expressions of possession; and also on obligatory rules, e.g. do-transformations in English, obligatory subjunctive in French and German, etc. If the learners have a common language background, items of the N. type can easily be written either from a formal contrastive analysis of the two languages, or from knowledge of typical errors.

At intermediate and advanced levels these kinds of items become less useful, because they are too easy. The basic points have been learnt, at least in principle. Then one has to construct items where all the alternatives are correct in themselves, but only one is possible or is the most likely in the context:

O. I can't talk to you now; ....

    a ( ) I'm working
    b ( ) I work
    c ( ) I am worked
    d ( ) I'm to be worked

P. If you go and look in the hall there might be ....

    a ( ) a present for you
    b ( ) the present for you
    c ( ) present for you
    d ( ) any present for you

When all the alternatives are correct in themselves, one or two may not be very convincing as distractors. The passives in O. are not all that good, but there are only two tenses to choose from to indicate present time, simple present and continuous present. In diagnostic testing one has to include many such points with only two real alternatives, and one has to accept that the extra items act more or less as camouflage. In attainment testing it is often possible to avoid testing the two-choice points and concentrate on those where there are three or four genuine possibilities. P. is an example of at least three reasonable alternatives with indefinite, definite and zero article. There are three members to choose from in this natural set; the fourth alternative—any—is much weaker. It may be useful to undertake an extended form of item analysis to see if too many alternatives are mere passengers. Usually item analysis is done in terms of counting correct and incorrect answers (see Appendix), but one may also count how often each of the distractors has been chosen. If nobody chooses a particular distractor, it is obviously useless and should be changed.

Sometimes it is difficult to find contexts which rule out all except one alternative. This happens particularly when it is the choice of one member of the natural grammatical set which gives the precise meaning to the context-sentence. Examples are modals and prepositions.

Q. .... to go to Glasgow tomorrow; there's a meeting I ought to attend.

    a ( ) I will have
    b ( ) I shall have
    c ( ) I may have
    d ( ) I have

There is no difference in probability here, only slight differences in meaning (I'm ignoring artificial classroom rules about will/shall). Obviously not all modals fit all contexts, but it is almost impossible to find contexts which distinguish between more than a pair of them at a time:

R. Mother thinks you .... go home now; it's rather late.

a (x) should
b ( ) would
c (x) ought to
d ( ) could

S. My brother always held his back straight, so that people .... think he was taller.

a (x) should
b (x) would
c ( ) could
d ( ) ought to

The most rewarding items to write at this advanced level, using only real-language distractors, are those involving choice of tenses. It is vitally important to secure native agreement; there is no point in being so obscure that nobody else can see what you are driving at.

But, as always in testing, the sin is not to be impure but to be inefficient. Any point of grammar can be tested; if necessary by mixing up two distinct grammatical points, or even by slipping in a non-language distractor. There seems no other way of testing, for instance, the placing of adverbs:

T. a ( ) Always on Fridays I wash my hair.
   b ( ) Always on Fridays I am washing my hair.
   c ( ) On Fridays I always wash my hair.
   d ( ) On Fridays I am always washing my hair.

The selection of grammatical points for testing depends on the purpose. In diagnostic and achievement testing the grammatical basis is given by the syllabus or textbook. In proficiency testing it is important to have a good linguistic description available, not because everything has to be included, but so that the test constructor can *decide* what to leave out, instead of just omitting things through inadvertence or ignorance.

Grammatical points should be selected for testing for their importance in the language (their general applicability, their frequency, their importance as constituents of more complex structures), for the level of difficulty which is appropriate and for the possibility of finding good, unambiguous and economical contexts and good and sufficiently convincing distractors. Still, the criterion is not in the validity of the appropriate grammatical analysis; it is the statistical analysis which tells you whether you've got a good test or not.

6.3 Lexis[1]

The study of lexis is concerned with the possibility of co-occurrence of words. *A round table, a square table* and *a square meal* are all possible co-occurrences or collocations in English, *a round meal* is not. The testing

---

[1] Ingram, following Halliday (1961), makes a distinction between vocabulary, i.e. lists of words, and *Lexis,* the formal part of vocabulary, analysable into *collocations* and *sets* [Editor].

of lexical collocations is not very advanced, perhaps chiefly because the study of it is not very advanced either. It is clearly bound up with the study of what variety of language is appropriate in what set of circumstances, but our knowledge of this is more intuitive than explicit. Another reason may be that past excesses, errors and trivialities in teaching 'idioms'—which are a special case of collocations—have put many present-day teachers off the subject.

I have occasionally devised small sub-tests on the lines of

U. The crime was.. during the night.	V. I was too late, so I .... the bus.	W. We are here dealing with the law of ....
a ( ) committed	a ( ) lost	a ( ) falling returns
b ( ) done	b ( ) missed	b ( ) smaller returns
c ( ) made	c ( ) omitted	c ( ) vanishing returns
d ( ) performed	d ( ) retarded	d ( ) diminishing returns

It can be great fun thinking up items like:

X. May I offer you a ...., Your Highness?
  a ( ) fag
  b ( ) nail
  c ( ) cigarette
  d ( ) gasper

But it is all too easy to end up in parody or cliché:

Y. Have you finished with the ....?
  a ( ) bloody shovel
  b ( ) spade
  c ( ) digging aid '
  d ( ) manually operated instrument for shifting earth

Z. This is the most .... crime known to Scotland Yard.
  a ( ) gross
  b ( ) naughty
  c ( ) fiendish
  d ( ) dastardly

However, I believe that such sub-tests could be usefully developed, for testing students who have to learn and use particular language varieties. I am not thinking of technical terms or labels, but of the semi-technical language which specialists use. Surgeons *perform* an operation, treasurers *present* the accounts, and so on.

6.4 *Vocabulary*

The most important reason why people are not so interested in testing lexis is that vocabulary testing is so successful. Vocabulary testing as we all know consists of having the candidate indicate the meaning of a word, by synonym, by opposites, by definition, or by context, in the foreign language or in the mother-tongue. It is not a pure test and linguists and direct methodists are not very interested, for their various reasons. It is, however, the nearest thing we have to a foolproof test, i.e. a constructor-proof test. The statistics, both item-analysis and correlation figures, are nearly always good. This is very odd, because the sampling of vocabulary items is purely quantitative. Knowing one vocabulary item doesn't imply knowledge of any other vocabulary item. With grammar it is different; if a candidate can choose correctly between a pair of tenses on one occasion, we have some justification in assuming that he will choose correctly between the same pair of tenses on another occasion. All we can assume about vocabulary is that if a candidate knows the meaning of say 80 out of 100 items in a test, he is likely to know a great many more vocabulary items from the general word stock of the language than a candidate who only gets 20 out of 100.

There are of course a few elementary precautions to observe. The first concerns related languages, and is relevant mainly to proficiency testing. In a test intended for candidates from many language backgrounds one must be careful not to favour a particular set. In English the danger is to include too many Latin-derived words, which will favour speakers of the romance languages.

This will not usually arise in achievement testing, where learners tend to share a mother-tongue, and I doubt if anybody would include a vocabulary section in a diagnostic test.

The second danger is to forget that one is testing language and not intelligence. Admittedly vocabulary testing is also one of the most valuable sub-tests in intelligence testing, admittedly there is a substantial correlation between language learning and intelligence, but the aim here is still language testing. This means excluding items which are failed by natives whose education and status is equivalent to the test population.

AA. I retained this item for at least one test revision too many:
OSTENSIBLY

a ( ) showily
b (x) seemingly
c ( ) demonstrably
d ( ) wittingly

because I couldn't bear to give up an item which I knew the correct meaning of and *lots* of natives failed. (My mother tongue is not English.)

Many people dislike the notion of testing vocabulary in isolation. I don't mind, if the technique works. It is most economical to print and read single words, so what you lose in face validity you more than gain in test economy. The only information I have concerns 15 items, mostly phrasal verbs, presented in isolation and in a minimal sentence context:

BB.	CC.
KNOCKED DOWN	He was KNOCKED DOWN late last night.
a ( ) struck to the ground	a ( ) struck to the ground
b ( ) beaten smooth	b ( ) beaten smooth
c ( ) hammered in	c ( ) hammered in
d ( ) flattened	d ( ) flattened

Forty students answered the items in both presentations, a week apart. The repeated items were distributed among new items. The correlation was ·88.

All the same, items which do not consist of a single word may work better with minimal contextualization, and I now usually place phrasal verbs and other multi-word expressions in simple sentences. The aim is to give only grammatical information, not the sort of context which will allow the candidates to infer the meaning:

He was KNOCKED DOWN late last night.
Not: He was KNOCKED DOWN by a bus.

6.5 Context

Context enters into all language behaviour, even into what may look like an exercise in pure motor-perceptual skill. Lieberman (1963) showed that when skilled phoneticians listened to sentences of an unknown language—it was in fact English with the words blurred by machine—they could distinguish only two degrees of stress. As soon as meaning was restored, when the sentences were heard in the normal way, they could hear the usual four degrees of stress again.

Whatever the philosophical implications behaviourally, meaning does not exist independently of the other levels of language, and cannot be taught or tested in isolation. Of course the degree of contextualization of any test varies with the level of language which is tested and with the actual test technique employed. The meaning component of the triplet phoneme test—one word spoken, three words written—is not large, but it is there. I had to reject the triplet—*woad—warred—word*—because many people did not know the meaning of woad and so could not reach the auditory decision fast enough, though the spelling of woad is entirely regular and can represent only one pronunciation.

The contextualization of grammar items with real language distractors is greater than the contextualization of items with distractors which are wrong in themselves.

The greatest amount of contextualization is given in the least pure tests: reading speed, passage completion, spoken and written comprehension. There are two absolutely safe generalizations to be made:

(1) The more contextualized a test is, the less diagnostic it is; and

(2) The more contextualized a test is, the more reliable it is, and therefore, the greater its chances of working near its true validity.

This does not of course mean that testing should consist only of highly contextualized sub-tests, but it is necessary to be aware of the inherent unreliability of low contextual formats, so that one can compensate, for instance, by increasing the number of items.

7. CODA

Some things can be measured accurately and objectively, e.g. time and distance and weight and heat. Some things can be counted without disagreement, e.g. right and wrong choices from a limited number of alternatives. This is a cruder form of measuring, and it is what we do in testing. But some things cannot be scored in this way, they have to be judged as good enough or not good enough to merit a particular rating. This is the usual examination procedure.

We cannot test the productive aspects of language behaviour, but we often judge them. Attempts are continuously made to improve these judgements.

The most successful efforts have been made in the field of pronunciation. This is no accident, phonetics/phonology is the most developed part of linguistics. Strevens, originally a phonetician, McCallien, a very experienced teacher, and Taylor, a psychologist, worked out a scheme of judging the pronunciation of Ghanaian students, on the basis of phonological comparison, teaching experience and test-technical requirements. The judges were secondary school teachers. Agreement was sought by calling in the examiners for two days' intensive training in the judging of sounds and sound patterns, with discussion of disagreements and re-evaluations until a high examiner inter-correlation was reached. Only one point was judged at a time. When the candidate read out the sentence 'There is a ship in the river' the only thing he was marked for was his ability to make the ship/sheep distinction. Other phonological features were similarly sampled, judged and counted.[1] This is as near as you can get to 'objective' testing without actually being objective. This is possible because the subject has been so successfully analysed and described. The success of this technique depends on how well the examiners have been trained, and on how well the standards of judging can be maintained.

There is no comparable technique for judging the learners' ability to express themselves in spoken and written language, i.e. employ the productive modes for communication. This is a much more complex activity, reaching beyond linguistics, and without a proper theory of language behaviour we cannot analyse it into smaller units for sampling and counting, in any meaningful way.

[1] A full description and discussion of the McCallien Test is given in Chapter 10.

Job sampling seems to be the only technique available. The only way to find out how good people are at writing essays is to have them write an essay. The validity of the job sample is assumed, the task is to try to improve the reliability of the judging.

Some examiners advocate using marking schemes; awarding out of 50 for 'language', 25 for skill in logical composition, 10 for spelling, 5 for neatness, etc., and adding it all up in the end. There is no evidence that this is any more valid or reliable than the overall impressionistic marking of experienced examiners.[1] Since these marking schemes are entirely *ad hoc*, this is not surprising.

The only way to increase the reliability of the marking is to have several judges, whose marks are averaged. This is what they always do in athletics. They measure what can be measured with the most accurate instruments; but what cannot be measured—e.g. style in figure skating—is judged by a minimum of three judges, in important events often five or seven or even nine.

The judging of essays would be perfectly adequate provided that:
(1) Three experienced examiners judged each essay. This may sound prohibitively expensive, but the verdicts reached, for instance, at university entrance level are vitally important both for the individuals and for the nation. Economies may possibly be made by speeding up the process of impressionistic marking. Experiments are needed to show if time spent on each essay could be shortened without significant loss.
(2) The examiners are trained to use the same marking scale. This sounds superfluous, but though all examiners know the official scale extremely well, they may not all use the same sections of it. Practically everybody is reluctant to use the extreme top and bottom marks, some people use mainly the top two-thirds of the scale, others the lower two-thirds, etc. Periodic tests should be carried out to check any divergencies or idiosyncracies developing in individual examiners.

In writing, we can assume that the job sample is valid, more or less. The direction of communication is one-way, so the result is almost completely dependent on the writer alone. But in speech the process of communication is continuously back-and-forth; each person is both speaker and listener in rapid alternation. The speech situation is therefore inherently dependent on at least two persons, and a candidate is judged on a performance which is only a part of the total situation. This must affect the validity profoundly. Since the other participant is also the judge, the reliability must be suspect too. It is no solution to introduce more judges, because they necessarily change the interview situation still further. More judges can be used if the conversation is taped, but tapes give only an incomplete record of any occasion.

[1] But see p. 28 and p. 31 in Chapter 2.

From a practical point of view, judging tapes is a very time-consuming business, it has to be done at intervals, because one's judgement goes off very quickly, usually after about an hour, or an hour and a half, and after that it becomes physically impossible to sit and listen in a booth any longer.

The success of an interview depends very largely on whether examiner and candidate manage to establish contact quickly. The degree of this happening can be increased in two ways:

(1) Choosing examiners who are good at establishing contact. Some sort of apprenticeship system would seem to be the only way of finding and training such people—certainly there is no test to do it.

(2) Choosing productive topics of conversation. This was first tried by Rulon at Harvard in 1943, who ran courses in German and Russian for the American Army. He predetermined the 'conversational yield' of a number of topics, by finding out how much the soldiers found to say on each, in their own language. Then he picked the best for the oral examinations (Rulon, 1944).

The aim is to assess individuals from a population fairly and truly. Testing and examinations are only means to this end. Testing cannot be efficient or useful unless the tester knows why he is testing and what he is testing, so that he can devise appropriate techniques. Analysis of subject and purpose make it possible to devise appropriate techniques; statistical follow-up shows whether one in fact has been able to do so. I prefer to use quantitative objective testing techniques whenever possible because the amount of error can be discovered. But there is no point in trying to impress oneself and others by using pseudo-quantitative testing formats, in processes which defy analysis, nor is there any point in pretending that what cannot be tested objectively cannot be real.

6

Language Aptitude Testing

Paul Pimsleur

The purpose of an aptitude test may be summarized in two words: prediction and diagnosis. The following article will describe and discuss these two concepts, their applications in the schools, and how they are served by a recently published test.

I. PREDICTION

The majority of schools in the United States make decisions every year which are based upon prediction. They decide which pupils are to begin a foreign language the following year, and which language they are permitted to take. These decisions are then justified in terms of the school's estimation of how well the pupil is likely to do in learning a foreign language. Very often they base their estimation on the child's IQ, or else on his grades in English (native language). How relatively ineffectual and unreliable these methods are may be seen by glancing at Table 1, which shows the correlation between the frequently used

Predictor	Correlation with language marks[1]
IQ	r = ·46
Marks in English	r = ·57
Average of marks	r = ·62
Aptitude test	R = ·62
Average + Test	R = ·72

TABLE I

[1] The first line of entries, for example, may be read as follows: 'The correlation between IQ and language marks was ·46.' As the reader may already know, correlations can vary between +1·00 (a completely positive correlation) and −1·00 (a completely negative correlation). For purposes of prediction, one tries to come as close as possible to a perfect positive correlation.

A further point: the small letter 'r' signifies a correlation between just *one* predictor and the criterion, while a capital 'R' signifies that a *multiple* (several part) predictor was used.

Reference is made to this chapter on p. 15 of the Introduction.

predictors on the one hand, and the students' actual success in the language class on the other

Table 1 indicates clearly that both IQ and English marks are distinctly inferior to other methods which could as well be used by the schools—in particular, the *average* of marks. Schools ought at least to take the student's marks in several of his chief subjects into account, rather than English marks alone, since they have the former available without additional testing.

There is, however, a still better method. Notice what happens to the correlation when the average of marks is used *in conjunction with* an aptitude test. The figure rises to ·72, which is a considerable increase in the accuracy of prediction.

We must realize that considerably more is at stake here than just statistical numbers. The higher the correlation, the fewer pupils will be put into classes for which they are not well suited. The less likely it will be that a pupil will be excluded from a class in which he would have succeeded, or be put into one in which he will not succeed. Schools should equip themselves with the best possible means for selecting the correct classes for their pupils, not only in fairness to the majority of pupils, but also out of consideration for those few whose sole chance of excelling academically may lie in their talent for languages. They are almost certain to be overlooked, unless a highly specialized method of selection is employed.

2. DIAGNOSIS

Diagnosis is a matter of finding out as much as we can about an individual student, in order to counsel him effectively. In terms of foreign languages this will usually mean that we want to identify the 'under-achiever' as early as possible—if possible even before he has begun language study. The 'under-achiever' is not just the all-around weak pupil who does as poorly in languages as he does in his other classes, but rather the pupil who does really *less* well in languages than in his other classes. Such a pupil may have an average mark of B (second from highest), but attain only D in French; or he may have an average of C but fail to even pass his French course. A relevant investigation (Pimsleur, Sundland, and McIntyre, 1963) has shown that most language classes contain between 10 per cent and 20 per cent such students. These cases are often particularly vexing for all concerned—teacher, pupil, and parents—because the student's marks in language suddenly and unexpectedly turn out to be below the performance usually attained by him. We can do a great deal to help such pupils, if we can identify them early, before they have lost so much ground that they cannot any longer catch up, and before they have developed such a complex towards foreign languages that even the best teacher cannot break through it. In order to make this early identification possible, we need a diagnostic test.

A further conclusion from these considerations is this: we need to know just what abilities are required for learning a language well, before we can predict who will do it. This explains why we analyse aptitude so thoroughly—because the more we discover regarding aptitude the better we can understand individual differences among pupils learning languages, and the more chance we have of turning these differences to advantage.

3. HISTORY

The history of foreign language aptitude testing can be described very briefly, since this type of testing only really began a few years ago. Although there have been a number of tests since the 1920's (mostly known by their author's names: Stoddard, Symonds, Luria and Orleans, etc.) these were mainly concerned with predicting a particular type of achievement, namely the analytical manipulation of the written language, which today is quite *passé*. A very different type of test is required to establish who will be adept in *understanding* and *speaking* a foreign language. Only one other test of this type has appeared until now, apart from my own: the Modern Language Aptitude Test (MLAT) by Carroll and Sapon.[1]

4. PIMSLEUR LANGUAGE APTITUDE BATTERY (Pimsleur, 1966a)

The following will serve to introduce the reader to the test under discussion here, by means of a brief description of its six parts.

Part 1: Major Subjects

Following the instructions of the taped voice, the student fills out on his answer sheet his most recent marks in English, Mathematics, History, and Science. (1 minute)

Part 2: Interest

The student indicates, on a five-point scale printed on his answer sheet, just how interested he is in learning a foreign language. (2 minutes)

Part 3: Vocabulary

A 24-item test of the pupil's command of the vocabulary of his native language. (6 minutes)

---

[1] A description of the Modern Language Aptitude Test is given at the end of this chapter. Reference is also made to it in the Introduction (p. 15) [Editor].

Part 4: Language Analysis

The student sees a series of foreign forms (in Kabardian) and their English equivalents. From these he is to conclude how other things would be expressed in this language. (15 items, 12 minutes)

Part 5: Sound Discrimination

The student learns three foreign words from the tape (in Ewe); they are similar in sound but not identical. He then hears sentences spoken in Ewe and has to tell which of these three words was contained in each sentence. (30 items, 8 minutes)

Part 6: Sound-Symbol Association

The student hears nonsense words of two- or three-syllable length and must choose, from among four printed words, the correct spelling of the one he heard. (30 items, 9 minutes)

The entire Battery can be administered in about 40 minutes. All instructions and time indications are given on the tape.

5. RELIABILITY AND VALIDITY

The two most important questions concerning any test are 'Is it a reliable test?' and 'Is it a valid test?'

Reliability relates roughly speaking to its exactness as a measuring instrument (regardless of *what* it is measuring). In the case of a desk ruler, for example, we might ask whether it is reliable to the nearest eighth of an inch, or sixteenth, etc. Other factors being equal, a test is more reliable, the *longer* it is. To establish the reliability of the Pimsleur Language Aptitude Battery, it was given to 1,201 students in the seventh grade, to 979 students in the eighth grade, and to 1,765 students in the ninth grade. The respective reliability coefficients for Parts 3 through 6 of the Battery were ·85. ·89, and ·89. These figures are quite acceptable, especially in view of the fact that the Battery has purposely been kept short, so that it can be given in a single class hour.

The question of validity is concerned with how well a test examines that which it is designed to examine—in this case, language aptitude. Proof of validity can be given when the test results are compared with the actual achievement of the students in language classes; the resulting figures are termed validity coefficients. The Manual for the Aptitude Battery reports 31 such coefficients ranging from a low of ·25 to a high of ·79. The median validity figure is ·52. These results can be considered quite satisfactory, whether one compares them with other tests of language aptitude, or with aptitude tests in other fields.

6. DISCUSSION OF DIAGNOSIS

The theory on which the Language Aptitude Battery is based, an empirical theory, arrived at by analysing experimental data, treats language aptitude as consisting of three factors. The first is Verbal Intelligence, by which is meant familiarity with words in the mother tongue (tested by the Vocabulary part) and also the ability to manipulate verbal material analytically (tested by Part 4: Language Analysis). The second factor is the motivation for learning a foreign language, for which the test of Interest is designed. The third factor is Auditory Ability and is measured in two different aspects by Parts 5 and 6: Sound Discrimination and Sound-Symbol Association. Auditory Ability, which has not been heretofore recognized nor accorded its true importance, was found in a recent investigation (Pimsleur, Sundland and McIntyre, 1963) to be the factor which distinguished students who achieved normally from those who were under-achievers. It appears that auditory ability is often responsible for differences in people's ability to learn foreign languages which cannot be explained by intelligence or motivation.

Diagnosis concerns itself with the individual; it aids in detecting beforehand the strong and not-so-strong points of each student, so he can be helped as early and as much as possible. If we look at some actual cases, we can see how the test accomplishes its task of diagnosis. Consider the first case:

	Case 1: Pupil R.P.			
	Vocabulary	Lang. Anal.	Sound Discr.	Sound-Symbol
+2	x	x		x
+1			x	
Average				
−1				
−2				

The pupil's results for the last four parts of the Battery are marked on the diagram by x. The distance between the x and the horizontal centre line shows approximately how far above or below the class average the result is. In this case, that of an Ohio junior high school girl, the results for all four parts are well above average. The diagnosis based on these results was that this pupil would be one of the very best. Later this was corroborated by her teacher, who said that this girl was one of two best students in the class.

It must be mentioned that this investigation was carried out by correspondence, so that neither the pupil nor the teacher was personally acquainted with the diagnostician. The diagnosis was made without knowing anything about the pupil except the Battery scores. And similarly, the diagnosis was not presented to the teacher until *after* the pupil had received final grades.

	Case 2: Pupil D.J.M.			
	Vocabulary	Lang. Anal.	Sound Discr.	Sound-Symbol
+2				
+1	x			
Average		x		
—1			x	x
—2				

The next case, that of schoolboy D.J.M., was more complex. His results in the first two tests, designed to measure aspects of his verbal intelligence, were about average, while in the last two tests, which measure auditory ability, he was distinctly below average. The diagnosis was made accordingly: he would not be an outstanding pupil in any aspect of language learning, but his written work might be slightly better than his oral work. Said in other words, his low scores on the auditory ability tests (the last two) lead one to expect he may do poorly in oral work. This, too, was later corroborated by his teacher.

	Case 3: Pupil C.C.			
	Vocabulary	Lang. Anal.	Sound Discr.	Sound-Symbol
+2				x
+1			x	
Average				
—1	x			
—2		x		

The case of C.C., a French student in a Florida college, was totally different. The test results indicated she would do better at audio-lingual work, such as comprehension of the spoken language, pronunciation, and speaking, than she would at grammar or translation exercises. This diagnosis proved to be essentially accurate, as this pupil received a C for her written work, but a B for her oral work.

	Case 4: Pupil M.E.			
	Vocabulary	Lang. Anal.	Sound Discr.	Sound-Symbol
+2				
+1			x	
Average		x		
−1	x			
−2				x

Another girl in the same French class, M.E., seems to have average ability for foreign language study, apart from the unusually bad score in the last test. The diagnosis was made that she probably would have difficulty in her audio-lingual work. As it turned out, the girl received a B for her written achievement, but an F (failing grade) for her oral work.

These cases illustrate typical applications of the Language Aptitude Battery for diagnostic purposes. Accuracy in both prediction and diagnosis will increase as more practical experience is gained and as the test profits from the studies presently under way. I believe it can fairly be stated, however, that the Battery is the only means currently available by which such predictive and diagnostic information can conveniently be obtained.

Editor's Note

In his discussion of Aptitude testing Pimsleur limits himself to the Language Aptitude Battery (LAB) which he and his associates have constructed. Mention has been made in Chapter 1 (Introduction 6.2) of the Modern Language Aptitude Test constructed by Carroll and Sapon. It will be pertinent to describe this test more fully than was done in the Introduction, in the light of Pimsleur's discussion.

The Modern Language Aptitude Test (MLAT) was devised by Carroll and Sapon after a five-year period of research work (1953–58) at Harvard University. The five tests of the final MLAT were selected from a number of language tests which were used during the research on the basis of fairly low inter-correlations and of contributions to predictive validity. About 5,000 subjects were given the experimental tests, coming from high schools, colleges and adult short courses.

The factor analysis performed on the results vindicates, Carroll considers, the claim that the five tests are measuring distinct abilities. These abilities are represented by his four factors, viz. phonetic coding, grammatical sensitivity, rote memorization ability, and inductive language learning ability. Here follows a brief account of the five tests:

1. *Number Learning:* this tests rote memory for recall of numbers in an artificial language learnt through hearing them repeated on tape. The test numbers are rearrangements of the digits in such a way that though the student will have practised the parts he will not have heard the complete number before. (*Example:* write down in figures the number given in words in the new language.)

2. *Phonetic Script:* this measures the ability to associate sounds with symbols (cf. Pimsleur's Test No. 6). Carroll and Sapon claim a high correlation with the ability to mimic speech sounds, etc. (*Example:* underline the word you hear: tik, tiyk, tis, tiys).

3. *Spelling Clues:* the student is given word clues as to pronunciation of the stimulus and asked to select a synonym from a set of choices. The test measures verbal knowledge to a considerable extent. (*Example:* which choice is a synonym of the word pronounced like this: *ernst:* shelter, sincere, slanted, free, impatient.)

4. *Words in Sentences:* a test of grammatical sensitivity. A choice must be made of a word or a construction similar to a model one. It is not clear how much skill in this test is a reflection of formal grammar teaching. In use this test seems to be the most valid and robust of the battery. (*Example:* which italicized part of 2. corresponds syntactically to the italicized part of 1: 1. *London* is the capital of Europe. 2. *He liked* to *go fishing* in *Maine.*)

5. *Paired Associates:* this tests rote memory for Kurdish vocabulary. This makes it similar to Test 1 except that the emphasis is on visual rather than auditory memory. (*Example: hij:* frog, fall, cold, draw, book.)

Carroll and Sapon take no account of motivation nor of general academic attainment, both of which Pimsleur wishes to assess in his LAB. They put a great deal of emphasis on thinking, which means that in comparison with Pimsleur's test the MLAT is heavily intellectual. There seems to be little theory behind the composition of the MLAT. These five tests, says Carroll (1959) were 'relatively uncorrelated . . . showed good validity and made unique contributions to the prediction of success in foreign languages'. The lack of a construct (see Chapter 1.3) makes it very difficult to interpret the factor analysis in terms of anything except combinations of tests. Even so the fact is that the MLAT works; it shows consistently good predictive validity in a variety of situations and it contains content validity.

It will be obvious that both the LAB and the MLAT make use only of listening and of reading tests. Neither attempts to test the production skills. Arguments as to practical difficulties elsewhere in this volume indicate the reasons for this but it does seem necessary that experimental aptitude work (as opposed to a selection instrument) should grapple with production.

The MLAT is available commercially in a long and a short form. The long form contains all five tests and takes about 70 minutes to administer. The short form is made up of tests 3, 4 and 5, i.e. the reading tests only, and takes about 30 minutes. Norms and other statistical information are available in the Manual.

7

Testing Spoken Language:
Some Unsolved Problems

G. E. Perren

The following pages do not attempt to catalogue all the techniques used to test spoken language, still less to suggest new ones, for useful suggestions would need to be specific to particular languages and imply detailed study of where, how and why they were being taught, as well as appropriate linguistic description of the skills involved in speaking each language. The aim is rather, in a broad sense, to question some of the assumptions which underlie testing techniques and perhaps help explain why satisfactory tests of spoken language are at present so rare. Such examples as are given refer mostly to testing English as a second language.

Ability to speak and understand a language requires the generalized use of highly complex skills, but is probably the most highly rated and widely useful aspect of language proficiency. It is claimed that preliminary oral ability makes reading and writing in a foreign language easier to learn, and certainly fluent speech represents a more fundamental control of the language for practical purposes than any skills which are related entirely to written forms. Linguists, language teachers and laymen are probably in comfortable agreement about the primacy of speech. However, there is far less agreement as to how far particular speech skills can be isolated and validly tested separately from those skills normally associated with writing and reading.

From the testing as well as from the teaching point of view, a good deal of misunderstanding has no doubt arisen from the assumption that language proficiency can be categorized in terms of four skills—hearing, speaking, reading and writing—which can then be taught and tested independently. Any analyses of teaching, and certainly most attempts at objective testing, show that while there may be four such aspects of the use of language, the skills involved overlap, are often integrated and are certainly not specific to any one aspect. For some limited purposes it may indeed be useful to separate language abilities into those associated primarily with the written form and those

Reference is made to this chapter on pp. 15–16 of the Introduction.

associated primarily with the spoken form.[1] (A moment's reflection shows that writing skills must embrace some reading skills, while speaking skills must embrace some listening skills.) A division into literacy and oracy is, however, merely a convenient distinction according to the physical media employed rather than a separation of skills according to any valid linguistic or pedagogical categories.

In tests of spoken language, it is therefore to be understood that auditory and oral abilities are often so closely involved with each other that they cannot be separated, while apart from the media employed there may sometimes be little linguistic difference between skills involved in oracy and literacy. In practical terms this means that all the theoretical problems of language testing are likely to be present in a concentrated form when trying to measure performance in spoken language. For there are very considerable technical problems in trying to measure, within a limited time, the display of an array of integrated skills used in relation to an unpredictable (and often uncontrolled) social situation. Moreover, in a sense not applicable to the written medium, spoken language is fugitive. It cannot be re-scanned and reassessed in context like writing; even a recording used for repeated playback cannot include the full social context in which significant utterances occur. A limited isolation of certain skills specific to either written or spoken language may be possible, but oracy can no more be measured by the ability to identify (or produce) phonemes than literacy can be measured by ability to read (or write) letters of the alphabet. Similarly, reading a passage aloud may display skill in pronunciation, but as a pre-requisite assumes reading skills which may have no connexion at all with speech.

Too often at present the selection of material for tests of spoken language appears arbitrary or based on old-established and now unfashionable teaching conventions; while in achievement tests the validity of tests depends on the validity of the material taught, in proficiency tests some fresh thinking may be necessary. In the following pages, *tests* refers to proficiency tests unless otherwise indicated.

Objective tests of spoken language available at present often appear extremely unsatisfactory. Those that exist are frequently criticized as being (variously) invalid, unreliable, too long, too short, too difficult to score, or harmful in their backwash effect on teaching. (There is also the common argument that the *lack* of tests of spoken language has a harmful effect on teaching by reinforcing emphasis on the written

---

[1] Indeed, there may be some justification for the use of such a term as *oracy* in opposition to *literacy*, as suggested by Andrew Wilkinson (1965, pp. 13–14), *oracy* designating general ability in the oral skills and *literacy* general ability in the use of the written language. (*Editor's note:* See Chapter 8 of this present volume where Wilkinson describes his tests of oracy.)

medium.) Interesting attempts have been made to measure certain speech skills at the more elementary level, but at advanced levels progress remains slow. Until recently there was indeed little effort to construct objective tests of speech, and today it still seems premature to claim 'that the problem of objective testing of speaking ability has largely been overcome in recent years' (Pimsleur, 1966b, p. 205). It all depends on what is meant by speaking ability. It might be more accurate to say that as a result of serious attempts to construct objective tests of speech, only now are we becoming aware of the problems involved. Perhaps before accepting claims made for new tests we should search critically for assumptions about the nature and composition of speech skills which underlie them.

Effective testing requires first that we have a clear notion of what we are trying to test and secondly that we have adequate sampling techniques on which to base a choice of items which can be reliably scored. When the aim is to test anything so embracing as the ability to understand and use spoken language, the first requirement is very difficult to meet, while the second at present remains largely experimental. The danger lies in accepting a definition of language ability which is arbitrary or too narrow, merely perhaps to permit the use of techniques which are more respectable psychometrically than they are linguistically.

It is common form in educational testing for the test constructor to ask the teacher for a specification of exactly what is to be tested. When faced with this question the teacher of spoken language is hard put to it to provide a satisfactory answer. He may have no very clear definition of language itself and thus be forced into making his own definition of language ability empirically. There are dangers in this, for a teacher often, by bitter experience, becomes more conscious of his pupils' deficiencies than of their success. Thus he is more sensitive about what his pupils cannot say than of what they can say accurately. He refers to his own inventory of pupils' past errors, from which he concludes that certain skills are lacking. He thus tends to define language ability from experience of its breakdown rather than of its success, in negative rather than positive terms. If he turns to the linguist for useful definitions, he may find them too wide or too abstract to be of much help, ranging from those which see language as the distinguishing feature of human society to those which precisely delineate the formal structure of language in terms required for its scientific analysis. Certainly general statements that language is a form of social behaviour or a system or systems of communication do not much help teachers either to decide their priorities in teaching or to understand the relative importance of particular skills in relation to overall competence in communication. In short, to the teacher who is preoccupied with the linguistic shortcomings of his pupils, the linguist may seem to be too exclusively concerned with contemplating how well a language works when it is already mastered.

The gulf between linguistics and language teaching cannot always be bridged easily—although this is precisely what effective testing requires. Achievement tests ought to test what teachers believe they teach; but they should also assess performance in what linguists agree are valid linguistic categories. Proficiency tests must measure the skills required by a carefully defined (and therefore limited) employment of language at known levels in particular social situations. The criteria of proficiency in spoken language should not be abstracted from a theoretical construct of *la langue* (i.e. the language system) but rather from a practical analysis of *la parole* (i.e. actual speech) (de Saussure, 1915).

Applied linguistics—in the sense of applying to language-teaching the findings of modern linguistic studies—seems by no means to be a simple addition of teaching method to linguistic data. The interests of linguists and language teachers are not the same: the linguist may be seeking to discover or elucidate the pattern which he is sure must underlie what is obviously a sophisticated working system of communication, while the teacher is seeking to establish a restricted version of such a system. The teacher wants precise inventories of component skills rather more quickly than the linguist is prepared to supply them. When it comes to establishing effective standardized tests, there is sometimes a third force—often unsympathetic to both—the administrator, who wishes to arrange students in tidy categories according to their predicted skill in performing undefined tasks. This, however, need not deter teachers from constructing useful tests of achievement for their own purposes, or, indeed, researchers from using experimental methods to define language skills through measuring them. At present language teaching could be helped more by efficient tests than by almost any other agency.

If the language-teacher turns to those practical studies which underpin linguistic theory—such as phonetics—he may at present get comparatively little help in his search for a working definition of what to test. Phonetics concerns itself with describing the physiological or acoustic features of utterances and may even provide useful guidance in how to teach the articulation of sounds. But within the larger field of linguistic description the features catalogued or described by phoneticians are themselves subject to linguistic analysis to determine their relevance, and are subject to criteria arising from the assumption that phonetic description occupies a defined and probably subordinate place in the hierarchy of linguistic studies (Firth, 1957, p. 145; Haas, 1959). Thus, when the teacher asks the phonetician what he should teach and test, and what are the relative importance to skill in communication of the items he teaches, the linguist may object that the phonetician is more interested in the trees than in the wood and cannot be relied on to rate the importance of various phonological skills in relation to communication. More important, phoneticians normally offer only detailed descriptions of how certain people *do* speak, while the teacher really wants a description of how they *must* speak in order to be understood. Similarly, linguists have hitherto been mostly concerned with the description of languages as they are used by native-speakers, when teachers might find more useful norms in descriptions of them when used effectively as second or acquired languages. To the teacher (and to the tester) a realistic model of proficiency might well be what the competent foreigner has found it worth his while to learn, rather than what the native 'does'. But in language teaching and language testing the criterion is usually assumed to be that of native speakers without further definition. Terms such as 'native-like skill' are commonly used at the top end of rating scales, but what exactly do they mean? What kind of native, speaking about what, and to whom?

In short, most language teachers, and perhaps especially the expatriate teachers of their own mother tongue, have been faced with the task of teaching a complex form of behaviour, which for their purposes and for those of their pupils, has not been adequately analysed. From his experience of error the teacher notes the need for 'intelligible' pronunciation, for a 'conventional' syntax, for an 'adequate' range of vocabulary, and he proceeds to teach these by isolating items which appear to be teachable in an order assumed to be on the scale *easy—difficult* or *useful—less useful*. He probably has no clear view about the relative importance of these skills to the total 'command of the language' which he is trying to establish. He remains an opportunist, if not an empiricist, largely because no scientific discipline has yet provided him with adequate theoretical basis for his practical task.

Despite the lip-service which nowadays is almost universally paid to the primacy of speech—and by extension, to teaching oral skills—the evidence of syllabuses and teaching programmes at all levels often discloses a concept of language to be learnt in hierarchical layers: a preliminary layer of oral instruction, overlaid by a stratum of reading ability—to be topped by a slab of writing to hold down firmly the whole complex of skills. The concept reveals an interesting confusion of linguistic and educational conventions. For although oracy is now admitted to be the more complex, literacy is traditionally the more respectable.

Although testing oral ability is relatively easy in the early stages, it becomes increasingly difficult as competence increases. As soon as original communication (as distinct from mimicry or identification) begins, the real difficulties arise. Often we can only judge what the testee *wants* to say by what he *does* say—which makes it extremely difficult to establish independent criteria of success, for overall competence in spoken language must be judged ultimately in terms of intelligibility and communication. But intelligibility is not merely the production of identifiable sounds in a conventional order; it depends on a situation which includes a particular listener. The meaning of what is said must be the final criterion, and it can only be judged by reference to a context of situation and audience. A learner may, for example, be able to say the sounds of English recognizably, and even combine them into words and sentences with appropriate prosodic features of stress and intonation, according to recognizable patterns. But the real test of whether he can speak the language is whether he can say something which is understood by the listener as relevant to a particular situation. If in a conventional 'free conversation' test, the tester (or examiner) asks 'What did you do during the vacation?' and A replies 'I am quite well, thank you', while B says 'I work for getting money. I was waiter in hotels, also I wash dishes'—how do we rank A's and B's relative competence in spoken English? A produced a syntactically (and probably phonetically) accurate, but in the situation meaningless, reply; B has made all kinds of formal errors but has nevertheless communicated something relevant and comprehensible in terms of the situation. We may assume that A does not understand the question while B does, but what is being tested—pronunciation, auditory comprehension, commonsense, or what? Nothing which can be isolated among these factors (and others), whose relative importance to the whole act of communication can easily be decided. The problem of meaning and relevance is fundamental, for signals must add up to meaning in an integrated relationship. Attempts to assess ability in spoken language objectively in terms only of sounds or signals, independently of the meaning they are being used to convey, could be misleading, unless we are quite certain first of the relative importance of each to particular acts of communication. Because of their overlappings and compensations, and the essential redundancy of speech, this seems almost impossible. We are thus thrown back on making informal guesses and fairly arbitrary judgements about which isolable and testable skills should be sampled as reliable indices of ability. The only alternative is the overall 'impression' method of assessment, which is seldom reliable without a great expenditure of time by highly skilled testers.

It has been noted above that in testing spoken language a clear distinction between auditory and oral skills is not always possible, or even desirable. However much psychometricians may desire to 'test one thing at a time', language nearly always makes use of several things

at once when it conveys meaning. Nevertheless, for descriptive purposes we can conveniently separate testing techniques under those
requiring *auditory comprehension* and those requiring *speech production.*

TESTS OF AUDITORY COMPREHENSION

To standardize presentation, the use of recorded material is of course
valuable. But in a number of languages, and especially in English, this
raises the question of which pronunciation should be employed. No
doubt that of a native-speaker (but what kind of native-speaker of
English, for example?) would be recommended by many. On the other
hand, in areas where either English or French have been adopted as
naturalized second languages (as in Africa or India), there may be
good arguments for presenting a locally acceptable second-language
form. At higher levels of attainment it seems that there are good
arguments for presenting in one test a variety of forms, since it seems
that an aspect of competence is ability to understand freely not merely
any single 'recommended' form of a language but also other major
varieties. Thus, at an advanced level, a student of English might be
expected to understand British, American, Australian and perhaps
educated Indian or African varieties of pronunciation: a student of
German might be expected to understand regional lexical variants, a
student of Spanish both Iberian and South American varieties, etc.

The integrated skills of understanding the spoken language can
perhaps be tested on the same lines as those commonly used for the
written medium, by presenting recorded stretches of speech followed
by multiple-choice questions on the meaning conveyed, although both
the signals used and the process of comprehension may be much more
complex, because of the redundancy of speech (Rivers, 1966). At first
sight, however, this appears a realistic and valid test of general proficiency, in which there would be a self-adjusting balance of the
factors involved. Experience has shown, however, that such tests are
often unreliable. Two special factors may contribute to this: memory
span, involving the ability to hold and recall a succession of sounds or
sentences; the influence of previous knowledge of or interest in the
content of what is said. Both of these factors may be regarded as extra-
linguistic by some. They seem to be interrelated (Lado, 1965) and
both are doubtless important in contributing to competence at an
advanced level. The factor of content interest is not of course confined
to tests of spoken language, but also applies to tests of comprehension
of written language.

At the other extreme, tests such as those of phonetic discrimination
are widely used, in which apparently a single skill is isolated and can
be reliably tested. While such tests may be appropriate and valid at
elementary levels, their degree of relevance to a 'total command' of

spoken language becomes less certain at advanced levels, when the dependence of the listener on segmental phonological features may be reduced by his increased ability to interpret prosodic or other contextual clues to meaning. The beginner's inventory of phonetic recognition may be crucial to him, when small variations in pronunciation can easily obscure meaning; the advanced student or native-speaker has a wider tolerance of variations and may well 'read-in' corrections or interpretations of sounds without realizing it.

There are also other problems affecting such tests. Estimating the functional load of particular phonemic contrasts in many languages is still largely a matter of guesswork. The relative frequency of occurrence of particular phonemes (according to sample counts) is not necessarily a reliable guide to their burden in the speech of any particular person. It could be argued for example, that in British English ə being most frequent therefore carries the greatest load, and therefore is most essential for the foreign learner both to identify and produce. But many of the occurrences of ə are in weak forms of words such as *a, the, to* and so on, which themselves carry little information. There would indeed be no great loss to comprehension in English if weak forms realized in ə were regularly replaced, as they often are, by strong forms in ei, iː, uː, etc. There is always a danger, too, of confusing criteria in tests of features of pronunciation: is the norm to be 'native-like' performance or is it to be an acceptably 'intelligible' second language standard? Both are equally difficult to define, except empirically, but they are different.

Comprehension of stress, pitch or 'intonation' can all be partly tested by a variety of techniques, many susceptible to objective scoring. But having effectively isolated such features which can be sampled through test items, we are still left to decide on the weighting which they should be given in any overall assessment of ability to understand speech. If, for example, we decide that a test-battery should include sub-tests of phonemic discrimination, perception of stress and perception of pitch—combined if necessary into tests of understanding meaning conveyed by intonation contours—we still have no reliable guide to their relative importance as contributions to total understanding in normal speech. Even if performances in tests of particular skills are then correlated with overall performance in a test of comprehension (in which all are used together) this may not give us much guidance because other major factors, such as those mentioned above, appear to be present. Not for the first time must we recall that the meaning of an utterance is often more than the sum of its parts. Hitherto factorial analysis does not appear to have yielded any very clear indication of component skills in terms in which they can be individually tested. The pattern of relevance may vary considerably with different languages.

TESTS OF SPEECH PRODUCTION

The most difficult problems arise when trying to construct tests of ability to speak a language—in so far as this can be separated from ability to understand it. It has occasionally been argued that there is a sufficiently high correlation between performances in auditory and oral tests for separate tests of production to be largely unnecessary, but more evidence than is available would be needed to convince most teachers of this. Reference has already been made above to some of the problems which arise from traditional 'conversational' tests. Suffice to say that although the ideal of a test based on free conversation is very attractive, the problems of sampling, and reliable scoring are almost insoluble, unless a great deal of time and many standardized expert testers are available. No free conversation test can ensure that the material to be scored (i.e. the utterances by the testee) can be standard or made thoroughly comparable. Different people will speak differently about the same subjects or in response to the same stimuli. If conversational tests are recorded, scoring can be based on pooled or multiple assessments, but for good reliability quite long passages are required and scoring takes proportionately longer.

Reading aloud (recorded or scored 'live') is commonly used as a test of pronunciation and has the advantage of providing carefully chosen standard material, but, of course, it involves skills other than those required in speech. It is not by any means certain that pronunciation used when reading aloud is representative of pronunciation used in free speech; certainly it does not provide the opportunities for selection and choice which are an essential component of communication skills in free speech.

A number of devices have been tried to elicit from testees comparable examples of the display of oral skills. Repetition or mimicry of utterances presented on tape or 'live', responses to fixed questions about pictures, free description of pictures, narration of events presented in pictures, have all been used.[1] Prepared questions, the answers to which were scored by a formula giving credit for a fluency factor (i.e. number of words spoken in relation to errors made), have been tried (Dodson, 1963). However, it seems that two basic problems as noted by Lado (1961, pp. 95, 247) remain: efficient and reliable tests of spoken language are likely to be too long and too expensive for general use, while sampling by tests of partial production cannot yet be fully objective. To these can be added the problems of identifying and validating the relative importance of skills which can be isolated and separately tested and of establishing acceptable criteria of performance

[1] Cf. for example *MLA Co-operative Foreign Language Tests* and *MLA Proficiency Tests for Teachers* (French, German, Russian, Italian and Spanish), Educational Testing Services Inc.

for integrated skills, based less on linguistic analysis than on a study of effective achievement by learners. For most purposes mother-tongue standards ('native-like skill') are either too remote or too vague to provide a very useful reference point on a measuring scale. We are thus often left with the ability to make fine discriminations about things which may or may not be important, and only unreliable judgements about things that we know *are* important. Only the critical examination of the results of a great deal more experimental testing than has yet been done will clarify these problems.

8

The Testing of Oracy[1]

Andrew Wilkinson

Tests of oracy may be of two kinds. On the one hand there are those which set out to assess the candidate's ability to express his thoughts and feelings and to communicate these to others. These are tests of *oral expression* (OE). On the other hand there are those which try to assess his ability to understand what he has heard. These are tests of *listening comprehension* (LC).

ORAL EXPRESSION

The first problem in designing a test of oral expression is to select an appropriate speech situation; for various reasons not all speech situations are available for this purpose.

I. SPEECH SITUATIONS

Not all speech is intended to communicate. Oaths and exclamations of frustration and annoyance come into this category quite frequently; so do muttered threats like 'You just wait, Jack' or 'Silly old besom!' and their originator would often be very embarrassed if an audience overheard. Usually, however, a speaker addresses his words to an audience of some kind, ranging from an individual in conversation to millions by TV. From one situation to the next he will adjust his mode of speech—perhaps slightly, merely a matter of tone, perhaps considerably, so that the register and style is greatly altered. (Register and Style as used here refer to variations in language according to the different uses needed by speakers and to the relationships between speakers, cf. Halliday, McIntosh and Strevens, 1964.)

The utterance of a speaker is determined by what he wishes to say, his aim (conscious or unconscious) in saying it, his status in relation to his audience, and his assessment of an attitude towards them. In all utterances intended to communicate, these factors operate, but in some speech situations a further factor is important—the immediate and

[1] It must be remembered that Wilkinson's chapter is concerned exclusively with the Lɪ or mother-tongue situation.

Reference is made to this chapter on p. 16 of the Introduction.

continuous response of the listeners; in other speech situations this is largely or completely absent. We shall call these two situations as follows: the first, the Reciprocal Speech Situation (RSS), the second, the Formal Speech Situation (FSS); and speech in the first Reciprocal Speech (RS), in the second Formal Speech (FS). These are not distinct categories; rather they are two poles between which many situations containing elements of both are to be found.

1.1 Reciprocal Speech Situations

Conversation is the normal RSS. In conversation the responses a speaker receives tell him whether he is communicating; the responses do not need to be words—other signals, looks, nods, grunts, can be quite sufficient. Acting on these the speaker may continue, or may repeat or rephrase his point if he judges it to have been missed. The contributions of the others may bring a new direction to the conversation, or introduce a new topic. In either case they will serve as a spur to further utterance on the part of the first speaker. This interchange is the essence of conversation; it serves to advance the communication between the speakers, and also by supplying a constant feedback, to help them judge whether they are still on the same wave-length. The two are bound in a reciprocal relationship. In a very real sense the listener creates the utterance of the speaker and vice versa.

The same conditions often apply in conversations or discussions among more than two people, whether these are casual, or have some definite purpose—in educational situations such as evening classes, in the host of committees which meet to further the working of some organization, whether it be the government at national or local level, the church, business, the union or professional association, or the darts or poultry club. If these discussions succeed at all and are not dominated by one loquacious and insensitive member they have the characteristics of the RSS to a large extent, with the common purpose—and perhaps a good chairman—giving direction to the utterances.

1.2 Formal Speech Situations

The reciprocal speech situation then is one in which the immediate and continuous response of the listener(s) may modify the mode of utterance. The extreme opposite of this is represented by radio and television where the form of the utterance, even if it is spontaneous, cannot be modified in that way. Thus a serious talk addressed to listeners at home may have many FS characteristics. On the other hand utterances addressed to listeners in the studio, as in a broadcast discussion, have many RS features, where the editing has not tried to shape them in the direction of FS.

Outside broadcasting and similar media the FSS is fairly common. It is particularly to be found in the sermon, which—to some extent for historical reasons—is nearly always a one-way communication. A major-general addressing troops lined up on the parade ground will not look for smiles for his witticisms or vocal support for his exhortations; a head teacher speaking in morning assembly will be surprised at more than a very limited range of audience responses. A common form of FSS is the lecture used in higher education as the normal mode of teaching. Its success will depend on such factors as the suitability of the matter for the listeners, the clarity of utterance—but it will also depend on how sensitive the speaker is to the responses of the audience. A good speaker will often know whether he has them with him by the signals they give. In other words this type of speech situation is not completely formal but has elements of reciprocity. If the lecture is followed by questions and discussion an RSS has developed.

Other types of speech situation which are Formal to a greater or lesser degree include public debate, speeches at dinners, weddings, and receptions; they include the performance by actors of a play at a theatre. The RSS could not continue without the participation of more than the first speaker; the FSS clearly can, though audience participation is welcomed in many cases. Actors are held to their form of words by the script, but their delivery of them would be lifeless, were not the audience sending back messages of enjoyment.

2. TEST SITUATIONS

A large number of common speech situations are excluded to the test constructor. In examinations so far conducted, or being experimented with, the following have been used. The first three (a–c) are in the field of RS; the next five (d–h) are in the field of FS.

(a) *The Interview*. The candidate holds a discussion with an adult, usually for about ten minutes. The adult may be a stranger to the candidate, and would probably be the examiner; or he may be the candidate's teacher, in which case the assessment will probably be done by a third person, perhaps in the room, or perhaps with a tape-recording of the interview. Conversation often arises from a short passage the candidate has read aloud; or it may be on any subject the interviewer finds him willing to talk on.

(b) *Group discussion*. A small group of candidates, usually not more than six, are given a choice, or free choice, of subject. The examiner may be present in the room from the first, or he may be called in when the discussion has warmed up: assessment by tape alone would not seem to be possible because of the difficulty of distinguishing voices. Very little experiment has been done with such tests, but it would seem probable that—with average candidates at least—a leaderless group might very soon dry up; the effect of having an adult to prompt the discussion, or of appointing a chairman from the candidates, might be looked into.

(c) *Seminar.* The candidate gives a talk which he has prepared beforehand, but which he has not learnt by heart, to a small group of his peers, preferably round a table. He must not read his matter, but may have with him a few notes. After his talk has finished he must be prepared to discuss it with the group. This situation has many of the characteristics of (b), i.e. it is partly an RSS, with resemblances to the talk or lecturette (d) below which is more formal. The examiner would need to be present, or observe on closed circuit TV.

(d) *Lecturette.* The candidate gives a talk to a group of his fellow candidates, as under (c). His audience is some feet away from him, and thus he must have developed some of the arts of the public speaker in knowing how to project himself, and will stand to address them. He may use pictures, objects, models, diagrams, to illustrate his points as long as his communication is predominantly oral. Questions and discussion may follow; the examiner is present in the room.

(e) *Recitation.* The very word has dropped out of use in the English classroom, partly as a result of the reaction against learning by heart some years ago, partly because of a distrust of the kind of material which used to be considered appropriate for the exercise. Recitation, perhaps under a new name, would be the delivery of a piece of memorized poetry or prose using at least some of the arts of the actor.

(f) *Dramatic or semi-dramatic group activities.* These include choral speech, the enactment of a ballad, or a scene from a play, free drama involving words. There is an audience, probably of other candidates. The time taken should not exceed the total of that which would be assigned to the candidates individually.

(g) *Debate.* The debate used in various public-speaking festivals has the competitors in teams of five—a chairman, and proposer and opposer with their seconders. An audience is present, but questions from the floor are not normally admitted. As far as one is aware this form of speech situation has not been suggested for examining at CSE or GCE level; but a case could be made out for taking into account any speech work the candidate has been engaged on during the year (see (i) below).

(h) *Reading aloud.* By far the most common FSS which has been suggested for an oral examination is reading aloud. Very few of the examinations the writer has come across omit it. The candidate is given a few minutes to study a piece of prose, and then must stand to read it to the examiner, from a distance of say 15 feet. The passage may be a set piece provided by the examiner, or it may be from a book known to the candidate and brought along by him. Sometimes one of the literature set books is used as a source of passages. The candidate is not usually required to possess the newsreader's technique of being able to read a previously unseen passage after the merest glance through it. Doubtless this would be difficult for some candidates, but it is hoped that oral work will increase in all types of institution and standards consequently improve; and if this happens the device should prove useful; certainly it would be worth while experimenting with it.

(*i*) *General speech work.* The examination of speech need not take place in a particular situation on a particular day. In an educational institution all the speech work of the candidates over a prescribed period could be taken into account in a process of continuous assessment.

3. MARKING SCHEMES

It seems likely that similar conditions apply to the marking of spoken English as to written work where the researches of Hartog and Rhodes (1936), Wiseman (1949) and Britton (1963) suggest that an impression mark has advantages over a system of code marking. Hitchman (1966) drawing on American research and his own experience prefers a combination of the two. Certainly all markers should have had training in the recognition of the qualities which go to make up their judgements even if the judgements are by impression on specific occasions. In the CSE experiment conducted by Southampton University examiners were asked to study lists of itemized qualities beforehand and reliability coefficients between an examiner and his observer varied between $\cdot785$ and $\cdot877$ depending on the speech situation used. (Schools Council, 1966.)

In the RS and FS situations outlined earlier as being usable for examining, the following basic elements would seem to require consideration, whatever credit is given to each.

(*a*) *Voice.* The instrument itself. Its *range*, whether too high or too low, whether used within its range, its flexibility; its *tone*, whether, e.g. whining, nasal, strident; its *accent*—how this adds to or detracts from the utterance; whether it is so broad as to interfere with communication.

(*b*) *Content.* What is produced. *Ideas*—what thought and appositeness do these show; interesting, or dull and commonplace? *Vocabulary and turn of phrase*—extent, exactness where necessary, vividness. *Register*—whether the kind of English used is appropriate to subject matter.

(*c*) *Delivery.* How the utterance is launched. *Clarity*—distinctness and articulation of words. *Projection and volume*—whether they reach the listeners. *Physical stance*—whether the position of the speaker is the most helpful in aiding his communication (and, incidentally, shows due courtesy to the audience).

(*d*) *Fluency.* The progress of the utterance. *Coherence*—whether the words and phrases are put together in acceptable groups; whether these groups are built up into relevant wholes in terms of delivery rather than content. *Sensitivity*—speaking at a suitable speed, allowing pauses where necessary; use of appropriate speech rhythms.

Stabilizers, utterances such as *er-er, mm, you know, sort of*, can have a positive or negative function. Positively, they may: steady the candidate to enable him to choose an effective word or phrase; be a springboard to creative utterance he would be self-conscious about otherwise; act as echo-sounders. Negatively, they may: irritate the listener; be a sign of incoherence, a cry even of despair (in these cases they are sometimes called *stopgaps*, or *fillers*). It is important to recognize which is the case.

(*e*) *Reciprocity*. Relationship with the listener(s). This will naturally vary with the nature of the speech situation. *Contact*—the ability to contribute to a conversation so as to involve the other(s), to gain the interest and attention of an audience. *Flexibility*—the ability to adjust one's utterances in the light of responses received. *Style*—the forms appropriate to the people being addressed—neither over formal nor over familiar.

In the FSS's where the material is given, as in passages for reading aloud, or a play, the above categories are in general appropriate, with some modification, except that credit can no longer be given for content. Instead the element of Interpretation is introduced.

(*f*) *Interpretation*. This is largely a new item, though obviously it overlaps with Sensitivity (*d*) a little. It consists in the appreciation of mood, content, and intention of the material, and the way this is brought out.

Existing marking schemes tend to confine themselves to a few items. The English Speaking Board assesses on a five-point scale each of the items, *Voice*; *Clarity*; *Vocabulary* and *Composition*; *Audience Control and Relationship*; *Imagination, Sincerity, Spontaneity*. The Brighton CSE Examinations have used *Voice*; *Pronunciation*; *Delivery*; *Language*; *Fluency*. The NUJMB[1] uses, for the interview, *Speech in Conversation*; *Command of Language*; *Communication*; and for reading aloud *Speech in Reading* (Voice, Articulation, Pronunciation); *Interpretation of Reading* (Delivery, Communication). The examiners are given guidance on the marking sheet under each heading, with an indication of the range in which good, fair and poor marks in each category might be expected to be given. Thus under Voice in conversation:

[1] Northern Universities Joint Matriculation Board.

Successful maintenance in conversation of reasonable standards of voice and speech	7–10
Fair	4–6
Poor voice. Too many colloquial contractions, substitutions, dropped h's for the semi-formal occasion	0–3

Other specimen rating scales and mark sheets are given in Hitchman (1966, appendix 2).

The common practice of examining boards is to take more than one measure of each candidate, and this is clearly necessary. A description of the main batteries currently in use is given by the present writer elsewhere (Wilkinson, 1965, Ch. V).

4. SUGGESTED CRITERIA FOR OE TESTS

The following criteria would seem to be appropriate for tests of oral expression:

(i) Do they set out to test the kind of spoken English which, under normal circumstances, the candidate will need to use?

(ii) If not, is there some other justification for including them?

(iii) Are the tests such as to have a beneficial 'washback' effect upon teaching?

(iv) Are they valid?

(v) Are they reliable?

(vi) Are they administratively practicable?

These criteria will now be discussed in more detail.

(i) *Common usage*. Of all speech situations the RSS is by far the most common, even with professional speakers. Conversation is most frequently between two individuals, but often between members of a group, particularly at meal times. In terms of usefulness an RSS test is therefore of first importance. The major problem with any type of interview test is the very large part played in it by the interviewer. In business and education interviews have been shown to be unsatisfactory as predictors of future success; the relevance of this may be that the contribution of the *interviewer* is very important. A sympathetic interviewer might win speech from stones who are in any other situation unspeaking; an unsympathetic or clumsy one is likely to inhibit all but the most orate candidate. Even with a good interviewer the situation would seem to militate against the testing of all but a narrow area of the candidate's oracy—his ability to be interviewed.

And this is in fact largely admitted in the Instructions to Schools, 1961, issued by the Durham Examining Board:

Because of the inequality of status of the participants—the Examiner must remain an Examiner and the candidate a candidate—the situation is as much an interview as a conversational one and to this extent a candidate's performance . . . is a measure of his performance in interview.

A second RSS test is the 'group discussion' in which several candidates discuss a topic which they have previously been made aware of. There is a good deal to be said for this; discussion, between two or several people, whether as conversation at home, or an essential part of the work in class, is constantly taking place. The slightly more formal atmosphere of the classroom prompts the discussion towards an acceptable form of Classroom rather than Playground English. The stresses in such a situation may well be less, since the candidates support one another and authority does not play a dominant part. This is an RSS in the way that the interview is not. There are, however, administrative and other difficulties, which will be looked at later.

A third form of test is what has been called earlier the Seminar. This has both RSS and FSS elements. It consists of a candidate giving a short talk (FSS) to others in a fairly intimate atmosphere, say round a table, and then leading a discussion (RSS) upon it. The conditions are such, however, that the talk has some of the characteristics of a prolonged utterance in an RSS—it might use echo-sounding devices and sense the non-verbal responses of the listeners. Thus it is well within the category of Common Usage whilst to some extent testing FS and RS skills. Experiments suggest that the difficulties in using 'group discussion' and 'seminar' can be overcome by close-circuit TV. The Manchester experiment (1966) successfully employed examiners circulating amongst pairs of conversing candidates.

(ii) *Other Usage.* The more Formal a speech situation becomes the less one can justify using it in testing by saying that the candidates are normally involved in it, or will be in future. For the ordinary person the occasions for participating in public debate, or for giving a public speech are practically non-existent. Reading aloud is very popular in speech examinations, yet it is not a skill which is ever employed extensively. Again participation in drama is confined to a very small proportion of the population. One reason for including these in an examination would be that they involve skills which are closely related to RS skills, so that to test the one is to give a measure also of the other. A second reason would be that, though they are not very closely related they are in other ways valuable. Now on the first point: nothing is known for certain about how specific speech skills are, but it seems likely that they are fairly specific. Clearly there are common elements in all speech and training in one *may* transfer to another though not automatically. Thus reading aloud may sensitize children to meaning, and its communication in intonation, pitch, rhythm, pace. But reading aloud is not 'speaking' English; the spontaneous creative element is lacking, the matter is probably highly literary. (At Manchester (1966) it was found that of the four types in the trial, 'conversation' and 'discussion' fell together as against 'reading aloud' and a 'prepared talk'.) Reading aloud is, however, a sufficiently similar activity in some ways to justify some place in a speech examination; and because (and this is the second point referred to above) it is a way of coming to terms with literature. Similar advantages can be claimed for dramatic activities of various kinds—plays, dramatic recitation. But that does not mean they are equally appropriate for an examination in spoken English. The subject is, after all, speech, not speech and drama; very many highly orate people would be at a complete loss on the stage.

(*iii*) '*Washback*'. The 'washback' of an examination is the effect it has on teaching in the school taking it. All too often the effect has been bad; designed as testing devices examinations have become teaching devices; work is directed upon what are—in effect if not in fact—past examination papers, and consequently becomes narrow and uninspired.

The refreshing thing about most tests in oral English therefore is that they are virtually impossible to cram for. If a candidate is to give a talk, and writes it out beforehand, he will not be permitted to read it. If he memorizes it, this will be much more apparent than with written work. If the candidate is given only one well-directed question from the examiner or the audience he finds his prepared text is useless; he is thrown upon his own resources and will have to answer spontaneously. In any case he can only memorize Content; the other qualities are the result of extended training.

The best way to ensure that children speak well is for them to participate in a variety of speech activities of all kinds.

(*iv*) *Validity*. Insufficient work has been completed on the validity of any type of oral expression test. We need to know more about which type best reflects the candidate's speech ability, as measured by other criteria—such as speech work continuously assessed, or the estimate of one or several teachers. It is not known whether we can speak of the candidate's speech ability as a general factor, or whether it can only be defined in relation to specific situations. In the Southampton experiment validity coefficients—correlations with teachers' estimates— were between ·344 and ·565 (Schools Council, 1966, p. 21). At

Manchester (1966) the correlations were between ·436 and ·687 in
four different tests. The highest correlations, between ·7 and ·8, are
claimed by Hitchman (1966, p. 63).

(v) *Reliability*. Tests of oral expression can never be standardized item
by item, and marked purely objectively, as can verbal reasoning tests,
and for that matter tests of listening comprehension. It seems likely
that they will be less reliable than tests of written expression at least
for the time being as there is no general agreement on the part of
teachers as to standards in speech. Work carried out in the Department
of Education, University of Leeds, 'shows that the views held by
teaching practice supervisors, heads, and school staff, concerning
successful and unsuccessful speech vary to such an extent that very
little in the way of a common denominator between them can be
discovered. The idea that . . . internal examining might safely be left
to the English staff of a school has been severely shaken by other
investigations (see TES, 22nd June 1962, p. 1285; and Wise, 1963).
     The problems of reliability are bound to be many at first, until a
body of experience is built up; and even then exact parity cannot be
hoped for, especially since it is highly desirable that schools shall
experiment with a large variety of speech activities, and attempt
varied types of test. The teacher's estimate mark in particular will be
one in which a high degree of subjectivity enters. Amongst comparatively small groups of schools or candidates, with examiners and
moderators holding common assumptions, experience suggests that a
considerable amount of agreement is possible. The Southampton
experiment gives a reliability coefficient between 'observer' and
'examiner' present on the same 'topic' situation of ·837; the 'assessor'
using tape correlates with the 'observer' ·591. Hitchman gives a figure
of ·75 for 'competent examiners under properly organized conditions'
(p. 63).

(vi) *Administrative practicability*. The larger a test battery becomes the
more difficulties it presents in administration. An important reason
that reading aloud followed by interview with the examiner has become
the most common form of test is that it is swift (10 minutes) and does
not disrupt school activities. It can also be taped for moderating. It is
claimed this can reduce the time of the actual test to five minutes
(Household, 1963). It would be a pity, however, if administrative
convenience became the over-riding factor. Group and seminar tests,
and tests requiring an audience are probably much more valuable and
merit extra time and trouble. The present writer has been involved in
an experiment conducted by Bernard Bryan for the East Suffolk

NATE in which close-circuit television was used to assess a group test. It would seem that in this device lies the answer to many of the problems which have so far beset the assessing of this type of test.

LISTENING COMPREHENSION

Little attention has been paid to listening in education in this country. A summary of the research carried out in America has been given elsewhere by the present writer (1965). It is sufficient here to mention the general findings; that it is an inefficient function despite the amount of time that is spent in listening in educational situations; that it can be improved by training: and that it seems to involve a specific listening factor (Spearritt, 1962).

This section will describe two listening tests: one, a widely-used American one for college students; the other one constructed in this country with the CSE[1] in mind.

1. THE BROWN-CARLSEN TEST

The best-known American listening test is the Brown-Carlsen (1953). It consists of five parts. In Part A, Immediate Recall, subjects are asked orally questions like '4. In the series of numbers 6–9–4–4–8–2 the fifth number is ....'. Part B, Following Directions, has questions like '28. Subtract the next to the smallest odd number from the next to the largest even number. The number one less than that is ....' (a group of numbers and letters is presented visually to the subjects). Part C, Recognizing Transitions, asks whether a sentence is *introductory*, *transitional*, or *concluding*: no. 41 is 'A somewhat similar treatment is taking the murderous sting out of whooping-cough' (where 'similar' is the main reference back, 'whooping-cough' that forward—transitional). Part D, Recognizing Word Meanings, has paired questions on the pattern: '56. What does *turn* mean in the sentence, "One good turn deserves another"?' and '47. What does turn mean in the sentence, "She knew how to express every turn of emotion"?' (multiple choice dictionary definitions are provided visually). Part E is Lecture Comprehension; a speaker delivers a fifteen-minute prepared talk, reading it aloud. One part is:

With a terrified roll of his eyes the boy ran to obey, placing the jade bowl on the flagstone, close to the mistress of the house. Then he stood back, holding a looped whip in his hand, as, from under the white napery of the table, there slithered a long bloated thing, yellowish-brown with black and white marks. The cobra approached the milk and the native boy fell on it and killed it.

[1] Certificate of Secondary Education.

The talk also contains a literary quotation, part of which runs:

In my feelings, her beauty merged in some subtle way with that of the birds and furnished the inspiration for my poem 'Egrets', which describes her as being 'kin to their slim hauteur', as being 'gentle and yet far away as wings upon wild water'.

The administrator of the test has the job of presenting the material to the candidates, predominantly by reading it aloud to them. Questions are then asked to test comprehension of the text. These questions which demand written answers, relate to interpretation as well as vocabulary meanings.

2. THE BIRMINGHAM TESTS

The work carried out at Birmingham University Department of Education from 1963 onwards was commissioned by the Ministry of Education and responsibility was later transferred to the Schools Council. The project[1] was to prepare a Listening Comprehension (LC) test for students of 16 years old between the 40th and 80th percentile of ability for use in the CSE examination.

There is a difference in emphasis in the Birmingham tests from that in the Brown-Carlsen and other LC tests. The reading aloud of the items and passages by the administrator would seem to limit very much the nature of what can be tested; features which only exist in the spoken language—intonation for instance—cannot be used because there is no guarantee that the various administrators will utter them the same way. Further, the Brown-Carlsen passages are of a literary nature, and literary material does not communicate with the recipient in the same ways as spoken material, with its empirical structures, reciprocities, stabilizers, etc. In the Birmingham tests it was felt to be important that a listening test should not be of literary material read aloud, but as far as possible of genuine spoken language recorded as uttered. This does not mean that some of the items might not conceivably occur in a reading comprehension test—speech and writing of course draw on a common stock of language. But even these common items are involving in some sense the ability to listen in the LC test. The question to ask about them is not whether they could occur in a reading comprehension test, but whether they test understanding of something which frequently occurs orally. Thus one often receives verbal directions as well as written; one often meets the advertising register in television as well as in newsprint.

For these reasons it was decided that the whole of the test material should be recorded on tape. The questions were also included on the

[1] The research fellow throughout the project has been Mrs Dorothy Atkinson; the help of Dr Alan Davies in the earlier stages is gratefully acknowledged.

tape. Answers were of the multiple choice (usually triple) kind and the alternatives were given in an answer booklet, the subject having to mark his choice. The intention was to make the marking completely objective.

3. A BIRMINGHAM TRIAL TEST

The sections in the test were as follows: (*a*) Content, (*b*) Detail, (*c*) Transitions, (*d*) Word Meaning, (*e*) Ambiguity, (*f*) Deduction, (*g*) Intonation, (*h*) Register, (*i*) Style. Of these the first two, which consisted of passages of continuous or conversational utterance, were clearly the most important and this was reflected in the loading of the marks. To some extent the other sections were subsumed in them. Only to some extent, however, because the occurrence of any one particular speech feature—an irony, an ambiguity, a stylistic usage— is not necessarily frequent in any one piece of utterance, and is seldom courteous enough to occur in close proximity to other such speech features for the convenience of the test constructor. The first two sections therefore are of continuous utterance, the other five are of individual items designed to test understanding of specific features. A full description of the test with demonstration items has been given elsewhere by Atkinson (Wilkinson *et al.*, 1965) and thus it will be appropriate here to give an outline only.

(*a*) *Content.* The listener might be expected to understand the major and minor ideas, to infer as well as to recall, to be aware of the direction of the utterance, of the profession or attitude of the speaker, to interpret figurative language. A passage of unscripted narrative is used punctuated by comments and prompts from other speakers. The questions are asked on the tape after the passage has ended; and an appropriate time of a few seconds is given for the answer to be ticked in the answer booklet.

(*b*) *Detail.* Correct recall of facts is often important, particularly in a learning situation. Thus this test is concerned more specifically than (*a*) with the remembering of particular items. A three-minute passage of exposition is played, and the subjects then have four minutes in which to *read* the questions and tick the correct alternatives.

(*c*) *Transitions.* The question in effect asked is: Whereabouts in an utterance do you think this sentence occurs—at the beginning, during or at the end? Thus 'A funny thing happened to me on the way to the Forum' is clearly introductory. 'For instance there's the case of Ruth Ellis' points both backwards and forwards, and thus occurs during an utterance. One needs to be able to recognize signals which inform one as to the progress of an utterance, especially if one joins it part way through, as frequently happens. A question occurs on the tape after each item.

(*d*) *Word meanings.* Word meaning is contextual. Subjects are asked to distinguish which meaning of a particular word is intended in a specific context. 'I'll give a pound' has at least four meanings leaving out differences which could be brought about by intonation. Two of these meanings (£1 and 1 lb.) are likely; a third (pound = animal pen) is quite possible, and so is a fourth in the famous story of the boy who offered his pound (of pulling power) to launch the lifeboat. A question occurs on tape after each item.

(*e*) *Verbal ambiguity.* Many common utterances involve a choice of alternatives. They present a problem or series of problems, to be solved before the intended meaning is hit upon. 'I'll never not love you' is one example, and the question would ask whether or not he would continue to love her. A question occurs on the tape after each item.

(*f*) *Rapid Deductions.* One commonly deduces the subject, person or thing under discussion from contextual clues though it is not actually mentioned. 'He made a flying start from the standstill position.' Aeroplane or racing car? From the vocabulary (aeroplanes are never described as making a 'flying start') clearly the latter. A question occurs on the tape after each item.

(*g*) *Intonation.* Under this head are included meanings brought about by changes in tone or emphasis. 'Light house-keeping' is not the same as 'light-house keeping', nor 'What *are* you doing?' as 'What are *you* doing?'. Questions follow individual items on the tape.

(*h*) *Register.* Different groups of people, especially occupational groups, have their own vocabulary (and to some extent grammar). Some advertising attempts to appropriate a medical or a poetic vocabulary. Subjects might be asked to distinguish between the appropriate and the appropriated. Questions after each individual passage.

(*i*) *Style.* The sense of felt relationship between two people in a particular situation is indicated by the language they use. Examples are seen in the use of titles, surnames, Christian names, endearments; but these things are only indications and may easily be absent. 'I lay a somewhat different emphasis from Mr Jones' in the board meeting, might be 'You're talking nonsense, Harry' in the pub, where the whole form of words is different. Subjects are asked to consider appropriate and inappropriate utterances (questions after each item).

4. TRIAL TEST RESULTS

The test was standardized by several trials. Standard deviations indicated good discrimination. Other measures of IQ, oracy by teacher's estimate, and written composition, were taken. In the final trial correlations with the measures were as shown in Table 1.

School	IQ	Oracy (teacher's estimate)	Composition
A	·61	·23	·20
B	·76	·40	·48
C	·53	·55	·44

TABLE 1. Oracy LC test validity correlations in three schools

Apart from the two low correlations in school A where there were special difficulties the correlations were very satisfactory, and were fully supported by figures in the previous trials. Too high a correlation would indicate that the test was measuring something already being measured in another way; such as by an IQ test; too low a correlation, especially with linguistic measures, would suggest invalidity. The predictions of the teachers on oracy are necessarily based on the expressive than the receptive ability of their pupils. Full results are given by Wilkinson and Atkinson (1966).

5. CRITERIA FOR LC TESTS

Similar criteria to those set forth for tests of oral expression (p. 123) are appropriate for tests of listening comprehension.

(*i*) *Common usage.* Is the English employed in the tests the kind which is normally heard? The range of utterance people hear is much wider than that they employ; and thus it is appropriate in LC tests to include both RS and FS. In the RSS test reciprocity is necessarily not with the listener *to* the tape, but with the listener *on* the tape, but exhibits the same speech features.

(*ii*) *Other usage.* Tests which do not test normal RS and FS are those which use mainly literary material read aloud, such as the Brown-Carlsen.

(*iii*) *Washback.* The washback of oral expression tests will be in terms of speech *activity* in the school. The washback of LC tests will be in terms of increased *awareness* of the spoken language, and how it is used in different circumstances. The awareness of language may be expected to have two educational effects; linguistically, it may result in a greater interest and skill in the use of words; and, socially, in less anxiety in a variety of speech situations.

(*iv*) and (*v*) *Validity* and *reliability*. In LC tests of the type envisaged, validity and reliability are guaranteed by the standardization (i.e. pretesting) and completely objective marking.

(*vi*) *Administration*. There are no administrative difficulties with a test of the type envisaged. Ordinary examination conditions, with freedom from interruption, and a good tape-recorder, are all that is required. In common with other speech tests they can be administered at a time most suitable to the institution concerned.

9

Tests in Education

D. W. Grieve

1. THE SCHOOL CERTIFICATE EXAMINATION

1.1. Initially, it was disquiet about certain aspects of the current School Certificate Examinations which led to this inquiry. In view of the general economic and social importance attaching to the award of the School Certificates, as well as the opportunities for higher education open to those whose performance in the examination is satisfactory, it is perhaps true to say that the examination for this Certificate is one of the most important single 'events' in the West African educational calendar. To say this is perhaps a sad reflection on the values of the schools and of society, but, once more, there is little to be gained by pretending that facts are not facts: shutting one's eyes to them will not, unfortunately, make them go away. It is right, therefore, that this particular examination should be the subject of special scrutiny.

1.2. Disquiet about the School Certificate Examination manifests itself in various ways:

(1) School teachers are unhappy about certain aspects of the syllabus and about various papers set in different years. They are also puzzled on occasion by rather odd results. Inevitably there is some suspicion of the competence of the Council's examiners and of the procedures followed in marking and awarding;

(2) The universities are dissatisfied with the low standard of English of many entrants who have scored reasonable marks in the examination but are handicapped in their University studies by their inability to read with understanding or to write clearly;

(3) Conversely there is in some quarters a feeling that the examination in English Language is an artificial barrier to the progress of pupils whose performance in other subjects is wholly satisfactory. It is felt, therefore, that this examination, by preventing good students from proceeding to studies which would lead to higher professional qualifications, is an obstacle to the progress of countries which need as many professionally qualified people as they can get;

Reference is made to this chapter on pp. 16–17 of the Introduction.

(4) The officers of the Council feel that while an examination in English Language is necessary, some better means of measuring attainment in language than that currently in use might be found.

1.3. It is interesting to note that in 1961 the Secondary School Examinations Council in the United Kingdom had set up an English Language Examining Committee to inquire into very similar complaints in this country; by courtesy of Sir John Lockwood I have been able to attend the meetings of this Committee, which have given me a most valuable insight into current developments in the United Kingdom and an opportunity to discuss common problems with many of those engaged in the teaching and examining of English at this level. The report of the English Language Examining Committee (HMSO, 1964) is expected very shortly; its conclusions regarding the GCE at 'O' level (the nearest equivalent in the UK to the School Certificate Examination) are, briefly:

(1) The examination is unreliable (from this it must follow that it is invalid);

(2) The standard of performance accepted for a pass is much too low;

(3) The backwash effect on teaching is thoroughly bad;

(4) The training necessary to pass the examination does not contribute significantly towards teaching children to read extensively or intelligently or to write well;

(5) The examination encourages artificial forms of language use, primarily because the composition topics fail to connect with the candidates' fields of interest and are such as to demand artificial inventiveness on the part of candidates rather than the power to use language on subjects of interest to themselves;

(6) Examiners compensate for their own subjectivity by marking composition within a relatively narrow band of marks. As a result the trivial questions on grammar and vocabulary—which do not test anything very effectively—come to assume a disproportionate importance when it is a matter of discriminating between pass and fail;

(7) Comprehension tests are frequently trivial in nature;

(8) Précis, with its uniform requirement of a reduction to 'one-third of the original', and its insistence on the use of the candidate's own words, cannot be regarded as a fair test of understanding and is not conducive to good teaching;

(9) The questions on grammar and vocabulary in their present form do positive harm. Such questions are often based on a few usages which may be common enough in some varieties of the language, but have traditionally come to be regarded as 'incorrect' in all;

(10) In particular, these questions foster a false concept of the absolute 'correctness' of a given usage, without reference to context.

1.4. Paragraph 1.3 contains part of a considerable list of weighty criticisms directed at current examining practices in the GCE. It has been quoted here because these criticisms seem to be even more relevant to the School Certificate Examination as it exists in West Africa at present. The following additional points relate in particular to this latter examination:

(1) To all intents and purposes, it takes no account of the fact that English in Africa is a second language; as an examination of language skills it is therefore largely irrelevant;

(2) Its effect on teaching is quite calamitous, except where an able and courageous teacher feels able to ignore the examination and teach English regardless of examination requirements;

(3) It has little discriminatory power; very good and very bad candidates are picked out from the mass, but the examination results provide little reliable information about the remainder;

(4) The examination encourages a thoroughly artificial kind of language use, which is particularly undesirable in a situation where the pupils have little opportunity of hearing and reading good modern English.

1.5. These criticisms may be severe, but they are not necessarily a reflection on the Examinations Council, which inherited this examination from the Syndicate only three years ago and has naturally followed the pattern set in previous years. If any blame attaches to anyone for the continued existence of this most unsatisfactory examination, it is to the West African Universities, which have not only insisted on the maintenance of a 'GCE or equivalent' entrance qualification in English Language, but have, since their inception, failed to institute any effective research either into modern English usage in West Africa or into comparative studies of English and West African languages: research which if begun some years ago might by this time have provided the information which could have formed the basis of more satisfactory examinations.

1.6. The most striking thing about the School Certificate English examinations in West Africa at present is that their syllabuses, in so far as they can be said to exist, are almost the same as those for the GCE in the United Kingdom. A comparative study of the syllabuses current in West Africa and in the United Kingdom quickly shows that the nature of the West African syllabuses differs but little from that of their UK counterparts, and, in particular, no mention at all seems to be made of the fact that English is not the mother-tongue of the candidates. There is a striking contrast here with the practice of the Welsh Joint Committee, which provides *three* papers in Welsh: Welsh 01, for candidates whose first language is Welsh, Welsh 02, for candidates offering Welsh as a *second* language, and Welsh 03, for candidates offering Welsh as a *foreign* language. Whether one thinks these examinations in Welsh are good or bad is beside the point: the fact is that their content is different and takes account of the different uses the candidates will make of the Welsh language, as well as the different problems they have met in learning it, and, moreover, *all* are equally acceptable as 'O' level passes in Welsh. There is no question of the candidate who takes 02 or 03 being regarded as having an inferior qualification: for practical purposes he, like the candidate who passes 01, has an 'O' level pass in Welsh.

1.7. The fact that the School Certificate Examinations in English Language take no account of the special learning problems of African students in learning English naturally invalidates them from the start. Even if there were no public disquiet (and there is in fact surprisingly little), to a professional examiner or a professional linguist the examinations would be worth very little because they are very largely irrelevant.

1.8. A further defect of the School Certificate syllabuses as they stand is that they tell the teacher and the candidate practically nothing that he wants to know. For Paper 1, for example, we are told 'account will be taken of subject-matter, arrangement, general expression and command of English'. The questions one immediately wants to ask are 'How much account of each?' 'What is meant by general expression and how does it differ from command of English?' 'How much command of how much English?' 'What is the vocabulary range expected?' 'What structures is the candidate expected to know and to be able to use?'

1.9. The 'syllabuses' for the so-called 'language' papers (Paper 2 in the West African School Certificate (WASC) and Paper 3 in the School Certificate of the West African Examinations Council (SCWAEC)) are similarly uninformative. There is no indication of the nature of the passages to be set for précis and comprehension, and no information as to the *range* of language likely to be required. The list of 'types' of question listed is insufficiently precise in terms of both lexis and grammar. The only grammar questions mentioned are:
　(1) turning direct into indirect speech (or vice versa);

(2) synthesis and exercises in sentence construction (candidates will be expected to distinguish between a phrase, a clause, and a sentence, and to recognize the grammatical function of words, phrases and clauses in their context);

(3) detection and correction of errors of expression.

From this, one does not know whether to expect full-scale analysis and parsing as well as synthesis (it is certainly not ruled out by the syllabus), nor can one tell just how complex the sentences used as the basis for the test are to be. There is a similar lack of information about the lexical questions: 'the rewriting of phrases or sentences' could mean almost anything, and there is no delimitation even in the most general terms of what the required lexis will be. In comparison with the teacher of other subjects, the teacher of English is told singularly little about what he and his charges are expected to do.

1.10. This is perhaps more important than it might seem, because in the absence of a detailed syllabus teachers are driven to past question papers to find out just what is expected of them, and very often these question papers are used for teaching purposes. In order to avoid accusations of unfairness, therefore, examiners are driven to setting similar types of question each year, and over the years papers become extremely stereotyped—a stereotype which is reflected all too often in teaching. The absence of a detailed prescription which would serve as a guide to examiners, moreover, means that the selection of material for testing may be quite arbitrary, as it very often is. Such arbitrariness cannot but be unfair.

1.11. In the following sections it is proposed to examine in some detail the actual tests of which the School Certificate Examination is made up. In passing it may be noted that where criticisms are made—e.g. of précis—they apply equally to other examinations where similar testing techniques are employed: the defects are not exclusive to the School Certificate Examination. The assumption underlying the discussion is that the purpose of these examinations is to measure skill in the use of English: the extent to which the student has mastered the learning problems involved.

2. THE SCHOOL CERTIFICATE EXAMINATION—OPINION IN THE SCHOOLS

2.1. As no major changes can be introduced in an examination such as that for the School Certificate without at least the acquiescence of the teaching profession, an attempt was made to ascertain the views of school staffs on various questions relating to School Certificate examining. This was done by means of a fairly detailed questionnaire, and follow-up discussions wherever it was indicated that these were desired.

It is encouraging to note that the majority of schools responded to this invitation to make their views known, and as a result it was possible to form a fairly accurate view of what teachers thought about the examination.

2.2. In this report I shall concentrate on the answers to what seem to be more important questions. These were:

(1) III.4. *What, in your view, should be the primary function of English Language papers at this level?*

Some replies—fortunately few—were based directly on the nature of the examination tests: 'To test the ability to write compositions and answer comprehension questions on a passage' and so on. Most, however, went further than this and spoke of the ability to express oneself clearly, concisely, and correctly, and the ability to understand what is read. It is noticeable that none made any reference to 'communication' as the purpose of composition exercises (though perhaps this was what was meant by 'expression'), and few made any reference to the use of language skills in real life. From some answers, it seemed that many teachers—though by no means all—regarded the teaching and examining of English as a closed system, with the teaching of English looked on primarily as a preparation for the examination. In fact, of course, the teaching of English should be a preparation for the use of it in real life, and the examination should be an incidental test of one's ability to use it. If this is accepted, the examination should be (a) as accurate a measure as possible of the extent of one's control over the language; (b) an opportunity to show how effectively one can use it in real life situations. In more precise terms, the examination should be a valid and reliable measure of

(a) the ability to communicate ideas, feelings, and attitudes;
(b) the ability to understand the ideas, feelings, and attitudes of
    others as expressed or implied through the written word;

and all the tests which go to make up the examination should be framed with this objective in view.

(2) III.5.(1) *Do the present papers, in your opinion, fulfil this function?*

It is possible to present the answers to this question in tabular form:

	Ghana	Sierra Leone	Gambia
YES	18	6	2
NO	15	4	0

TABLE I

A few others said, 'Partly'.

It will be seen that there is a fairly even division of opinion: there is no evidence that African teachers voted one way and expatriate teachers the other. To the next question:

(3) III.5.(2) *If NO, state briefly in what ways you consider they fail to do so.* A variety of answers appeared. Most significant perhaps, was that of the percipient teacher who said that the papers as set did not distinguish between those candidates who had little or no command of English and those who simply failed to meet the examiners' requirements in the special techniques called for. This is, of course, true, and is an indirect way of saying that the papers do not in fact test skill or attainment in English, but something else (mastery of examination techniques). Of the more detailed comments, most common were the complaints that the comprehension question ought to be compulsory, as it is in Nigeria, that the questions on the content of passages were often trivial and those on phraseology often too difficult, that précis was a poor indicator of attainment, that the grammar questions were redundant, as a knowledge of grammar was already being tested through composition and précis, and that such grammar questions as were set appeared to be traps for the unwary rather than genuine tests of language. Several replies stressed the inconsistency of the précis test from year to year in terms of content: sometimes candidates hardly had a chance because the material was so unfamiliar. One answer showed very clearly that the writer felt that there was no consistent standard but that the standards fluctuated from year to year. (There can of course be no such thing as an absolute standard, but this does not mean that annual fluctuations are inevitable or desirable: all it means is that the general standard of an attainment examination must inevitably follow the general trend of achievement set by the population examined over the years. One may expect a decline or rise over a period of say, ten years; one does not expect fluctuations from year to year.) Many of the replies indicated that it was not so much the *form* of examination that was objected to as the material chosen for inclusion in it. Some thought, however, that the English Language paper should be a sort of General Paper at 'O' level, and one answer in particular complained that the papers demanded 'merely arbitrary knowledge in a purely linguistic context'. What other kind of context the complainant expected to find in a language paper he did not say.

In contrast to the answers to III.4, several here stressed the failure of the papers to take into account the practical uses of language in everyday life, and more than one observed that the 'language' questions in Paper 3 (i.e. questions on vocabulary and grammar) did not in any way reflect the candidates' ability to read and write English.

It will be seen that many teachers are alive to the defects of the existing examination as a test of 'expression' and understanding, even though different teachers put particular emphasis on different defects. If we added up all those complaints which had substance, we should have a formidable list indeed.

(4) III.5.(3) *If NO, state briefly the form which you would like to see the papers take.*

The answers to this question to some extent overlapped those to the previous one. Particular points made were:

    (a) Comprehension should be compulsory;
    (b) Précis and grammar should be omitted;
    (c) The papers should stress the *practical* uses of language;
    (d) Paper 3 should concentrate on the correction of common errors in speech and writing;
    (e) Objective questions might be set;
    (f) Poetry should be included in the comprehension test.

(5) III.5.(4) *Do you consider the present papers a fair test for candidates whose mother-tongue is not English?*

	Ghana	Sierra Leone	Gambia
YES	17	7	2[1]
NO	16	3	3[1]

TABLE 2

It will be seen from the answers to this question that rather less than half the teachers in the three countries were aware of the special defects of the examination as applied in a second-language situation. What the table does not show is that most of the affirmative answers came from relatively well-established schools, many of them with second- or third-generation literate pupils. It seemed to be the teachers from less well-established schools, trying to cope with much less sophisticated pupils, who were most acutely aware of the unsatisfactory nature of the examination, even though they could not say exactly why it was unsatisfactory.

The responses to this question are not, of course, surprising. Few teachers of English have had any linguistic training, and so few can

[1] There are only three recognized secondary schools in Gambia, but two voted 'Yes and No'.

pin-point the genuine learning problems of their pupils except in a superficial way through a study of so-called 'Common Errors'.

(6) III.5.(5) *If NO, why?*
Many of those who answered this question missed the main point and concentrated on difficulties of 'background'. This, of course, is not a linguistic difficulty at all. It is a problem of cross-cultural understanding. A native English speaker has the same sort of difficulty in reading in English about a culture wholly different from his own: his verbal understanding may be perfect, his understanding of the underlying concepts neglible. Although these 'background' difficulties do cause a great deal of trouble, and indeed can invalidate a test, in themselves they are not especially significant in the *second-language* situation. What is important in this situation is the linguistic element: lexis, structures, the requirement in terms of writing, and so on. Such unfairness as there is in the examination stems from the lack of system in the choice of this material, which in turn derives from the absence of a detailed prescription of requirements in the form of a syllabus. In Paper 3, for example, 30 out of 50 marks may depend on a knowledge of six words, six structural items, and a few metaphors, all chosen on no recognizable principle. To the native speaker at the same level, with his incomparably greater experience of the language, such items probably present little difficulty: for the second-language speaker on the other hand, it is really a matter of chance whether he has come across these particular items before or not. This is where the unfairness really lies, if there is any.

More relevantly, a number of answers pointed to the difficulty of précis for the second-language learner (though here again some objected not to précis as such but to the unsuitability of particular passages).

(7) III.6.(1) *Would you welcome a detailed syllabus in English Language?*

	Ghana	Sierra Leone	Gambia
YES	16	4	0
NO	16	6	3

TABLE 3

(8) III.6.(2) *If YES, indicate briefly the form which you would expect such a syllabus to take.*
An alarming number of those who wanted a syllabus expected it to be a detailed exposition of the work to be covered each year or even

each term. This is, of course, quite outside the scope of an examination syllabus, which should be a prescription of what the candidates are expected to know at the end of their course: how they arrive at the end-point is a matter for them and their teachers. One answer suggested that a list of the structures that candidates would be expected to know would be useful, together with a rough idea of the situations they would be expected to have the vocabulary to describe (this is close to the idea of defining registers suggested earlier). Several suggested an expansion of the existing syllabus, with a number of examples of the forms that tests were likely to take. (Certainly any future syllabus must include at least specimen questions.) Several answers also suggested, with justice, that the syllabus should include a clear indication of what the examiners were looking for.

Perhaps because of a certain ambiguity in the wording of the question, there seemed to be some confusion between teaching and examining syllabuses, many teachers rightly rejecting any suggestion of the former. It is not the business of an examining body to lay down what shall be taught year by year, or how it shall be taught. That is the business of teachers, inspectors, and others more directly engaged in the field. The trend of certain discussions after the receipt of the completed questionnaires led me to believe that had this distinction been made clearer in the question, there would have been a majority in favour of a detailed *examination* syllabus, delimiting the field in which the candidates would be examined.

(9) III.7.(1) *Would you welcome the introduction of an objective element into the examination?*

	Ghana	Sierra Leone	Gambia
YES	20	4	3
NO	10	4	0

TABLE 4

In addition, there was one gentleman who remarked, 'We do not understand this jargon here.'

(10) III.7.(2) *If NO, please state your reasons.*

A variety of reasons were advanced against the use of objective tests, more particularly:

(a) that it was possible to score well by guessing;
(b) that objective tests did not test the use of language;

(c) that they would encourage memorization and rote learning;

(d) that they would become stereotyped and mechanical;

(e) that they tested neither expression nor comprehension.

As objective testing has already been discussed in some detail,[1] here it need only be observed that all these charges, except possibly (e), might well be laid against the existing kind of question set. No doubt much of the distrust of objective tests which exists arises from the very unsatisfactory tests which have hitherto been used in Common Entrance and Middle School Leaving Examinations. It remains necessary to convince the sceptical that, like most other things, objective tests are of many kinds, some good and some bad. So far West Africa has seen only the bad ones.

(11) III.8.(2) *Does the allocation of marks to each element of the existing papers reflect your view of their relative importance?*

The majority of those who answered this question wished to reduce the allocation to composition and increase that to précis (despite the almost universally admitted unsuitability of précis as a test at this level).

(12) III.15.(1) *Has your teaching of English been helped or hindered either (a) generally by the present English Language papers or (b) by any specific part of them?*

	Ghana		Sierra Leone		Gambia	
	Helped	Hindered	Helped	Hindered	Helped	Hindered
Generally	17	5	4	3	3	—
Composition	21	1	8	—	3	—
Comprehension	12	4	5	3	2	—
Précis	9	16	6	2	2	1
Other questions	19	8	2	4	2	—

TABLE 5

(13) III.16. *In your opinion, what would be the effect on (a) your teaching of English, (b) examination results, and (c) your pupils' real skill in*

[1] Grieve is here referring to Chapter 12 of his Report [Ed.]

English as a medium of communication if (1) *the précis question were omitted,* (2) *the questions on vocabulary, figures of speech, and grammar were omitted?*

(a) The answers to question (1) were surprisingly inconsistent. Most thought that teaching would be more enjoyable, that there would be more time for reading, composition, and appreciation, and the examination results would improve if précis were no longer an examination requirement. Yet 25 replies were to the effect that real skill in English would fall and only 8 that it would improve as a result. This is puzzling when we consider that no fewer than 19 replies stated that précis was a hindrance rather than a help in teaching English. It is also difficult to understand why the extra time spent on composition, appreciation, and reading should result in a fall in the standard of English. Some, of course, boldly stated that the elimination of précis from the examination would make no difference: they would still teach it. This attitude is at least understandable. What is less comprehensible is how a body of responsible teachers can vote in favour of the abolition of a particular test if in fact they believe that such abolition will result in lower standards.

(b) The answers to question (2) were, on the whole, that it would make little difference to teaching but that examination results would be worse. (This is probably true, as it is usually possible to pick up marks fairly easily on at least one of these questions.) So far as the effect on skill in English is concerned, nineteen considered that the elimination of these questions would have an adverse effect, one thought that it would provide an opportunity to examine the same elements more intelligently by means of objective tests, three expected an improvement and the remainder thought that there would be little or no difference.

2.3. It proved remarkably difficult to summarize the answers to the questions put to the schools on the questionnaire, and the answers discussed above show that on many matters of importance there was a fairly even division of opinion, an impression borne out by the answers to the remaining questions and by discussions. With the exception of the elimination of précis, no major change would seem to have the very active support of the majority of the teachers in any country, and if any major change is contemplated it would be necessary first to persuade the teachers of the necessity of it.

2.4. In view of the reports I had at second-hand before visiting West Africa of considerable discontent over examination results, I think it should be placed on record that neither the answers to this questionnaire nor further discussions with teachers were such as to lend any credence to such reports. Few schools found serious discrepancies between results and expectations (though there were naturally some), and fewer still had had occasion to make complaints to the Council or to ask for an investigation into the marking of their scripts. All said that their queries were promptly and satisfactorily answered, and it was evident that the reports which had come to me had been much exaggerated.

2.5. On the other hand, I think it ought also to go on record that in my view the schools are possibly too satisfied with what can only be described as an unsatisfactory examination. Even when invited to make general comments not related to any specific questions, only two raised the question of reliability, and none that of validity. Many were frankly puzzled that any inquiry at all had been thought necessary, and, while the Ghana Association of Teachers of English had been active over the past eighteen months in trying to secure modifications to the scheme of examination and syllabus, most of the changes suggested were relatively slight, suggesting that there was no quarrel over the objects of the examination or even with its techniques (except for précis), but only disagreement over the details of the approach and selection of material.

3. ENGLISH AND THE OTHER SUBJECTS OF THE EXAMINATION

3.1. The original intention of the inclusion of item (4)[1] in the terms of reference of the inquiry was to provide an opportunity for a discussion of the retention of English Language as a compulsory subject. In fact, this intention was soon overtaken by events, as in January 1963 the School Examinations Committee decided that English Language should no longer be compulsory in SCWAEC, and that a similar step should shortly be taken in relation to WASC. It is therefore only necessary to say here that I myself noted this decision with considerable pleasure. The lifting of this compulsion should reduce the extreme pressure on English teachers and should also make it possible ultimately to require a rather higher level of performance for a pass: the element of compulsion seems inevitably to depress standards in a subject, as examiners are naturally loath to fail a candidate whose whole Certificate result, and whose future, therefore, depends on passing in that subject. The fact that English has been a compulsory subject may well have been a contributory factor in establishing such a low pass standard.

3.2. The pressure for the abolition of compulsory English Language arose primarily because it was felt that many able candidates with a

[1] (4) To consider the examination in English Language in relation to the examination as a whole.

satisfactory performance in other subjects failed to gain a Certificate because of failure in English Language. Study of the relevant figures shows that some candidates were certainly so affected, although their numbers were relatively few (Table 6):

	Credits	1960	1961	1962
(1)	Five or more	48	46	26
(2)	Four	58	45	52
(3)	Three	82	79	68
(4)	Two	134	177	146
(5)	One	216	264	299
(6)	Number of candidates who would have qualified for a certificate but for their failure in English Language	216	220	196
(7)	Balance of 'failed' candidates (i.e. number of candidates who would have failed even if they had passed or did pass in English Language)	606	902	905

TABLE 6. Numbers of SCWAEC candidates failing in English language and gaining in other subjects the number of credits shown

It will be seen that there were roughly 80–100 candidates each year who gained four or five credits or more (i.e. four or five GCE passes or more) but gained no Certificate because of failure in English Language, while in 1962, roughly one-sixth of the overall Certificate failures (as against 25 per cent in 1960) were due to failure in this subject. If one had confidence in the English Language examining procedures and results these figures would not necessarily cause any alarm, but it is certainly disturbing to think that so many full Certificate failures were due to failure in an unreliable and invalid examination. In the circumstances, the position of those who sought to retain, or seek to restore, English Language in its present form as a compulsory subject would seem to be untenable.

3.3. Table 7, showing correlations between English Language and other subjects, is interesting in that it shows that for SCWAEC, with the exception of English Literature, English Language correlated more highly with the science subjects than with the arts subjects.

As science students are probably more highly selected than arts students, this would bear out the hypothesis that, although English Language is not a very good test of language skill, it is a reasonable test of general ability. (The difference between science and arts subjects is less noticeable in WASC, however.)

	Eng. Lit.	Bible Know.	His-tory	Geog.	Maths	Phy-sics	Che-mis-try	Biol-ogy	Gen. Sci.
English Language	·534	·395	·348	·420	·375	·447	·405	·403	·415

Correlations between English Language and Other Subjects
A. SCWAEC 1962

	Eng. Lit.	Bible Know.	His-tory	Geog.	Maths	Phy-sics	Che-mis-try	Biol-ogy	Gen. Sci.
English Language	·429	·396	·293	·417	·377	·412	·503	·384	·309

Correlations between English Language and Other Subjects
B. WASC 1961

TABLE 7

3.4. A frequent cause of complaint in schools is that candidates who score highly in, say, English Literature or History, where one would expect the verbal factor to play a large part, frequently come to grief in English Language: the immediate suspect is of course the marking of the English Language papers. Surely, it is said, something has gone wrong here? (Significantly, it is rarely the high marks in Literature or History that are suspect!)

3.5. While it is true that these discrepancies are sometimes surprising, it must be expected that there will always be some divergence between the marks on the Language papers and those gained on the others. Underlying all such differences, of course, is the factor of unreliability of candidate performance. It is surprising how many schools overlook this: a particular candidate is good at English and must get a credit, but fails; there is something wrong with the marking. Much more likely is that there was something wrong with the candidate on the day of the examination. More particular reasons are:

(1) In subjects such as History, minimal communication is taken to suffice except for the very highest (distinction) grades;

(2) Most of the arts subjects depend on the regurgitation of gobbets of acquired knowledge; English Language depends on the flexible use of a skill; a more intelligent setting of questions in other subjects would probably reduce the number of surprising results quite considerably;

(3) A scrutiny of scripts shows that quite often candidates' language is better in their History scripts than it is in their Language scripts. This is not so surprising as it might seem, because (a) they are dealing with familiar material, and (b) words, phrases, and clauses are consciously or unconsciously repeated from textbooks and notes which have been assiduously studied for at least a year and probably two; the language is therefore very much more *mature* than it is in the Language papers, where the candidate, unless he is exceptionally lucky, has no prepared information and no notes. It is the difference between the reproduction of collocations learned over a period to fit a familiar context and making up one's own out of the raw material of the language: a much more difficult task.

3.6. Despite the admitted failings of the Language papers at present, and they are very great, the fact must be faced that an improvement in the Language papers would probably result in even greater discrepancies between results in Language and results in other subjects. The present Literature and History papers require little more than a capacious memory for facts, the one thing that a true Language paper will not test. If it is really desired to reduce anomalies between Language results and others, it will be necessary to effect improvements in the papers in other subjects as well, in particular to require candidates not only to assimilate and regurgitate facts, but to think about them as well.

3.7. Another factor which ought to be taken into account is the standard of language regarded as acceptable in other subjects. The impression I have gained in the course of discussion with examiners in subjects such as History is that their marking is based on factual accuracy and little else. In these circumstances the English teacher alone can do little to improve the standard of English of his pupils, because in the absence of any incentive there will be little or no transfer of skill from English Language to expression in the other subjects. For perhaps five periods per week the English teacher tries to inculcate good language habits: in the remaining thirty no one bothers. The influence which even the best teacher of English can have in these circumstances is therefore much reduced. Probably one of the most potent single influences for good which the Examinations Council could bring to bear on the general standard of English in West Africa would be a clear statement to the effect that English expression will be taken into account in *all* subjects into which the use of the English language enters. (The Northern Universities Joint Board does this.) It is therefore most strongly recommended that some such rubric be included at the head of the question paper in every relevant subject. The details of the working out of the scheme are a matter for the appropriate committees and panels of the Council, its officers, and its Chief Examiners. However it is done, there is little doubt that it will have a beneficial influence on the attitudes to and the use of the English language in the schools.

3.8. A related question which also formed part of the initial inquiry, but which again was overtaken by events, is that of the abandonment of subject grouping, and the adoption of a GCE-style subject examination with School Certificate standards. In view of the public interest in this question, it was included in the questionnaire circulated to schools and referred to above. The answers were:

		Ghana	Sierra Leone	Gambia
Satisfied with present arrangement in principle	YES	19	5	2
	NO	11	5	1
Would prefer GCE-style examination with SC standards	YES	13	6	2
	NO	16	4	1

TABLE 8

These figures of course do not tally. The only conclusion one can draw is that whereas there is no overwhelming desire for change, at the same time there would be no very strenuous opposition if change were felt to be desirable on grounds other than that of teacher-opinion. My own view is that it is no part of the function of an examining body to lay down which combinations of subjects shall be taken by pupils. This is a matter for Ministries of Education or, we hope, increasingly for the schools themselves. The 'good general education' which is the stated goal is to be attained through the atmosphere and attitudes to work prevailing in the secondary school rather than through the fixed study of a certain group of subjects for an examination. At its best this system means that certain pupils are forced—for Certificate purposes—

to study certain subjects for which they have neither aptitude nor inclination, and while it is undeniable that in school, as in real life, we all ought sometimes to have to do some things we have no particular liking for, there cannot be any true educative value in struggling year in and year out with a subject for which one has no feeling at all. An average School Certificate which duly records that the pupil has studied subjects chosen from a given number of groups and reached a certain level of attainment in them is not really evidence of a general education, for this depends not on the subjects one studies or even on the level of achievement attained in each, but on the attitudes one has developed through study, and this is something that cannot be recorded on any certificate because it cannot be measured. The abolition of grouping would not *force* schools which wished to maintain it to give it up; it would merely make it possible for those which no longer desired it to plan more flexible curricula and timetables, and also for pupils to follow up interests without necessarily turning them into subjects of examination.

3.9. In saying this I am aware that the results which the Norwood Committee hoped would come from the introduction of the GCE in place of the School Certificate have not in fact come about: schools have become even more examination-dominated than ever before; it seems almost a subject for local pride if the town Grammar School has a boy or girl pupil who is about to enter for ten subjects at 'O' level at the age of 14; there is also a growing habit of taking the three 'O' level subjects required for University entrance at an early age and so 'getting them out of the way', thereafter concentrating on the 'A' level subjects on which University scholarships and entrance depend. In examination-ridden West Africa the temptations to ignore all but examination subjects will be very strong indeed, but surely this is a challenge to the teaching profession? In any case, I cannot believe that ignoring a subject altogether is educationally any worse than a five-year grind at it, directed solely towards passing an examination. 'Discipline' is not necessarily related to the distasteful.

3.10. In view of the foregoing I am wholeheartedly in agreement with the Council's recent decision in principle to introduce a GCE-style examination in a few years' time.

10

Oral English Testing in West Africa

Alan Davies

In the spring of 1965 the writer was invited by the West African Examinations Council to visit West Africa for the purpose of reporting on the possibilities of introducing a compulsory Oral English Test at the School Certificate ('O' level) stage. This chapter consists of the larger part of the Report ('Oral English Testing in West Africa: Report of a Preliminary Study, April–May 1965') submitted by the writer to the West African Examinations Council. The Report begins with a brief description of the background to the visit including the recommendation made by D. W. Grieve[1] that an oral English test be made compulsory. Dr David Harris, author of Chapter 3 of this volume, was to have accompanied the writer with the purpose of producing a joint report but he fell ill and was prevented from taking part. He did, in fact, prepare a set of recommendations, printed as an Appendix to the Report (but not included in this volume).

As well as other discussions and visits the writer visited 16 secondary schools, 2 primary schools, 8 universities and 4 teacher training colleges while in West Africa. The body of the Report proceeds as follows.

I. THE PRESENT SYSTEM OF EXAMINING ORAL ENGLISH

1.1 Introductory

The present examination in Oral English employed by the West African Examinations Council (the *McCallien Test*) has been in use for some 10 or 12 years. For reasons of administration that will be outlined below (most of which are self-evident, and the realization of which did, in fact, serve to precipitate the WAEC's arranging of this survey now being reported) the McCallien Test cannot, as it stands, be made compulsory. Since the WAEC has decided on a *compulsory* test of Oral English, a new test is essential. However, this is an argument which relates purely to the *administration* problems of Oral Testing, and administration, though of great practical importance, is not the only way of evaluating a Test. It could be argued that a test which has sound linguistic content and which has a firm psychometric backing should not be rejected simply because its administration on a large scale would not be feasible. It is necessary, therefore, to discuss

[1] See Chapter 9 of this present volume.

Reference is made to this chapter on p. 17 of the Introduction.

the McCallien Test both from the 'how it is done' approach (its administration) and from the 'what it contains' approach (its linguistic content and statistical analysis).

This section will deal with the administration of the McCallien Test; the next section (section 2) with the Test from the linguistic and psychometric points of view.

1.2. Candidates and Examiners

At the last examination in Ghana, Sierra Leone and the Gambia for which figures are available (May 1964) some 1,250 candidates took the optional Oral Test. This was about 50 per cent of the total GCE candidates who would have taken the Test had it been compulsory (i.e. all those who took the English Language written papers). In the 1964 examination in Nigeria (November 1964) there were some 2,500 candidates for the Oral Test, representing 20 per cent of all possible candidates. Thus of all West African candidates in 1964 about 25 per cent took the Oral Test.

In all four countries something like 50–60 examiners were involved in applying the Test in 1964 (20 or so in Ghana, about 10 in Sierra Leone and 20 or so in Nigeria). Thus if the Test had been compulsory in 1964 the total number of examiners needed would have had to be about 200. However, the total number of possible candidates in 1964 is no prognostic of how many would be sitting for a compulsory test in say five years' time. Here the situation in Nigeria, as is well known, is very different from that in the other three countries. From figures suggested in conversation to the writer it seems likely that while the total number of candidates presenting themselves in 1970 in Sierra Leone, Ghana and the Gambia will be at most doubled, in Nigeria it may be five times as many. These figures are at best wild guesses but they do suggest the difference of the administrative problems for Nigeria and for the other three countries: they suggest that to apply the present test about four times the present number of examiners would be needed in Sierra Leone, Ghana and the Gambia for a compulsory McCallien Test in 1970 but 20 times the present number in Nigeria. The figures suggest that while properly qualified examiners might be found in Sierra Leone, Ghana and the Gambia in 1970, in Nigeria they could not possibly be.

But it is very doubtful if they could be found even in the first three countries. In the 1965 (May) examination observed by the writer the Ghana examiners were either all members of staff at one of the three university colleges or had had a close connexion with or training from Mrs McCallien herself. The Sierra Leone examiners were all members of the staff at Fourah Bay. It seems unlikely that the examining body in either Ghana or Sierra Leone could be quadrupled or even doubled, so to speak overnight. It is, of course, possible that an examiners' training course similar to those run by the WAEC in other subjects would be of value (and indeed Mrs McCallien has held such courses in the past); but it did seem to the writer that a good deal of at best phonetic training and at worst expertise in Spoken English were called for in the demands made by the test observed this year.

Other administrative problems, such as time spent per candidate, distances to be covered by examiners, finance involved in carrying out the examination, seem of less importance to the writer than the central one, as he sees it, of examiner adequacy and examiner supply. The present test (for the candidates who take it) is administratively workable: there are the examiners, the distances are covered (probably as great as for a compulsory test, certainly in Sierra Leone, perhaps less so though still considerable in Nigeria); the money is found. If the examiners were available it would be equally workable administratively on a compulsory basis.

This suggests that the present examiners are themselves adequate to the job, and therefore raises the important question of whether the McCallien Test is, in fact, examinable by any but professionally trained phoneticians; this question will be taken up more fully in Section 2. Here we are concerned with it from, as it were, a consumer point of view; and indeed it was suggested to the writer in several conversations (particularly in schools) that the present examiners were not all adequate, that being a native speaker of English or being a staff member of a University English Department was not a sufficient reason for selection as an examiner. If this were so, if some examiners were less efficient or adequate than others, their weakness should appear in the test statistics—if the test allows for such statistics. Of course this criticism is essentially subjective and impressionistic and may arise from a refusal to accept external judgement (in the shape of test discrimination) on one's own pupils in what is, after all, a mode of behaviour, the spoken language, an affair highly personal and often emotional. But it is surely important that the consumers of examinations, of Oral English no less than anything else, should be reasonably satisfied and should be assured of the competence of those who examine their pupils.

These administrative considerations were, of course, well known to the WAEC and its Working Parties before the writer's visit to West Africa. The Grieve Report had pointed them out in general terms; the two Working Parties had already begun drafting schemes for a new test partly because the McCallien Test would not be administratively feasible much longer. Both Grieve and the Working Parties were motivated towards a new test for other than administrative reasons; these will appear in Section 2.

However, it should be noted that during the writer's visit the two Working Parties were still thinking in terms of using trained examiners, somehow, for some part of a new Test. Somehow Oral production, the candidate's ability to speak, to produce English, should, it was felt, be tested if only for 3–5 minutes; and this would need a trained examiner. This point will be taken up again (Section 2) but the writer does want to emphasize here that trained examiners are trained examiners in Spoken English, however brief the time devoted to each candidate: that it seems unclear that all present examiners have the required competence and highly unlikely that even 100–150 examiners with the necessary *phonetics competence* (and the writer would put the demands at no less even for a modified and shortened McCallien Test) could be found in West Africa in the next five years.

It is only right to state that both the Chief Examiner for Ghana and the Chief Examiner for Nigeria thought that sufficient trained examiners could be found, the first for the present McCallien Test, the second for a modified and shortened form. These are serious professional views and need to be respected; but they do seem to the writer little more than guesswork, to assume that the present examiners are all competent, and to accept that examiners for the McCallien Test need not be professional phoneticians, a view which the writer does not share.

1.3. Attitudes to the McCallien Test

Before going on (in Section 2) to discuss the McCallien Test internally, as it were, it seems relevant here to set down some of the attitudes towards it met by the writer in West Africa. These all came from direct or indirect consumers: candidates' teachers who are concerned directly and members of University staff who take on the candidates after they have left school or if they do not do this are inevitably involved in the total ambience of Spoken English in West Africa of which the McCallien Test forms an important part.

It needs to be remembered that it is *attitudes* not facts that are being reported in this sub-section, that no structured analysis of them was made and that they were often quite random (in the sense that the same person might voice two conflicting attitudes). The fact remains that the writer did make contact with a number of the professionals in West Africa most closely concerned with Spoken English and that, therefore, their opinions themselves bear on the total situation and are part of it. These attitudes will be mentioned here under four headings: African and non-African; Improvement in Spoken English; Validity of the McCallien Test; and Wash-back on Schools.

1.3.1. African and non-African. In all three countries visited there was a clear, if crude, distinction between the opinion of the Africans professionally involved with Spoken English towards the McCallien Test

and the non-Africans. All the opposition criticism came from the non-Africans. Of course some Africans found parts of the Test to criticize but in the main were satisfied with it. The non-Africans (above all the *British*) were usually doubtful and often sceptical: that is not, of course, to say that approval for the Test was confined to the Africans. It was not. Some non-Africans were as whole-heartedly in favour.

This general African approval is not substantiated with fact (the non-African does have, as will be seen later, some solid basis in fact); but once again it is their opinion that is the important fact. Any new test must be seen by them to be doing at least what they reckon the McCallien Test to be contributing at the moment. No less will do.

1.3.2. Improvement in Spoken English. Whether Spoken English has improved or deteriorated in West Africa is problematic, and will, in any case, be taken up again in Section 3. As far as the McCallien Test is concerned in this issue there are two relevant questions: has the McCallien Test served to improve Spoken English? How far can the Test be used to assess Spoken English diachronically?

To both questions the three possible answers, Yes, No or Doubtful were all given. The fact is, of course, that unless this Test is used itself as the measure there is no other objective way of knowing what has happened to Spoken English in the last 15 years in West Africa. Since the McCallien Test exists alone, with no criterion against which to measure it, no *valid* proof that it does itself measure Spoken English effectively, then it does seem to the writer that the *Doubtful* answer to both questions is the only tenable one.

1.3.3. Validity of the McCallien Test. This again is a matter to be taken up later (Section 2). Here we are concerned with *attitudes* towards validity. If a Test is valid then it measures in fact what it is intended to measure. One method of estimating validity is to discover how closely the test *results* of a group of students agree with what, say, their teachers think they should be. This is exactly what several school Principals— in all three countries—complained of: that their students were being misplaced according to their real competence in Spoken English. Of course their criticisms had no objective value: they were not arguments against the statistical validity of the Test. But once again they indicated a lack of confidence in the Test's results and therefore in what the Test stands for and its influence on what the schools teach.

1.3.4. Wash-back on Schools. This indeed is our fourth type of attitude. A good educational test, it is axiomatic to say, will always (and should) influence the teaching for which it serves as a goal and as a sample of terminal behaviour. It seemed impossible to discover whether the McCallien Test was having this beneficial effect and this for several reasons.

(1) The schools themselves where the Test was taken were unsure: some (very few) gave special teaching in Spoken English over a year or more in which the demands of the McCallien Test were borne in mind; others had no special Spoken English teaching but gave an intensive training for the Test just before it took place; still others gave no special preparation of any kind.

(2) Some sources felt that the Test could not have a beneficial effect since it concentrates attention on (and demands control over) features of Spoken English which most teachers in West Africa (many expatriates; most West Africans) could not realistically teach for, since they demand either some specialized phonetic training or that the teacher should himself be a native Received Pronunciation speaker.

(3) A test would need to be very comprehensive and of very far-reaching influence in the schools to counteract the gross interference on the students' English not only from the local vernaculars and the depleted Englishes of the towns but also from the English used around them in school by the other students and by the teachers of subjects other than English. It is from these, as much as from his *English* teacher (and above all during his Primary School years) that the student learns his English. What effect can the McCallien Test (indeed *any* test) have in this situation?

This may be a counsel of despair or of realism, whichever way one chooses to look at it. It certainly comes near to rejecting the whole idea of the testing at all of Spoken English. It says, in effect, in this language situation English is acting *in schools* very much as a *first* language, with its own momentum; you cannot assess it with a test which does not take the whole language exposure situation into account, certainly not one which concentrates so heavily on one restricted variety of English pronunciation (RP).

This suggests, of course, that what is needed urgently is a description of just what contrasts (both segmental and prosodic) are made in West Africa, whether there is tacit agreement about them and whether they serve adequately for the *English* needs of second language speakers there. This work on *Intelligibility* will be referred to later (Section 4); certainly it is high time that this job was done.

It should be added that nearly everyone to whom the writer spoke in West Africa was in strong favour of a test of Oral English. And it is but fair to say that the strictures mentioned above regarding the wash-back effect of the McCallien Test do not necessarily apply particularly to *this* Test. They would be made whatever the Test and are a kind of rejection of any kind of test; yet, paradoxically, their exponents recognize the need for some method of bringing attention to bear on Spoken English in schools and of improving its teaching. Even the most severe critics of the McCallien Test were sure that if it did nothing else this Test focused attention on the whole problem throughout West Africa.

2. DISCUSSION AND INTERNAL ANALYSIS OF THE MCCALLIEN TEST

2.1. Introductory

As will appear later in this Section, the McCallien Test is in fact more robust statistically than some of the criticisms noted above would suggest. Even so before going on to an internal analysis of the Test the writer wishes to make clear his admiration for Mrs McCallien's work in this field: it is, so far as he knows, the only partially objective test of Oral English in existence; it has set out to do what overwhelmingly needs to be done but which other workers are still declining to attempt, i.e. to set up a standard of Spoken English within one area, detail the likely problems, and then attempt to test their production. This may be labelled an impossible task (which explains others' reluctance) in our present state of knowledge but if it is, then Mrs McCallien's represents a brave and necessary attempt. Above all her Test has focused attention on the needs of Spoken English in West Africa and in some schools stimulated remedial work to be done. The writer endorses fully the appreciation given to Mrs McCallien's Test by D. W. Grieve: 'as it stands the oral test represents a considerable advance in thinking over any of the traditional techniques employed in the written examinations. Both productive and receptive skills are tested, and there is a high measure of objectivity in the assessment of attainment: probably as high as can be achieved when performance has to be assessed by a number of different examiners. This degree of objectivity has been attained by a careful analysis of the speech problems of children in West Africa and by the testing of a fairly wide sample of these problems in a variety of situations' (Grieve, 1964, p. 72).

This said it is, of course, important to know just how effective the McCallien Test is as a Test. The writer saw it as part of his task to look particularly at the statistical results (as opposed to the opinions and attitudes mentioned above in Section 1) of the Test in order to gain some idea of the relevance of the kind of item tested.

2.2. Arrangement of Discussion

This analysis will now be given in three parts: first a simple outline of a typical McCallien Test; second a description of its linguistic content with some evaluation of the Test from the point of view of content validity; third a statement of some simple statistical analysis performed for the writer on last year's results (1964) in Accra with a view to estimating the stability of the Test particularly from the points of view of reliability, construct validity and item validity.

2.3. Composition of a typical McCallien Test (May 1965 Version)

Part 1 (Production of English by) *Reading Test*

A Candidates have 10 minutes to prepare a Reading Passage of about 150 words. They then read this aloud to the examiner twice:
   (1) for production of segmental phonemes (20 items)
   (2) for production of stress and non-stress (10 items).

B In the 10 minutes' preparation time candidates must also prepare 10 short sentences (for which some measure of pointing is provided by italics and directions). They then read these aloud:
   (3) for intonation and emphasis (10 items).

Part 2 Comprehension

A The examiner reads a word containing a potential (or zero) phonemic contrast and asks the candidate to make up a sentence containing that word:
   (1) Phonemes in sentences (2 items).

B The examiner reads a word containing a potential (or zero) phonemic contrast as in A above and asks the candidate to spell it.
   (2) Phonemes in isolation (5 items).

C The examiner reads two stress-contrasting sentences where stress provides the only contrasting feature and asks the candidate to provide the stressed words in each sentence:
   (3) Sentence stress (2 items).

D The examiner reads a sentence involving marked stress and asks the candidate to suggest its meaning; (stress on pronominal):
   (4) Sentence stress (1 item).

E As in D above with stress on modifier:
   (5) Sentence stress (1 item).

F The examiner reads a sentence involving a fall-rise intonation pattern to signal uncertainty of some kind and asks the candidate to suggest its implications:
   (6) Sentence intonation (1 item).

Part 3 Conversation

The examiner engages the candidate in a few minutes (unspecified time, probably about 3–5 minutes) conversation in which he has the following rubric as a guide:

'Credit will be given for fluency, intelligibility, vocabulary and the use of idiomatic forms. The Examiner should avoid questions which can be answered by Yes or No, and he should endeavour to find some topic which will interest the candidate and induce him to respond. The candidate must not, however, be allowed to deliver a prepared speech.'

Weighting

The relative weighting of the three Parts is as follows:

Part *1*				
Production	A	1	Segmental Phonemes	20 marks
		2	Stress	20 marks
	B	3	Intonation	20 marks
	Total			60 marks

Part *2*
Comprehension

Total   20 marks

Part *3*
Conversation

Total   20 marks

Grand Total   100 marks

2.4. Linguistic Content of the McCallien Test

In the absence of any firm external criterion which can be used to validate a language test the test constructor must fall back on content validity. This is an appropriate enough procedure: he is, as it were, saying that his criterion is already determined by his linguistic analysis of the language problems in his situation, that he has sampled these problems adequately in his Test and that competence in the particular language skill he is testing is shown by control over these problems sampled in his items. This, it would seem, is what the McCallien Test is doing. In Grieve's remark already quoted it is based on 'a careful analysis of the speech problems of children in West Africa' (Section 2.1).

There can be no doubt that the Test does base its content on an analysis of the English learning problems for many speakers of West African languages. It is at these points (segmental and prosodic) that these learners have greatest difficulty.

However, there are three queries which may be raised over the linguistic side of the test.

2.4.1. Sampling.
For a test the validity of which is based on *content* alone how adequate is the sampling? In the particular version described above (2.3) there are 52 items plus the conversation. Of these 52, 40 are Production (20 phoneme; 10 stress; 10 intonation) and 12 Comprehension, of which 5 are spelling.

Sampling is inevitably a serious problem when a Test's validity is being justified on *Content Validity* grounds alone: but it would seem that receptive ability (or listening comprehension) is barely touched on in the Test, and that (as in fact the statistics bear out: Section 2.5) the McCallien Test is essentially one of *Production*.

2.4.2. Functional Load of Problems. Even if these language problems which are being sampled in the Test are the learning problems for West African speakers of English it is by no means clear how important they are, *functionally* as it were. Very many people in West Africa spoke to the writer of *Intelligibility* as the true standard of Spoken English there. Intelligibility is a difficult concept which has, so far as is known, not yet been precisely enough defined for it to be set up as a standard and tested. Certainly it is (International) Intelligibility rather than, say, RP, or some other L1 or even West African standard which needs setting up but how far can any of the problems which the McCallien Test incorporates be said to be obstacles to Intelligibility (or Communication, another rather vague term) until it is known (and described) what Intelligibility in this situation is?

From this point of view it would seem that Mrs McCallien's insistence on some kind of RP standard for her Test is sound policy. However unrealistic or inappropriate (see 3.2) RP may be it is, at least, fixed and known.

However, even if we accept RP as the only possible standard for such a test at the moment it is still uncertain how far inability to produce (or comprehend) the features of the RP that are being tested affects the ability to speak (or understand) English. These may be the *learning* problems but how far are they the *communication* problems? If we agree, as has already been argued, that Communication (or Intelligibility) cannot be tested at the moment and that RP is the only possible standard then it would seem that the McCallien Test not only sets up RP as the standard but also tests ability in RP and *that ability* (in Parts 1 and 2) alone, i.e. *not* necessarily ability in Spoken English.

Mrs McCallien herself, in a conversation with the writer, explained that it was an approximation to RP rather than RP itself which she exhorted her examiners to look for. It is not clear to the writer how production of approximations can effectively be assessed except by professional phoneticians. This leads on to a third query.

2.4.3. Examiners. The writer attended the April/May 1965 Oral Test Co-ordination Meeting in Accra on April 23rd and 24th and subsequently sat in on a number of testing sessions with various examiners both in Ghana and Sierra Leone.

D. W. Grieve points out (Grieve, 1964) that after the initial standardization there is little opportunity to check on the performance of individual examiners. This, of course, the writer agrees with. But it assumes that at least initially all examiners agree. This the writer found not to be the case. There were many differences of opinion at the Co-ordination Meeting on both the recorded voices on the first day and the live 'guinea-pigs' on the second. The examiners disagreed; their scoring seemed highly random.

Here it must be made clear what is involved in this disagreement. It is not the competence of individual examiners that is being criticized. Unlike the opinions of some schools mentioned above (1.2) the writer found all examiners he saw in action to be highly competent and deeply concerned; Nor is the co-ordinating procedure itself being criticized; this the writer found to be both professional and highly responsible. What is involved in examiner disagreement is the ability of every examiner to hear accurately each precise point at issue and without repetition. It is not only that the examiners could not hear an approximation to RP, it is that they could not test RP itself in production. (Of course professional phoneticians could do it, but even they might welcome the use of a tape repeater; asking the candidate to repeat live is not at all the same thing.)

What is being questioned here is just how accurately any test of segmental or prosodic features in production can be tested objectively. The whole point of the McCallien Test (and much of its merit) is that this should be done objectively; but to the writer it does seem that any serious belief that the Test achieves very great objectivity is unrealistic. Production of speech must be tested in any Oral Test but it may be queried whether it can be done accurately at the moment and whether, if it cannot be done accurately, it is worth doing at all.

2.5. Brief Statistical Analysis

The 'accuracy' of a Test may often be shown up in its statistical findings.

So far as the writer could discover the only statistical analyses that had been made of the McCallien Test were the norming distribution (which appears at the back of the two published versions of the Test: McCallien, 1958) and an early Item Analysis, mentioned to the writer by Professor A. Taylor of Ibadan.

With the much appreciated co-operation of Mr C. Modu (Deputy Registrar, WAEC, Ghana) four simple analyses were made of a random sample of data for the May 1964 examination in Sierra Leone, Ghana and the Gambia. The results of these four analyses with comments are noted below. The processed data is all presented in *Appendix 2.*[1]

2.5.1. Item Analysis (N = 100). The results of the Item Analysis are presented in *Appendix 2.*[1] Item Analysis gives some assessment of the *internal* validity of a test, that is of the discrimination item by item. For a language test an item discrimination of $+\cdot20$ or more is desirable. This Item discrimination is set out in the last column of the Item Analysis ($= r$). Here it will be noted only that the Test, on

---

[1] This refers to Appendix 2 of the original Report presented to the WAEC.

the basis of these figures, does well enough for a set of untried items. Only 10 of the 50 items would be rejected ($r < +\cdot20$), and these 10 *all* come from the Word List (production test of segmental phonemes). No analysis of this kind was made of Comprehension or Conversation.

However, on the basis of these figures, the Test is not without blemish. As will be seen below it is the Production part of the Test that matters, nothing else. For one-fifth of the Production items to be invalid is too large a proportion, particularly when the narrow band of total discrimination is borne in mind (see the Tables of Norms, McCallien, 1958).

2.5.2. The obtained measures are set out below (Table 1).

Part	Total Poss. Marks	Mean	Standard Deviation	Reliability (Kuder Richardson Formula 21) N = 100
1. Production	60	26·19	6·1	0·68
2. Comprehension	20	12·87	2·7	
3. Conversation	20	9·54	1·9	
Total (i.e. 1 + 2 + 3)	100	48·62	7·8	

TABLE 1. Obtained measures

Only Part 1 was analysed for Reliability. As will be seen (Table 1) its coefficient is remarkably high for what, on other grounds, seems so potentially unstable a test.

2.5.3. Inter-Test Correlation. The correlation co-efficients are set out below (Table 2).

	Parts			Total
	1	2	3	
Part 1	—	·014	·501	·912
Part 2		—	·012	—·576
Part 3			—	—·037

TABLE 2. Interpart correlations (N = 100)

These coefficients reveal several very acceptable aspects of the structure of the McCallien Test:

(1) Parts 1 and 2 (as is common sense) are testing different things: Production and Comprehension are not the same skill.

(2) Parts 1 and 3 (again as is common sense) have a shared component: Conversation includes some Production.

(3) Part 1 has a very large influence on the Total score: Production should play an important part in the total assessment of Oral English.

However, there are some not so acceptable aspects of the structure:

(1) Parts 2 and 3 have very little in common: if Production is Part of Conversation, so is Comprehension; but Comprehension and Conversation seem to share nothing in common.

(2) Neither Part 2 nor Part 3 has any influence on Total Score. Indeed Part 2 (Comprehension) has a relatively high negative coefficient: i.e. those who do well on Comprehension tend to do badly on Total Score. Conversation has no effect on Total Score.

This means that only Part 1 (Production) has any influence at all on Total Score. The only skill being tested by the McCallien Test, from the statistical evidence available, is Production.

There are several possible reasons: one is that both Comprehension and Conversation are not weighted sufficiently in relation to Production (totals of 20; 20; 60). Another, more important one, is that examiners tend to place candidates on Comprehension (and, more especially, Conversation) in a very narrow band: so that these two Parts (above all, Conversation) do not contribute to Total Score. This can be seen from the evidence of the Standard Deviations (in Table 1); in Part 3, two-thirds of the candidates vary from about 8 to about 11.

2.5.4. Comparison of Means. An attempt was made in the Ghana data to investigate if two very obvious variables in the Test situation had any influence on the results. The first was the variable of examiner (Ghanaian : British) and the second of secondary school teacher (mostly Ghanaian : mostly British). The results are presented below in Table 3:

	Means	N (pupils)
(1) Examiner Variable		
Ghanaian (N = 19)	50·25	886
British (N = 17)	51·11	562
(2) Teacher Variable		
Ghanaian (N = 27 schools)	49·88	1,010
British (N = 6 schools)	52·45	436

TABLE 3. Means by Examiner and Teacher L1

Although no statistical test of significance was applied to the means it seemed clear that there was no significant difference between the variables.

On the basis of these simple analyses it does seem that Part 1 (Production) of the McCallien Test possesses a certain stability: this cannot be said, for lack of evidence, of the other two Parts. Even though a number (10) of the items in Part 1 were seen to be invalid (non-discriminating) there is considerable accord in the small comparison of means. However, what this may imply is that the Test as a whole achieves this stability which seems apparent for Part 1 because examiners unconsciously weight their scoring for Part 2 and, particularly, Part 3 so as to bring their Total towards the Mean. A further analysis (as of the two variables above) for Part 1 alone would be necessary to provide any further evidence of the stability of this Part of the Test.

Even so, statistically, the McCallien Test stands up for itself against assault. It has a certain consistency and a certain stability within itself. However, there is one further statistic which does put a further query against the permanent stability of the Test. This is the percentage success at each cut-off point (Pass : Credit), for all four countries—Nigeria, Ghana, Sierra Leone and the Gambia. Not quite the same type of figures are available for Nigeria as for the other three countries: a certain over-all lack of periodic stability does emerge; between 1962 and 1963 in particular there are extreme differences. At the *Credit* level, for example, here are the sets of percentages for the two years:

	1962	1963
Nigeria	22·3	41·8
Ghana	26·3	22·5
Sierra Leone	31·8	73·6
Gambia	57·1	96·0

TABLE 4. Percentage success on McCallien at Credit level, 1962, 1963

Ghana alone remained in balance: but even Ghana had a difference at the *Pass* level from 67·4 to 78·2 per cent in these two years.

It seems likely that the reason for this lack of stability from year to year arises from a laudable desire for objectivity by using (especially outside Ghana) the same numerical score as an index of Pass, Credit, etc. The result of this is that quite different proportions are successful from year to year. The normal (traditional type examination) way round this problem is to vary the pass/credit mark so that a similar proportion achieves success from year to year. This is satisfactory in the traditional type examination because numerical scores have no significance beyond their one year. In an objective examination they must have since it is assumed that the norming sample (i.e. any one year's candidates) are representative of the total population (i.e. every year's candidates). The fact that the McCallien cut-offs do not possess the stability of similar proportions is a strong argument against the Test's claim to objectivity.

3. SPOKEN ENGLISH IN WEST AFRICA

3.1. Introductory

This is a major topic in itself and will be discussed briefly here only in so far as it bears on the more immediate question of Oral Testing. (It is realized, of course, that this topic has a major influence on Oral Testing because this is precisely what Oral Testing is about: until the parameters are drawn of Spoken English in West Africa any discussion of Oral Testing is at best haphazard and at worst futile. All the more reason, it is suggested, for the basic *applied research* mentioned below.)

3.2. Uncertainty

There seemed to the writer a great uncertainty in West Africa about Spoken English there. There was uncertainty about the standard which should be adopted and uncertainty too about the Spoken English situation at the moment: just how much is it used and how much needed, etc. There was much talk about *Intelligibility, Communication, Inter-Comprehensibility*, but these all seemed ideals rather than educational aims. When an attempt was made to have these ideals detailed they varied from the ability to understand and be understood by a student's colleagues and teachers to the ability for a student to be transported from his Oral Test direct to London and perform competently in Spoken English there at once.

There was a strong conviction that the condition of Spoken English is serious and worsening fast: for this (see above 1.3) there was absolutely no evidence save the opinion of those who have dealt with generations of students (whose opinion is conflicting) and those who were themselves students a generation ago (whose opinions have the natural halo effect, and who were, in any case, a highly selected student body).

There were conflicting views about the relative importance of Production and Comprehension: among university teachers (though not everywhere) it was generally felt that Comprehension was somehow a more immediate problem.

There was uncertainty about the emergence of a West African standard of Spoken English. This was often alluded to but once again it seemed an ideal rather than a realistic aim since it did not seem possible to say what it is. (This is not, of course, to suggest that it could not be a realistic aim; it might well be.)

In the main (again not everywhere) those most in favour of introducing a West African standard were themselves expatriates. Africans were very much more in favour of retaining RP as the standard to aim at. The writer was led to believe that this attitude was much more prevalent in Ghana among Africans than in Nigeria; this was just not so among those he met. In the main Africans in both countries were in agreement.

One very strong argument put up to the writer by two headmasters (both expatriates and of long standing in West Africa) was that, while there might be a lot to desire of their students' Spoken English, in point of fact by the time they reached the GCE *it was intelligible* where it needed to be; and this because it has to be. The very fact of existing in an educational atmosphere (in a secondary school, often boarding) for four or five years in which nearly every subject is taught in the medium of English ensured that the students' own Spoken English (both productive and receptive) had to become intelligible. It was, as it were, a fact of survival. They would therefore expect *all* their students to pass an appropriate Oral Test in English at GCE.

There are several holes in this argument: the two schools involved were old-established ones with a tradition of Spoken English and of expatriate staff (though the comparison of means (2.5; Table 3) would suggest that this does not matter); the two principals had been so long in West Africa that they had been exposed themselves to interference in their own (receptive) English and had achieved a tolerance of their students' English which is not open to newcomers or to foreigners (but this suggests that for *West Africans* themselves West African Spoken English is intelligible); this view says nothing of the wider demands of international intelligibility (though it may be doubted how reasonable—and realistic—it is to expect a West African GCE student to produce a Spoken English which is internationally intelligible though it is certainly reasonable to expect him to comprehend such).

3.3. Functions of Spoken English Teaching

This is not to suggest that no test is needed. Both principals were in favour of a test (for their own schools as well as for less favoured ones). But it does raise the question of what a Test ought to test and what is the function of Spoken English teaching in a second language situation where a child learns by activity (i.e. listening and speaking) all he needs for the *school environment*. The functions of Spoken English teaching (and therefore of testing, the one acting as goal, the other as preparation for that goal) seem to the writer to be threefold.

(1) To ensure that students make all the segmental and prosodic contrasts in English which are phonologically relevant in West Africa. (This cannot be tested—or taught—until there is some basic research and description: in the absence of this it seems that the teacher must fall back on his own approximation to RP and it is probably simplest for everyone if he concentrates on certain very simple and obvious phonemic problems (e.g. Vowels 4 and 5) as in the Word List of the McCallien Test.)

(2) Since it seems agreed among experts in West Africa that the real barrier to Intelligibility is *rhythm* above all; i.e. that West African English would be intelligible if it produced British English rhythm whatever its stress patterns and primary phonemes, then the second function of Spoken English teaching must be to ensure that students move towards a British rhythm in their English.

Both 1 and 2 suffer from the need to employ trained examiners to test control over these features. However, it seems at least possible that paper and pencil techniques could be employed for the simple contrasts mentioned at the end of (1) above and for testing competence in (2). It must be realized, of course, that such techniques have not been tried out, that whatever may be stated elsewhere *no one knows* the relation of performance in such techniques and skill in speaking. If they were to be employed *it is essential* that the proper experimental work be done first.

(3) To ensure that students' tolerance over Spoken English is not confined to their educational situation the third function of the teaching of Spoken English is to extend this tolerance mainly by exposure to as many varieties of material as possible. These varieties should extend on both Linguistic and situational axes so that students hear their teacher (and practise themselves) making use of grammatical, lexical and intonational features which they do not normally hear in their educational environment; and they hear a range of voices varying both as to field (subject matter), mode (talk, conversation) and style of discourse (formal, informal, etc.). These would need the use of disc, tape, radio and TV as well as, in favourable circumstances, outside speakers. *There is no reason at all* why these mechanical aids should not be used.

3.4. Research on Intelligibility

As to the first function mentioned above, that of producing those segmental and prosodic features which are phonologically important in West Africa, it may well be that the various pieces of research in hand (in e.g. Ibadan, Cape Coast and Zaria) on descriptions of educated West African English will be of value. It seems to the writer that acceptable radio announcers' pronunciation might well be used as models for the necessary descriptions. From the educational point of view the sooner such work is done the better; what needs to be stressed is that it ought to be done, that it does not much matter *whose* pronunciation is selected (among, say, good announcers) and that until it is done the satisfactory Spoken English teaching cannot be done.

4. AIMS AND DEMANDS OF A NEW TEST OF SPOKEN ENGLISH

All the evidence given in West Africa to the writer was firmly in support of there being some test of Oral English at the GCE Secondary School 'O' level. The writer accepts this, i.e. that there should be a test at this stage.

There is, of course, a great deal to be said for applying the test at an earlier stage, either just after or just before entrance to secondary school; the major influence on the Spoken English of West African children is exercised in the Primary School, and it is the teaching of Spoken English there that needs the radical improvement. It seems to the writer questionable how much remedial work can be done in secondary schools in what is, after all, an ongoing situation, in which English, of a kind, is already possessed and in which, in any case, there is so much interference on that remedial work from the English of other teachers and lessons and from outside the school. It may well be that after a new Oral Test has been made to function the WAEC would see fit to applying it at some earlier point in the Secondary School.

The writer takes it as axiomatic that a test should have a firm educational purpose. This seems especially necessary of a subject like Spoken English in a situation like West Africa where the needs are so great and the problems so many. A good test is needed: this test should, above all, have an educational (not an administrative) purpose. The issue is therefore seen as an educational/social one rather than an administrative or even a linguistic one.

4.1. Approach

This issue must be approached from three sides: that of *aims*, that of *demands* and that of *constraints*.

4.1.1. Aims. It seemed to the writer that those professionally involved in Spoken English in West Africa who were specially anxious for a new test had three aims in mind, and these aims were not always kept distinct. They were:

(1) to produce a streamlined version of the present test;

(2) to exercise a strong influence on Spoken English in secondary schools, encouraging the teaching of the subject and acting as a goal for that teaching; and

(3) to raise the standard of Spoken English throughout West Africa.

It was this third aim which seemed least distinct and which kept emerging as the real need, the real purpose of the whole operation and as equivalent to the second aim. It is not, of course. A good new test would assure aims 1 and 2 (since it would build on the virtues of the present system and, because compulsory, have an important educational wash-back) but it would not meet aim 3, at least not for a very long time, since it would be taken only by the highly selected GCE entry. However, if this word of caution is accepted, it can be said that a good test, competently applied, would be one step towards the all-round improvement everyone wants. It is, of course, in teaching and the supply of well-trained teachers that the real answer to this third aim lies.

4.1.2. Demands: Threefold. The new test will have three demands on it simply as a type of good test. Every good educational test must meet these demands. These are that it should be:

(1) Simple.

(2) Teachable.

(3) Beneficial.

By *simple* is meant that the test should be easy to administer, that there should be no doubt as to what is being tested (no doubt to the teacher, that is) so that a detailed syllabus can be provided and worked at; and that there should be no doubt as to its results, i.e. it will contain all the virtues of a sound objective test.

By *teachable* is meant two things:

(a) that the syllabus leading to it should be sufficiently detailed so that it can really be taught for, so that at the end of a Course of Spoken English students should have undergone some learning. One of the doubts about the present system is whether any learning at all (except for a few practice sessions) takes place.

(b) that it should be teachable by the real teachers, i.e. by the average English teacher in the ordinary secondary school, not only by the phonetically trained teacher in the old-established urban school. In this sense it must be realistically based on what teachers can do and what is available to them.

There are arguments against this, of course. They apply to the goal which it is legitimate to set up. But Spoken English is not like other subjects. Whereas it may be wise to devise an examination in, say, the new mathematics and assume that all teachers will learn enough by the time the examination starts, it seems reasonable to ask just how far a teacher can teach those features of Spoken English which he is incapable of producing or discriminating among himself.

This is an argument which has particular reference to the *production* of phonemic and prosodic features and will be taken up later. It is an argument which questions the educational value of setting up un-attainable goals: e.g. the production of RP (or approximate RP) phonemic contrasts.

By *beneficial* is meant the influence the Test has on the teaching in the secondary school of Spoken English. So much is essential—it would be hoped that this beneficial influence would extend in two directions: first to the primary schools and to the teacher-training colleges, above all to the latter for if the teacher trainers' speech is improved that of the primary schools inevitably will be also; second to the rest of the teaching in the secondary school (*all* the teaching which takes place outside the Spoken English—or just the English—class).

The implications of this demand of beneficial influence are that the Test should deal extensively with valid problems, that it should set up a goal which is both realistic (i.e. teachable) and appropriate (i.e. necessary), that it should discriminate meaningfully, so that those who do well really do possess a certain control over Spoken English which those who do badly don't; that it should, in short, possess both content and predictive validity, content in that it looks back to what are the linguistic problems of communication; predictive in that it looks forward to what effective teaching in Spoken English will do.

4.1.3. Constraints. These are heavy demands: they would apply to any educational test which is used as a compulsory instrument; they are even further burdened by the constraints on the setting up of an Oral Test in West Africa.

Assuming that a desirable Test, which meets the demands outlined above *could* be produced, there still remain these constraints:

(1) Supply of trained examiners.

(2) Administrative problems: distances and number of candidates.

(3) Use of machinery (e.g. tape-recorders) in tropical conditions. It is not clear how serious a difficulty this is (and, indeed, as will appear below, this Report recommends extensive use of tape-recorders) but it was one widely mentioned. The supply and servicing of electric equipment are certainly problems which must be faced.

These three constraints are all practical; the assumption (which—as has been made clear—the writer does not share) here is that a complete Oral Test of both production and comprehension *could* be designed. If the theoretical problem of designing a valid production test were overcome it would be immediately absorbed into the practical problem of making every examiner a professional phonetician.

4.2. Critique of McCallien Test in relation to Aims, etc.

These, then, to the writer are the *Aims*, the *Demands* and the *Constraints* on the testing of Spoken English in West Africa. It may be worth while, very briefly to examine how far the McCallien Test has met them.

4.2.1. Aims

(1) This does not apply.

(2) *Wash-back on schools*. Opinions were very conflicting. The writer's impression was that the Test had made some schools think about the need for improving Spoken English without giving very much help on how to do it.

(3) *Raising standard of Spoken English in West Africa*. Again opinions conflicted. There is no objective way of telling. It may be that the effect mentioned in (2) above has had no influence in those schools. But as the Test has not been compulsory it cannot be expected to have made a widespread impression. Some of the *school* teachers spoken to thought that there was little change.

4.2.2. Demands

(1) *Simple*. The McCallien Test may be simple to design and apply but there were many complaints that it was not simple to aim at. It may be (as was said in some places) that a few practice lessons would teach the tricks. If this is so then the Test does not meet Demand 2.

(2) *Teachable*. This was perhaps the major complaint in the schools. Apart from a brief note on what the Test tested there seemed little guidance to teachers as to what to teach. As the Grieve Report demonstrated all too clearly it is essential for a Language Test to be absolutely specific as to syllabus. The alternative, for teachers, is simply to go over and over past Test papers. This, it was clear, is exactly what schools have been doing for the McCallien Test. They can hardly be blamed therefore for training their students in the tricks.

(3) *Beneficial*. To some extent this has been dealt with under *Aims* above. It might be said here that the sampling in the McCallien Test (particularly in the *Comprehension* section, Part 2) has been very restricted. It might further be said that there is no evidence at all of the influence of the Test extending to any other parts of the school curriculum than the Spoken English lessons. (No attempt, e.g. has been made to look at and perhaps assess—and then influence—the Spoken English that goes on in, say, Physics lessons.)

It might also be regretted that no statistical analysis has been attempted (after the early years) on the results of the Test, particularly with regard to its effective discrimination in relation to some acceptable criterion, i.e. no attempt at validity (e.g. concurrent) with, say, teachers' estimates.

(The writer is very glad to note here his pleasure at the action of the Ghana Oral English Working Party at its recent meeting (19 May 1965) in minuting its decision to perform such a follow-up study on this year's results.)

4.2.3. Constraints

1. *Examiner Supply*. As has already been noted, this is already a serious problem.
2. *Administration*. Again a growing problem. As is obvious, both 1 and 2 here are problems which have acted as major constraints on any extension of the McCallien Test towards making it compulsory.
3. *Machinery*. This does not apply.

5. RECOMMENDATIONS

The need for an objective, standardized Test of Spoken English in West Africa at the GCE 'O' level is acute. There is every reason to hope that such a Test which takes into consideration the *Aims*, *Demands* and *Constraints* (above all the *Demands*) outlined in Section 3 above will go some way towards improving the standard of Spoken English. But it must be stressed that 'some way' may not be very far. It must also be stressed that a *single* standardized Test will not serve; that such a Test once produced will need to exist in several forms, that the work, in fact, of construction will be continuous and not once-for-all.

In the Recommendations, which follow, the necessary conditions outlined in Section 4 are accepted as necessary and determine the methods and type of test suggested. The Recommendations are divided into two parts: first what sort of Test; second who should be responsible for its construction.

5.1. Four-stage Approach

It is recommended that a four-stage approach (5.2–5.5) to the problem be made. The four stages should vary in length, i.e. will differ in time needed. They will be specified here proceeding from long-term to short-term.

5.2. Test of Production of Spoken English

As has been made clear throughout this Report no objective test of Production anywhere is known to the writer, except for the McCallien Test itself, with its defects. It is therefore recommended that research be put in hand to develop such a test, bearing in mind the needs of and demands on Spoken English production among educated West Africans.

Such a test cannot properly be instituted until some work has been done on just what variety of Spoken English is both teachable and possesses wide Intelligibility within West Africa and internationally. This leads on to:

5.3. Research on Intelligibility: towards a West African Standard

Such research is clearly not within the scope of this Report. At the same time it is supremely necessary because without it the teaching of Spoken English must remain based on RP (for want of any other model) and therefore both unrealistic and inappropriate. At the same time, also, no valid Test of Production can be designed until it is clear what the demands of Intelligibility are, what, in fact, is the expectation of the educational process in Spoken English, what is expected of students who have gone through a Spoken English course and what it is necessary for them to have learned.

Such research may well not be the function of the West African Examinations Council. This might well be a useful field for co-operation between the Council and the Universities. Several of the West African Universities visited by the writer mentioned their interest in the problem (e.g. Ibadan, Zaria, Cape Coast, Fourah Bay). Certainly it cannot wait very much longer. But this is more the concern of Part 2 of these recommendations.

5.4. Search for a Criterion

An external criterion, acceptable and demonstrable, is essential to any valid test. Not only would correlation with such a criterion be necessary for 5.2 above, it might also help with 5.3, by making an approach to Intelligibility from the *measurement* rather than from the *survey* point of view. If a follow-up of a test at 'O' level were made at, say 'A' level (to give a simple example) then there would be some evidence of some of the demands of Intelligibility.

But the criterion is more immediately needed for 5.5 below. Here it is essential that one be accepted very soon. It may be that the Ghana Oral English Working Party's minute of 19 May 1965 (see 4.2.2) will be the method to adopt here. In any case data for this criterion must be collected so that the validity of 5.5 can be assessed.

5.5. The New Spoken English Test: the immediate plans

A Comprehensive Test of Listening Comprehension (recorded: on tape or disc or radio).

A pilot test of partial-production.

A subjective assessment of communication.

5.5.1. Part 1: Listening Comprehension. It is recommended that a Battery of Listening Comprehension tests be constructed at once. These tests should range over large areas of the field of Listening Comprehension in English. They should be recorded on tape or disc (or broadcast— see 5.7 below) so that the situation is standardized, as far as possible, for all candidates. The candidate *hears* the stimulus and responds in *writing* on paper. They should sample on two axes: one, on the linguistic feature work sample axis; two, on the varieties of English pronunciation axis. Here follows a suggested scheme for the Battery with example items where appropriate: e.g.

Test 1 Phonemic Contrasts (RP system) (About 40 items)
　　Are these three words all the same, all different or two the same?
　　e.g. *Stimulus* (Voice reads)　　　　*Response*
　　　　　HAD　HARD　HAD　　　All different　1　2　3

		12
	2 same	13✓
		23
	3 same	123

Test 2 Intonation and Stress (RP system) (About 20 items)
　　Which of these three responses is correct?
　　e.g. *Stimulus* (Voice reads)　　　　*Response*
　　　　　　　　　　　　　　　　1. The news is probably exciting.
　　Have you heard the news　　　2. The news is probably not exciting.
　　about the Test Match?　　　3. You have received the news.

Test 3 Lecturettes (About 30 items)
　　Three short spoken passages (5 or 6 minutes) each on subjects within the school curriculum: e.g. History, Biology, Mathematics, each with 10 multiple-choice questions to follow. Three different pronunciations, e.g. Mid West American, General West African, Australian.

Test 4 Conversation in Situation (About 30 items)
　　One short play-like scene built up with realistic dialogue to create a situation in which such aspects of meaning as suggestion, implication, inference, future and part reference are involved. To be followed by 30 multiple-choice questions. About three or four voices, a variety of those found in West African educated circles (including one RP) could be employed. The situation should be as realistic as possible but cannot be abstracted direct from life.

5.5.2. Part 2: Partial Production. As has been pointed out above this will need extensive experimental work. It is recommended that as a start there should be two paper-and-pencil tests, e.g.

Test 1 Phonemes through Rhyme (About 30 items) (RP system)
The following words all rhyme, that is they have the same middle
and last sounds: Sight, Fight, Bite. In the following item tick all
the words which rhyme.
  e.g. Sit
      Seat ✓
      Feet ✓
      Sheet ✓

Test 2 Rhythmic Groups (About 30 items)
If you were reading the following passage aloud you would make
pauses in certain places. The diagonal strokes (like this /) in the
passage are there to suggest possible places to make these pauses.
Only some of these are correct. You are asked to put a circle (like this Ø)
round those which you think are correct.
Thus:
John's / a Ø person / you can Ø really / reØly on Ø.

Weighting. The total number of items in Partial Production is 60, and
in Listening Comprehension 120: it is recommended that the weighting
be in this proportion, the Listening Comprehension Battery being
weighted twice as heavy as Partial Production.
  Whether or not such tests of Partial Production have any validity at
all remains to be seen. It is, of course, essential that the usual experimental procedures in psychometric research be applied before either
of these two Parts of the total scheme is put into large-scale operation.
  5.5.3. Part 3 Subjective Assessment of Communication. The reasons for
including this non-objective measure in the recommended scheme
have been given above. Here it will be dealt with under Content,
Administration and Scoring.

  5.5.4. Content. A conversation between the candidate and two teachers,
one from his own school, one from a neighbouring school. The purpose
of the conversation, which should last between 5–10 minutes per
candidate, should be to elicit whether the candidate can perform
adequately within a restricted range of English question and answer.
It is recommended that, rather than leave the conversation free, there
should be an attempt to make such restriction clear. It is further
recommended that the method described by C. J. Dodson, in his
pamphlet *Oral Examinations* (Dodson, 1963), or some modification of it,
be employed. Dodson suggests that schools be issued, at the beginning
of a language course, with a long list of questions. (He suggests 500;
this is probably too many: 200–300 might be enough.) An easy example
from his suggested list is:
  'What is your name?'

and a more difficult one:
'What do you say when you buy something at the post office?'
It may well be that, as well as increasing the range of such questions, the list might include statements as possible answers to questions. The candidate would be asked to provide the question:
e.g. (Examiner says):
'I spent three weeks at the sea-side'
to which the candidate might reply:
'What did you do for your holiday last year?'
with obvious variations.

Dodson suggests a scoring scheme. If this suggestion is taken up it is recommended that this is not employed but that a simple, subjective one is used.

5.5.5. Administration. This should present no greater problems than ensuring that schools are supplied at appropriate times with lists of questions. The use of local (teacher) examiners should be no problem. This, of course, the West African Examinations Council would have to arrange just as it does invigilators for the written papers.

5.5.6. Scoring. It is recommended that this be on a three-point scale (Fail, Pass, Distinction), that this be recorded on the Certificate but that it be of weight only beneficially to candidates whose performance in Parts 1 and 2 is border-line (Fail-Pass).

Naturally use of this technique would need to be experimented with as part of the initial trials.

5.6. Critique of Recommended Scheme

It may be asked how far such a scheme would go to meet the Aims, Demands and Constraints of Section 4. An attempt is made here to outline the advantages of such a scheme (it must, of course, be borne in mind that this is intended as an *Interim* Scheme until such time as work on Intelligibility and Production Tests is sufficiently advanced for a Test of Oral Production to be incorporated in the total scheme).

5.6.1. Aims

(1) *Streamlining for group purposes.* The new scheme would achieve this streamlining. Parts 1 and 2 would be group tests: Part 3 would not need trained external examiners.

(2) *Wash-back on schools.* Since the range of Part 1 would be very wide it is to be hoped that the test's influence would be educationally strong. Part 2 would at least focus attention on simple but important problems. Part 3 would at least draw attention to the need for some work to be done in schools on developing the ability to converse with a stranger. A detailed syllabus would need to be provided.

(3) *Improving the standard generally.* If (2) above applies then there would be some measure of success with this one. But there can be but very cautious optimism here.

5.6.2. Demands

(1) *Simple.* Parts 1 and 2, as objective group tests, would have no problem of administration. It should not be difficult to specify to schools (by way of syllabus, explanatory materials, teachers' courses, etc.) exactly what is being tested.

Part 3 is a much more disputable field. It is included by the writer for three reasons:

to involve the teachers in the problem;

to make sure that real production (however uncertainly tested) is worked at in schools—i.e. so that it is not neglected by students;

to include the demand for communication with a near-stranger.

Most students will rate Average on this Part. But then so they should.

(2) *Teachable.* Here, it must be admitted, will be the major problems. There are two of them: first the availability of sufficient materials from external sources (recorded, radio and TV, outside speakers, etc.); second the competence of the normal teacher to teach what (as with the McCallien Test) he may not be able to do himself. Here there is wide open room for special in-service courses for teachers. But this second problem is not lightly dismissed.

Even so, there are certain advantages of concentrating, as this scheme does, on a Listening Comprehension Battery. Teachers will not be expected to make contrasts, either phonemic or prosodic, themselves, nor teach their students how to. What they will be expected to do is to perceive them and assist their students in perceiving them. This is not easy; but it seems common sense that unless both teacher and students can *hear* them they certainly cannot be expected to produce them. And the segmental contrasts account for under half the tests of *this Listening* Battery. The lecture and conversation situation tests would not depend so heavily on purely linguistic features and would, it is to be hoped, therefore, be more amenable to the competence of the ordinary teacher.

Part 2 will be more difficult but if it makes use of a restricted set of items then it is at least possible for teachers to acquaint themselves with them all. Part 3, if it makes use of some such method as that referred to above, is again teachable in the sense that all possible questions are known to the teacher.

(3) *Beneficial.* A Battery of Listening Comprehension Tests is not in any sense a complete Test of Spoken English. Opinions given to the writer varied as to whether Production or Comprehension was more

important educationally. As has been pointed out above, Comprehension inevitably must precede Production. At the same time within the educational process students must comprehend what they hear; it is arguable how much they must actually speak. And from the point of view of *varieties*, while a student should be exposed to the range of Englishes spoken throughout West Africa and in L1 situations (and while parts of the LC Battery will do just this, testing his tolerance over this wide range) all he *must* do in production is to make himself intelligible within his own educational environment. This, of course, is what Part 3, in a crude fashion, will attempt to discover.

There are, then, certain *theoretical* reasons for concentrating at the moment on Listening Comprehension. But it must be made quite clear that the main reason for this concentration in the immediate scheme is the practical difficulty of devising a valid Test of Production which can be applied by unskilled examiners.

5.6.3. Constraints

(1) *Examiner Supply*. Since Parts 1 and 2 are objective group tests this problem does not apply. And since Part 3 makes use of local teachers, not trained phonetically and certainly not professional phoneticians, it does not apply here either.

(2) *Administration*. The new scheme is designed to overcome administration problems.

(3) *Machinery*. It seems clear to the writer that no adequate Test of Spoken English of even the lame kind outlined here can possibly succeed without the widespread use of machinery. Tape-recorders or disc players (preferably the latter) must be made available. So must tapes and discs, in quantity, both for the Tests themselves and for teaching materials necessary as preparation for the Tests. Responsibility for preparation and supply of materials, both testing and teaching, *must* be accepted by somebody: the WAEC might well be the appropriate body to take this responsibility.

5.7. Radio

There seems every reason to hope that Television and Radio authorities in West Africa would be prepared to help again both with *Testing* time and with *preparation* time. Certainly the TV officials spoken to in Ghana and the Radio officials in Nigeria seemed most anxious to help in any way they could. It is not clear that TV could, at the moment, be used as the testing medium *throughout* West Africa but there seems no reason why Radio could not. It might be possible for the various Radio stations in West Africa to put out several special Spoken English programmes each week, culminating in the final Test session itself. Indications are that most schools have access to a radio receiver and that reception is generally good. There is here an important field for co-operation between the West African Examinations Council, the British Council and the various Schools Broadcasting Units. But the responsibility for supply of materials and the inception of such courses would seem to lie with the West African Examinations Council. It may be easier, for a start, to rely on tape recorders and to bring in candidates to centrally located schools for the testing sessions. But it is to be hoped that the Radio idea could be investigated and experimented with as soon as possible.

(The Report continues with recommendations as to the responsibility for test construction and finishes with a summary of recommendations and a set of acknowledgements. The Appendices contain a detailed itinerary; statistical analyses of the McCallien Test; and Dr Harris's Preliminary Report, referred to in the preamble to this chapter.

It should be stated here that the West African Examinations Council Oral English International Panel, at its meeting in Accra on 2 March 1966, disagreed most strongly with the writer's views on supply of and demands on Examiners in Sections 1.2 and 2.4.3 of this chapter. The Panel considered that examiners did agree among themselves [and see p. 154, last paragraph of 1.2 of this chapter] at the Co-ordination meeting and that a sufficient supply of qualified examiners could be found.)

11

Intelligibility

Keith Brown

This chapter describes a limited investigation using objective tests into some aspects of the mutual intelligibility of the pronunciation of three accents[1] of English. It was partly prompted by P. D. Strevens's statements in *Spoken English* (1956, pp. 33–4) that:

Tests with West African speakers and with speakers of Received Pronunciation suggested that whereas Received Pronunciation, when used between speakers of that dialect, was 95 per cent efficient, West African pronunciation used between speakers of West African, on the same material, was only 30 per cent efficient, while in the opposite direction, speakers of the West African pronunciation found Received Pronunciation about 64 per cent efficient . . . Without going into (the tests) in detail we can say that under the given circumstances the possibility of misunderstanding, or confusion, or ambiguity, or complete lack of comprehension, may be between ten and twenty times as great with the West African pronunciation as with Received Pronunciation.

The experiment from which these figures derive was conducted in the course of an enquiry into the most appropriate accent of English to teach students at the then University College of the Gold Coast (now the University of Ghana) and is described thus (Strevens, 1954):

A series of tests were conducted, using recorded lists of monosyllabic words, spoken by speakers of GCP (Gold Coast Pronunciation) and a speaker of RP. These recordings were played to audiences of RP speakers and speakers of GCP and the ability of the listeners to write down the words spoken was reduced to a percentage and taken as an indication of the 'intelligibility' of the speech under those conditions. . . . In order to check on the loss of intelligibility through the equipment used, similar tests were conducted by the same speakers in the presence of the subjects. In this case the average of RP speakers listening to RP rose to 98 per cent, while the average of GCP speakers listening to their own dialect rose to 61 per cent still leaving a significant difference.

We were teaching English at the newly-established University College of Cape Coast, Ghana, between 1962–64, and assuming that

---

[1] Accent is here used as a neutral form meaning 'manner of pronouncing' (cf. Abercrombie, 1956, ch. 4) and covering both suprasegmental and segmental features.
Reference is made to this chapter on p. 17 of the Introduction.

Strevens's sample was drawn from his students our experience was somewhat different. Like Strevens, we found that our students claimed to have no difficulty in understanding each other, and as far as 'misunderstandings . . . etc.' deriving from difficulty with the phonology of English were concerned (and this is the area that was tested) this seemed to be substantially true. Indeed they claimed that they often had more difficulty in understanding expatriate English-speaking staff, particularly new arrivals until they had grown used to their pronunciation. The same situation seemed to obtain with British staff, that once they had acclimatized themselves to Ghanaian pronunciations of English, purely phonological difficulties were comparatively infrequent in their contacts with students.

To investigate the mutual intercomprehensibility of some of the accents of English used on the campus a sample of our students took an objective aural perception test administered by an RP speaker and Ghanaian speakers with Twi and Ewe as their mother tongue. Two different accents of Ghanaian pronunciation of English were chosen, as they were perceptibly different, even though the differences were slight, and it seemed to us that students from the same L_1 background were somewhat more intelligible to each other than to students of other L_1's.

Our sample consisted of 45 students following the Preliminary year at the University College, preparatory to entering on a three-year General Degree course in the Faculty of Arts. The L_1 background of the sample was:

> Akan Language Group 30 (inc. 23 Twi/Fante)
> Ewe 9
> Etc. 6 (inc. 2 Ga.)
> ——
> 45

There were 3 women (in the Akan group), and 42 men. Most of the sample were mature students; average age $30 \cdot 5$ years, with little difference between the groups. 27 Akans and 8 Ewes had been teachers, mostly in local authority schools, before coming to the College and would return to teaching after graduation. Many did not have the necessary entry qualifications for direct entry to the degree course, and the preliminary year was designed to give them this. All, however, had a substantial number of passes at the West African School Certificate (WASC) 'O' level examination, including in all cases 'English Language', and in some cases 'Oral English'. Sixteen Akans and 6 Ewes had one or more passes at the WASC 'H' level. All the sample were asked whether at any time in school or teacher training college they had been taught English by a native English speaker, from any of the English-speaking countries, and whether they had ever received any systematic instruction in 'Spoken English' (i.e. pronunciation, etc.) as opposed to casual correction. They replied as in Table 1:

	Taught English by native speaker	Instruction in 'Spoken English'		
		By native speaker	By non-nat. sp.	Not at all
Akan	19	13	8	9
Ewe	3	3	3	3
Etc.	4	3	1	2
Total	26 (58%)	19 (42%)	12 (27%)	14 (31%)

TABLE 1. Source of teaching and instruction in English

First instruction in English, in all cases, was by a non-native speaker. At the College, 'English' was a compulsory subject, and included some, largely practical, instruction in 'Spoken English'.

There are two points that should be made about this sample, as they affect statistical measures on the results of the test. It is, unfortunately, rather small, particularly for comparative work. More importantly it is also rather homogeneous. This we had found to be true of their pronunciation both from an impressionistic assessment and from a variety of formal and informal tests administered throughout the year. That this homogeneity was rather general may perhaps be inferred from the results of written University examinations taken shortly after the test under discussion. In 'English Language', the mean for the same students was 44·51 per cent and the standard deviation 5·35; in 'History' the mean was 44·3 per cent and the standard deviation 4·4.

The test battery was based on RP, sampling in particular those areas of the phonology that comparative studies and teaching experience led us to believe would offer the greatest difficulty to native Twi and Ewe speakers. Substantially the same test was then read by the other speakers, and an attempt made to validate their performance afterwards from recordings of their administration of the test compared with recordings of their conversation.

Ideally one would doubtless wish to test the intercomprehensibility of different accents by tests based on the significant distinctions maintained within each accent itself. The decision to use RP as the basis for the native speaker's version of the battery can be justified on the same grounds as led Strevens to choose RP as the accent to teach in the University College of the Gold Coast (Strevens, 1956). When pronunciation is taught in Ghanaian schools, RP is usually the model chosen, as it is by those who have made comparative studies (e.g. Schachter, 1962). It is the basis for the McCallien test (cf. Davies, 1965b).[1] All of our students were familiar with it and most of the College staff spoke a version of RP. From a practical point of view it also happens to be our accent; we had been teaching the students and were administering the test.

In the case of the Ghanaian pronunciations, there is no description of the phonology of an accent of Ghanaian English, and even if there were it would not necessarily have been more useful than the method adopted. Accents of Ghanaian English vary to some extent according to the L1 of the speaker, and to a considerable extent according to the education of the speaker. At the best they are completely acceptable; at the worst their phonology differs little from that of the speaker's L1. With individuals too accent is far from stable. We found that distinctions made in the test were not always unequivocally maintained in conversation, and distinctions made in conversation with British staff were not always maintained in speaking to, for example, College servants whose accent was usually less acceptable than that of the students. Thus, even among so comparatively homogeneous a group as our students it would have been difficult enough to settle on an appropriate standard to use as the basis of a test. This is not, of course, to deny that there are numerous features of Ghanaian pronunciation that appear to have become institutionalized (particularly 'stress' patterns of certain items, and the pronunciation, often a spelling pronunciation, of certain words) and occur rather generally throughout our sample.

The battery consisted of three parts:

(1) *Phoneme Discrimination:* a set of 36 items, 18 vowels and 18 consonants, in which subjects were presented with groups of three words, all stressed monosyllables, and asked to decide whether one was different from the other two, and if so which one, whether all were the same, or whether they were all different. (Cf. Davies's *English Proficiency Test Battery,* forthcoming.) The only monophthong not tested was the unstressed ə. Important though this vowel is in English, we had found from other tests that our sample had little difficulty in the perception of this vowel in RP. Thus in a ten-item test of the recognition of weak forms in rapid speech only one item had a difficulty level below 75 per cent, and six had levels above 90 per cent. The mean score was 8·4 and no score lower than 6. Another ten-item test based on those items with strong and weak

---

[1] See Chapter 10.

forms (cf. Lado, 1961; Stress Technique 9.3) had a mean of 7·1 with most item difficulty levels above 70 per cent. The production of this vowel in Ghanaian accents of English is, of course, another matter. Most of the consonant items were based on contrasts where at least one of the three items was an alveolar, post alveolar or dental phoneme. These are among the most frequent consonant phonemes in RP and include most of those that caused difficulty in perception and production. Areas of general difficulty (e.g. voice in final clusters) can be tested with these phonemes as adequately as with others. A few clusters were also tested, but not many owing to the fact that a test of this sort is based on minimal distinctions and many clusters do not lend themselves to satisfactory testing by this method.

We decided not to ask our sample to identify individual words, as Strevens had done, as we wished to test a larger number of distinctions than would have been possible in this way. We had also discovered from other tests that our sample had no more difficulty in the perception of individual words than in the discrimination of minimal triplets. It also seemed to us, from evidence from other tests, that we were not merely testing to hear whether the sample could perceive differences; they were also able to identify the items being said.

To introduce some check on the reliability of the Phoneme test three items were each tested twice. Correlation of these test-retest items was ·96.

(2) *Placement of tonicity in sentences* ('Sentence Stress'): a set of 25 items: 15 in which subjects were asked to listen to a sentence which was also printed on their answer sheet and underline the syllable on which the tonic was placed, and 10 in which a difference in tonicity affected the 'meaning' of the sentence. Subjects were asked to choose the more appropriate of two possible meanings printed on the answer sheet (cf. Lado, 1961; Stress Technique 9.1). Only rising and falling intonations were used, and the placement of the tonic varied so that it fell at the beginning, middle and end of various sentences. Word Stress (cf. Lado, 1961; Stress Technique 9.1) was not tested as we had found from earlier tests that it was non-discriminating. There is also the special problem that many words seem to have acquired institutionalized 'stress' patterns in Ghanaian pronunciations, different from those of RP.

(3) *Rhythm and Intonation:* 20 items in which subjects were asked to listen to a sentence and decide on the more appropriate of two possible 'meanings' of this sentence, given on the answer sheet. Ten items concerned grammatical relationships between and within sentences (cf. Lado, 1961; Intonation Technique 10.8), and the other 10 the 'affective' meanings of intonation patterns; in these the choice presented the subject was as unambiguous as possible, usually only requiring

him to distinguish between a marked and an unmarked, neutral, intonation. (Cf. Lado, 1961; Intonation Technique 10.7.)

The test was administered viva voce to half the sample at a time by an RP speaker, an Asante Twi speaker from Kumasi and an Ewe speaker from Keta. In each half sample there were approximately equal numbers of Twi and Ewe students. KB read the RP version to both half samples to establish some control between them. A different Ewe and Twi read to each half sample so that we might have evidence from more than one speaker of each accent. All the Ghanaians were apparently average speakers of their groups, chosen at random. The whole sample was familiar with the speech of all the readers.

The Twi and Ewe speakers were aware of the nature of the experiment but were not rehearsed. They were asked to read the items at a normal conversational speed and, as far as possible, in the accent they would use in conversation with their fellow students. The vowel and consonant items were not uncovered for the readers until just before they were read to try and minimize the production of rehearsed distinctions. For the stress and intonation items each reader was told what answer would be marked correct on the answer sheet and asked to read the item accordingly. These items they were asked to study beforehand so that they should have an opportunity to decide how to read them and so that their reading should be as spontaneous as possible.

For each of the three readings of the phoneme test the items were identical, but the order of presentation was different. In the other tests, while the sentences remained the same the correct answers were varied.

Because of the time taken to administer, the test was only read in its entirety by the RP speaker. The other speakers omitted the second 10 items of the stress test and the first 10 items of the intonation test.

The Ghanaian speakers' versions of the test were recorded and their pronunciation then compared with recordings of the same speakers in conversation in an attempt to determine the extent to which distinctions which may have been drawn in the test were maintained under more normal conditions. In the test, most of the items kept distinct by the RP speaker were also distinguished by the Ghanaians, and within the test distinctions were maintained very consistently, e.g. in comparable items, or in test-retest items. Needless to say the exponents of the distinctions were not always the same as those of the RP speaker. Thus, for example, Ewe reader (a) consistently distinguished between voiced and voiceless final consonant clusters in the quality of the immediately preceding vowel (backer or closer or both with the voiced item) rather than by voice in the final cluster; Twi reader (b)

7

appeared to signal marked intonations by changes in voice quality or by extra large pitch movements rather than by the choice of tone pattern.

The only distinctions that were made in the test that were not found at all in the conversation concern stress and intonation—all the vowel and consonant qualities recorded in the test were also found somewhere in the conversation.

Some readers attempted, in some of the 'stress' items, a rising intonation in imitation of an RP rising 'question' intonation: this was ill understood in the test and not found at all in the conversation. Similarly the affective use of intonation seemed to be entirely avoided in conversation. Otherwise stress and intonation patterns of both test and conversation seemed to be very similar.

With the vowels and consonants it was sometimes clear that regular distinctions of the test were far from consistently maintained in conversation: this was particularly true of the ð-d and θ-t pairs, though in fact all four sounds are found somewhere in the conversation.

In some cases, however, it was not at all clear to what extent distinctions were being maintained. Undoubtedly certain distinctions (as for instance between long and short vowels) were less rigorously maintained, though far from entirely lacking, but a difference in the distribution of the phonemes makes it difficult often to judge. As Schachter (1962, p. 16) has remarked:

(There are) . . . mispronunciations that result not from a student's inability to produce the sounds of a given English word correctly, but, rather, from a misconception about what sounds actually do occur in the word. Thus a student may be able to pronounce the words *full* and *fool* perfectly, but may be misled by the spelling into pronouncing *wool* to rhyme with *fool* rather than with *full*.

Furthermore, it is probably true to say that there are few, if any, RP sounds for which our readers could not produce an intelligible substitute (certainly intelligible to their fellows, and to a greater or lesser degree 'acceptable' to native speakers) if necessary. But the degree to which their phonology systematically corresponds to RP varies greatly according to the situation and is probably maximal in the case of administering a test. This is not surprising and is certainly also true of RP speakers. If we may agree with Catford that 'some contexts provide so many clues to the speaker's intention that speech is hardly necessary at all . . . Contexts which provide us with a minimum of clues may be termed *crucial contexts*. The real test of the efficiency of an utterance is its intelligibility in crucial contexts' (1950, p. 14), then the fact that our speakers maintained more distinctions more consistently in the test than in conversation need not disturb us.

Owing to the homogeneity of the sample already commented on, we were not surprised to find that the analysis of the results showed that the test was not highly discriminating.[1] Thus there were rather more items with a low discrimination index, particularly in the Phoneme test than would have been acceptable in a normal proficiency test. Thus 3 Phoneme, 1 Stress and 1 Intonation items had discrimination indices below $+\cdot3$. However, 6 Phoneme, 14 Stress and 6 Intonation items had indices above $+\cdot6$, which seemed fairly satisfactory. Some of the items with low discrimination were deliberately retained, although we knew from earlier tests with similar items that they would not be discriminating, because we wanted a measure of the overall control of phonological distinctions, rather than one particularly related to areas of maximum difficulty. Further the test was to be read by others than an RP speaker, and the pronunciation of the others was to some extent an unknown factor.

Results are presented in Tables 2 and 3:

	Poss. total	Mean	S.D.
Phonemes	36	25·0	4·3
Stress	25	16·1	3·4
Intonation	20	13·7	2·7

TABLE 2. Means and Standard Deviations

	Stress	Intonation	Total
Phonemes	·19	·06	·64
Stress		·14	·73
Intonation			·59

TABLE 3. Inter-test Correlations

A comparison of means for those who had been taught English at some time by a native speaker and those who hadn't, reveals no significant difference between the performance of the two groups.[2]

[1] Davies's (1965b,) analysis of the results of the McCallien test for the WASC shows that this test, too, is not very highly discriminating. This may be due to faulty test design. It may, on the other hand, show a similarly homogeneous sample.

[2] Davies (1965b,) reports a similar result. See p. 163 of Chapter 10 of this present volume. Chapter 10 contains the bulk of Davies (1965b) referred to here and elsewhere in this chapter.

Table 5 (pp. 190–1) shows a detailed analysis of Means for the Twi and Ewe students only by speaker, half sample and sub-test. These obtained results are summarized in percentage figures in Table 4.

In the RP version there is a remarkable uniformity between the Twi results for each half sample. The Ewe (b) half sample is rather better than the (a) half sample. This is also shown in the performance of the Ewe (b) sample in all the other tests. The results for Twi speaker (a) are rather better than those for Twi speaker (b). With the Ewe speakers, (b) scores slightly better than (a) with the Ewe sample, and (a) slightly better than (b) with the Twi sample. We may infer from this that both of the Twi half samples are rather similar, but that the Ewe (b) half sample is rather better than the (a) half sample. Twi reader (a) seems to have been slightly more intelligible than (b). Both the Ewe readers make very similar scores.

		(a)	(b)	Total
Twi sample	Twi reader	80	86	83
	RP reader	72	72	72
	Ewe reader	74	70	72
Ewe sample	Ewe reader	76	79	78
	Twi reader	69	77	73
	RP reader	66	73	70

TABLE 4. Percentage Means and Totals (percentage symbol omitted)

It seems clear that for both half samples a reader from their own L1 is rather more comprehensible than anyone else. For the Twi speakers, both half samples show absolutely better scores with a Twi speaker than with any other speaker. For the Ewe sample, each half has a better score than for any other reader.

These results seem to us to be a truer reflection of the mutual inter-comprehensibility of the accents tested than those suggested by Strevens, and we would have been surprised if our results had been otherwise. Indeed considering that English as well as being the language of instruction is also the preferred language in a number of formal and informal situations involving students either entirely or primarily it would be rather alarming if 'the possibility of misunderstanding, etc.' were really between ten and twenty times as great with the West African pronunciation as with Received Pronunciation.

Our results do not lead directly to any conclusions about the intelligibility[1] of these accents among others than the sample tested. Thus no conclusions can be drawn about their intelligibility to other Ghanaians whose phonology in speaking English is more similar to that of their L1. Informally, but from observation of British staff and students speaking with College servants and others whose English was much less 'English' than that of our students, we would expect the intelligibility of both groups to fall, but that of the RP speaker to fall more sharply. This drop in intelligibility of the RP speaker is, of course, not only a matter of phonology but also due to the fact that the grammar and lexis of the servants' English is a lot less 'standard' than that of the students: but whereas the students themselves can accommodate themselves to this, as it is a type of English with which they are familiar, RP speakers are generally much less able to do so.[2]

Nor can any conclusions be drawn about the 'international intelligibility' of the accents. We were unfortunately not able to assemble a sample of RP speakers. For a true assessment of this we would certainly need to compare results from a sample of English-speaking residents in Ghana and in Britain, as the 'threshold of intelligibility' (Catford, 1950) would undoubtedly be higher for those resident in Britain.

Finally, it would seem to us that the main interest of our results derives from our sample. Homogeneous as it apparently is, it is drawn from those Ghanaians whose English has a crucial influence on the level of English spoken throughout the country, local authority teachers. And it is thus interesting to note that many of the results of Davies's (1965b) analysis of the McCallien test of Oral English for the WASC 'O' level examination appear to parallel our own.

[1] We do not make any claims that a measurement of the mutual intercomprehensibility of the pronunciation of various accents is the only, or even the criterial factor in intelligibility. We note, however, the findings of Carrol (1963) of an experiment in which 16 judges were asked to rate the English of three non-native speakers on a ten-point scale for ten 'speech characteristics'. The ratings were all impressionistic, but the judges were mostly professional and experienced phoneticians or language teachers. From his results it would appear that 'stress', 'intonation' and 'diction' (i.e. the pronunciation of segments) all correlate fairly highly with 'Intelligibility' (easy v. difficult to understand) and 'Englishness' (very English v. most un-English), and more highly with these two parameters than any of the others examined.

[2] Cf. the distinction drawn by Mafeni (1965) between 'talkee-talkee', the broken English used by expatriates in the belief that they are speaking pidgin and true pidgin. And note Strevens's remark: 'It has already been my misfortune to discover that in bargaining for fish, or endeavouring to hire a taxi to the nearest town, R.P. is a strong disadvantage and GCP a distinct asset' (1954, p. 84).

Group	RP Speaker		TWI Speakers		EWE Speakers	
	TWI	EWE	TWI	EWE	TWI	EWE
Test 1						
Segments Vowels (18)						
a	15·1	12·4	15·1	12·6	12·9	13·0
b	14·8	14·5	16·9	13·5	12·8	15·0
Total	14·9	13·5	16·0	13·1	12·9	14·0
Consonants (18)						
a	10·7	10·8	14·1	11·0	12·2	13·3
b	10·7	12·0	12·9	10·5	11·6	13·3
Total	10·7	11·4	13·5	10·8	11·9	13·3
Total (36)						
a	25·8	23·2	29·2	23·6	25·1	26·3
b	25·5	26·5	29·8	24·0	24·4	28·3
Total	25·7	24·9	29·5	23·9	24·8	27·3

Test 2 Stress 15 (25)	a	9·8 (16·5)	8·8 (15·4)	11·5	10·2	12·7	12·2
	b	10·1 (16·0)	10·0 (16·7)	13·0	13·0	11·7	11·8
	Total	10·0 (16·3)	9·4 (16·1)	12·2	11·6	12·2	12·0
Test 3 Intonation 10 (20)	a	7·9 (13·4)	7·8 (13·4)	7·4	7·8	6·7	7·2
	b	7·9 (14·2)	7·5 (14·5)	8·9	9·2	6·1	7·6
	Total	7·9 (13·8)	7·7 (13·9)	8·2	8·5	6·4	7·4
Total 61 (81)	a	43·5 (55·7)	39·8 (52·0)	48·1	41·6	44·5	45·7
	b	43·5 (55·7)	44·0 (57·7)	51·7	46·2	42·2	47·7
	Total	43·5 (55·7)	41·9 (54·9)	49·9	43·8	43·4	46·7

TABLE 5. Raw Mean Scores by Test, Speaker and Group of Subjects

The scores in rows marked a and b are for each half sample; those in rows marked total are for the whole sample. The figures in brackets for the RP speaker column show scores made on the full version of the test; the unbracketed figure shows scores made on that part of the test which is directly comparable with the corresponding scores under the Twi and Ewe speaker columns. The RP speaker was the same for both a and b; a different Ewe and Twi speaker read to each half sample.

Appendix. Item Analysis

Elisabeth Ingram

Elisabeth Ingram

INTRODUCTION

The principles of Test evaluation are described in Chapter 2. The methods of computing product moment and rank order correlations in order to estimate test reliability and validity are described in a number of books on statistics in education and psychology. But it is difficult to find instructions in print on how to do item analysis. Item analysis is a means of estimating how much information each single item in a test contributes to the information provided by the test as a whole. The data for item analysis are provided by the detailed test results of those individuals who have taken the test in a preliminary draft.

Two assumptions are made:

(1) that the test, however poor, gives a better measure of the capacity of an individual than any single item does; and

(2) that the individuals in the try-out group or sample get results which are like the results the individuals from a much larger group might have got had they taken the test. This larger group is the target population, which consists of all potential test users.

The test constructor attempts to justify the first assumption by careful job-specification and by subject analysis. In language testing the job-specification has to do with determining which language skills are to be tested, which stimulus-response patterns to employ, and what difficulty level to aim at. The subject is language, the methods of analysing language are drawn formally or informally from linguistics, recent or traditional.

Attempts to ensure that the second assumption is valid come under the theory of sampling. This is a large and difficult subject which I have no intention of dealing with, beyond making a few elementary points. In choosing a sample it is safest to get the advice of a professional statistician, preferably one engaged in educational work of some kind.

When the test is completed, it will measure certain skills possessed to a greater or lesser degree by members of the target population.

Reference is made to this appendix on p. 17 of the Introduction.

The target population includes anybody who might reasonably be expected to take the test in the future. The individuals who make up this population have certain characteristics which affect their performance on the test.

The test constructor evaluates the first draft of his test in the light of the analysis of the scores obtained by the try-out sample. He then revises the test, hoping that the second version will be more appropriate to the target population than the first one, and so on, until he reaches the final form.

The value of the information he receives at each stage depends entirely on whether the try-out sample reflects accurately all the characteristics of the target population which affect test performance.

If, for instance, the test is intended to measure how much English secondary school pupils in a given district or state (the target population) have learnt after three years' teaching, then the try-out sample must consist of secondary school pupils in this district who have been taught English for three years.

If the secondary school population consists of pupils aged between 15 and 17 years, then the try-out sample must have the same age distribution. If half the secondary school population speaks one mother tongue (L1) and the other half speaks another, then the sample must be made up equally of speakers of each language. The number of poor, middling and good pupils in the sample must mirror the number of poor, middling and good pupils in the population. If intelligence test scores are available the sample should be chosen to mirror the population in this respect. Since the teachers of English in the district must necessarily vary in competence, pupils in the sample must be taken from the classes of several teachers. The target population will possess many more characteristics. Some are obvious, for instance social class (caste, tribe) and family income. Others are less obvious, but they may all affect test performance. The test constructor should list all the important characteristics he can think of, and choose his sample according to as many as he can manage.

SIZE OF TRY-OUT SAMPLE

The try-out sample should be as large as possible. Other things being equal, a larger sample is more likely to mirror the characteristics of the population than a smaller one.

An important factor in deciding on sample size is the degree of *heterogeneity* of the target population. If the individuals in the population are very different from one another in a number of important respects, then a large try-out sample is needed. If, for example, the individuals in the population speak four or five different L1's, if the secondary school system is relatively new, or has recently been expanded, so that

pupils vary a great deal in age and previous experience, and the
teachers and schools vary a great deal in quality, then the population
will be very heterogeneous; and a large sample will be needed.

The target population may, on the other hand, be fairly *homogeneous*,
that is, it may consist of individuals who are rather similar to each
other. A district may possess a well-established secondary school
system, where selection for secondary schooling is uniform and orderly,
where the teachers possess the same qualifications and work according
to similar methods, books and time-tables, and where the pupils speak
the same L1 and are of the same age in each class. In such a district
the secondary school population can be said to be relatively homogeneous, though, of course, the pupils will still differ among themselves
in ability and interest and so will the teachers.

Theoretically the sample should be chosen to mirror the population
for all relevant characteristics, and should be large enough for all
statistics to be reliable and significant. But this degree of perfection
is rarely reached in practice. An amateur test constructor (whose
time is largely taken up by his professional duties) may have to be
content with very pragmatic solutions to the problems of sampling,
such as assuming that the intake in one year is representative of the
intake in other years, or even that a few of the classes in one year are
representative of all the other classes. The larger the sample, the
more time is needed for test administration, scoring and working out
the result.

Working within a fairly homogeneous population, the test constructor
may decide to use no more than 50–60 subjects for the first pilot
version of his test on his try-out group. On the other hand, if the
population is known to be very heterogeneous, he may need a much
larger number.

As stated earlier, item analysis is a means of estimating to what
extent any single item contributes to the information provided by the
test as a whole, on the assumption that the total score is a better measure
of the individual's capacity than the score (1 for success, 0 for fail) on
each item taken separately.

The total score gives a general indication of the capacity of the
individual in comparison with the others who took the test. Arranging
the scores from the highest to the lowest gives a picture of the distribution of the scores and provides a rank order of overall capacity.
The correct and incorrect answers for all items and for all individuals
provide the detailed answer pattern. Item analysis is carried out by
comparing the answer pattern with the over-all rank order, so as to
judge how suitable each item is for inclusion in the test.

Items are usually judged with respect to the total score. But it is
also quite common to compare the item not with the over-all ranking,

but with the rank order established according to part scores or subtest scores. It depends on the purpose of the tester.

There are several methods of item analysis, but they all begin by establishing the answer pattern.

EXAMPLE AND INSTRUCTIONS FOR ITEM ANALYSIS

Recording the answer pattern

Let us assume that you have a written test of English grammar consisting of 100 items, administered it to 60 pupils, scored the completed test scripts, and entered the total score on the front page.

Arrange the scripts in order of merit, and divide them into three groups with an equal number of scripts in each, to get the upper third of scripts, the middle third and the lower third.

Here 60 pupils have taken the test, so the total number (N) is 60, and there will be 20 scripts in each group; $n = 20 : 20 : 20$. If N is not a multiple of 3 it is not necessary to throw away any scripts; what matters is that the upper and lower group must have the same number.

For $N = 61$, $n = 20 : 21 : 20$; and

For $N = 59$, $n = 20 : 19 : 20$; and so on.

The safest way to have the groups divided correctly is to write down the number of scripts in each third, here $20 : 20 : 20$. Then, when all the scripts have been arranged according to merit, the first twenty scripts are counted off from the top, to form the upper third, the next twenty to form the middle, and the last twenty to form the lower third.

The total scores of the 60 scripts in the example is set out in Table 1.

Top Third		Middle Third		Lower Third	
Score	Frequency	Score	Frequency	Score	Frequency
85	1	64	1	53	3
81	1	63	2	52	2
75	1	62	3	50	2
74	3	60	3	48	1
73	1	58	5	45	3
72	2	57	2	42	2
68	2	56	2	40	2
67	2	54	2	34	3
66	4	—		31	1
64	3	20		29	1
	20				20

TABLE 1. Frequency table of total test scores arranged in thirds

Notice that three of the scripts with a total score of 64 go into the top group, as the 18th, 19th and 20th scripts in that group. There cannot be a 21st, so one of the four, chosen at random becomes the 1st script in the middle group.

The next step is to prepare some tally sheets, as in Fig. 1, where the names of the Test and of the School are, of course, illustrative.

ITEM ANALYSIS

Test: *English,*   School: *St. George's*   Date: *6 June 1968*
Grammar,   Standard: *V*
Draft 1 N: 60; $\dfrac{N}{3}$: 20 : 20 : 20

1 Item	2 Upper		3 Middle		4 Lower		5 Total	6 %	7 Diff.	8 E_{1-3}
1										
2										
3										
4										
5										
6										
.										
.										
.										
100										

FIG. 1

You need one row for each item, i.e. 100 rows in all. In the extreme left column write the number of each item.

Take the 20 scripts of the upper group. Student A has the highest total score, 85. Look at his answer to item 1. He has chosen the correct answer, mark this with a stroke in the row for item number 1 in the second column from the left. He also got the correct answer to items 2, 3, 4 and 5; mark the sheet in the same way. But he got item 6 wrong, so do *not* put a mark in the row for item 6. Items 7, 8, 9 and 10 are correct, so mark each of these rows, and so on for each item in the test, down to item 100.

Figure 2 shows a section of the left side of the tally sheet, after the first ten items for the top student have been marked off.

When you have marked off each of the 100 items for student A, treat the script of the second highest scorer, student B, in the same way, and similarly for all the other scripts in the upper group.

Item	Upper								
1	—								
2	—								
3	—								
4	—								
5	—								
6	—								
7	—								
8	—								
9	—								
10	—								

FIG. 2

For convenience of counting, every fifth tally is drawn across the preceding four, making gates representing five successful answers to one item.

When all the scripts in the top group have been tallied, add up the number of tally-marks and write the sum down in the next column, immediately to the left of the double line.

When the section of the tally sheet shown in Fig. 2 is completed, it will appear as in Fig. 3.

The column immediately to the right of the double line is used to tally the successful answers from the scripts in the middle third. This is done in exactly the same way as for the upper group.

Finally the procedure is repeated for the answers in the scripts of the lower third.

Item	Upper	
1	ЖЖ ЖЖ ЖЖ ЖЖ	20
2	ЖЖ ЖЖ ЖЖ ЖЖ	20
3	ЖЖ ЖЖ ЖЖ IIII	19
4	ЖЖ ЖЖ ЖЖ II	17
5	ЖЖ ЖЖ ЖЖ	15
6	ЖЖ ЖЖ II	12
7	ЖЖ ЖЖ ЖЖ III	18
8	ЖЖ ЖЖ ЖЖ ЖЖ	20
9	ЖЖ ЖЖ I	11
10	ЖЖ II	7

FIG. 3

When the successful answers to each item for each of the thirds have been tallied and summed, the sum of the successful answers for all the 60 scripts is obtained, and entered in Column 5 under the heading 'Total'. For item 1 of the example the figures are $20+18+12 = 50$.

Next the facility value (Column 6) of each item is established. This involves calculating and writing down the correct answers for each item expressed as a percentage of the maximum possible. For instance:

	Upper		Middle		Lower		Total	%
Item 1	20	+	18	+	12	=	50;	$\frac{50}{60} \times 100 = 83$
Item 6	12	+	10	+	0	=	22;	$\frac{22}{60} \times 100 = 37$

The percentage of successful answers in relation to the total possible answers (given in whole numbers because fractions would give a misleading impression of accuracy) indicates the facility value of each item. Here item 1, which is answered correctly by 83 per cent of the candidates, is a very easy item, while item 6, which is answered correctly by only slightly more than a third of the sample, is a fairly difficult item. Column 6, headed % in Fig. 4 (see p. 200), gives the facility value for the first 10 items of the example.

The last step in the item analysis is the estimation of the discrimination value of each item. This can be done by referring to Flanagan charts (based not on equal thirds but on 27 : 46 : 27 per hundred, or by computing the point Bi-serial correlation of coefficients (Guilford, 1956). I shall describe a very simple method of obtaining the discrimination index. This method is known as the Estimate of the first group in ratio to the third group, or E_{1-3}.

The basic idea is that the people in the upper third should get any item right more often than the people in the lower third.

The E_{1-3} formula:
$$E_{1-3} = \text{Difference}/n$$
where Difference = for any item, the number of correct answers in the upper third, minus the number of correct answers in the lower third, and
$n = $ Total $N/3$.

So in the example we get from Fig. 4:
For item 1: Difference $= 20-12 = 8$, $n = 20$, $8/20 = \cdot40$
For item 2: Difference $= 20-20 = 0$, $n = 20$, $0/20 = 0$
For item 3: Difference $= 18-15 = 3$, $n = 20$, $3/20 = \cdot15$

The Difference is entered in Column 7 and the Discrimination Index (E_{1-3}) in Column 8.

ITEM ANALYSIS

Test: *English, Grammar, Draft. 1*

School: *St. George's*
Standard: *V*

Date: *6 June 1968*

N: 60; $\dfrac{N}{3}$ = 20 : 20 : 20

1 Item	2 Upper		3 Middle		4 Lower		5 Total	6 %	7 Diff.	8 E_{t-3}
1	⊥⊥⊥ ⊥⊥⊥ ⊥⊥⊥ ⊥⊥⊥	20	⊥⊥⊥ ⊥⊥⊥ ⊥⊥⊥ III	18	⊥⊥⊥ ⊥⊥⊥ II	12	50	83	8	·40
2	⊥⊥⊥ ⊥⊥⊥ ⊥⊥⊥ ⊥⊥⊥	20	⊥⊥⊥ ⊥⊥⊥ ⊥⊥⊥ ⊥⊥⊥	20	⊥⊥⊥ ⊥⊥⊥ ⊥⊥⊥ ⊥⊥⊥	20	60	100	0	0
3	⊥⊥⊥ ⊥⊥⊥ ⊥⊥⊥ III	18	⊥⊥⊥ ⊥⊥⊥ ⊥⊥⊥	15	⊥⊥⊥ ⊥⊥⊥ ⊥⊥⊥	15	48	80	3	·15
4	⊥⊥⊥ ⊥⊥⊥ ⊥⊥⊥ II	17	⊥⊥⊥ IIII	9	III	3	29	48	14	·70
5	⊥⊥⊥ ⊥⊥⊥ ⊥⊥⊥ I	16	⊥⊥⊥ ⊥⊥⊥ II	12	⊥⊥⊥ IIII	9	37	62	7	·35
6	⊥⊥⊥ ⊥⊥⊥ II	12	⊥⊥⊥ ⊥⊥⊥	10		0	22	37	12	·60
7	⊥⊥⊥ ⊥⊥⊥ ⊥⊥⊥ III	18	⊥⊥⊥ ⊥⊥⊥ I	11	⊥⊥⊥ III	8	37	62	10	·50
8	⊥⊥⊥ ⊥⊥⊥ ⊥⊥⊥ ⊥⊥⊥	20	⊥⊥⊥ ⊥⊥⊥	10	⊥⊥⊥ ⊥⊥⊥ III	13	43	72	7	·35
9	⊥⊥⊥ ⊥⊥⊥	10	⊥⊥⊥ IIII	9	⊥⊥⊥ ⊥⊥⊥ III	13	32	53	−3	—·15
10	⊥⊥⊥ II	7	IIII	4	II	2	13	22	5	·25

FIG. 4

Interpretation of the discrimination index

The value of E_{1-3} can vary between $+1$ and -1. If all the people in the upper third got item 1 right, and nobody in the lower third did, the difference would be 20 and the E_{1-3} formula would read $20/20 = 1$. Item 1 would then discriminate between the upper and lower thirds in much the same way as the total score.

But we cannot hope to have tests in which every item has an E_{1-3} of $+1$. Professional test constructors tend to reject any item with an E_{1-3} of less than $+·40$, but one may have to be content with lower figures initially, particularly when testing phonology.

E_{1-3} values of 0 or thereabouts show that the item does not discriminate, that the upper and lower thirds score about the same number of correct answers. Items below say $+·2$ contribute very little to the discrimination of the total test.

Negative E_{1-3} values occur when there are more correct answers in the lower third than in the upper. Item 9 in Fig. 4 is an example of this.

1 Item	6 %	8 E_{1-3}
1	83	·40
2	100	0
3	80	·15
4	48	·70
5	62	·35
6	37	·60
7	62	·50
8	72	·35
9	53	$-·15$
10	22	·25

To evaluate any item, look first at the discrimination index (Column 8). Items 1, 4, 6 and 7 have acceptable E_{1-3}. In practice one would probably retain items 5 and 8 also. Testers must be optimistic. Item 9 is clearly quite impossible, so is item 2. Items 3 and 10 have rather low values.

TABLE 2
facility value and
discrimination

Next look at the facility value—FV—(Column 6), especially for items with dubious or low discrimination. Item 2 has no discrimination, a glance at the % column shows why. Everybody answered it correctly, so there can be no difference between the upper and lower thirds. The item is too easy, for this group anyway, but it may of course be perfectly all right for another group that knows less English. Sometimes, however, a few easy items are deliberately used at the beginning of a test, just to give people confidence.

Item 10, on the other hand, was answered correctly by only about 22 per cent of the students, so this is a very difficult item for the group.

Because the number of correct answers is so small, the difference between the upper and lower thirds must be small also.

Items that are very difficult and items that are very easy show small discrimination figures and contribute very little if at all to the total discrimination. It is difficult to give absolute limits, but it is uneconomical to include items that show a difficulty level of above 85 per cent and below 15 per cent. The limits for retention depend on how many better items you have, or have time to write and try out.

Items that are very easy or very difficult, and therefore have low discrimination, may be perfectly all right in themselves; they may merely be wrong for the particular group. Item 2 may be a good item for, say, Standard IV, and item 10 may be good for Standard VII.

But the answer pattern for item 9 shows that there is something very wrong about this item. The difficulty level is all right, but the discrimination is negative, i.e. there are more correct answers in the lower group than in the upper group. The item may be badly written, be unclear or ambiguous, it may have poor distractors, or it may be badly chosen, so that ability to answer it depends on other things than knowledge of English.

But a sample of 60, even if drawn in accordance with the most rigorously accurate sampling procedures from the target population, is not nearly large enough to allow one to trust the figures very much. This is because every statistic, including the E_{1-3} and FV, is subject, to sampling error. The smaller the sample, the larger the sampling error. For item 9 in Table 2 there were 10 individuals passing in the upper third, and 13 in the lower third. But another sample, drawn in precisely the same way, might have, for instance, 13 successful individuals in the upper third and 10 in the lower, and the total number of successful individuals might also be different. This is obviously true for all the other items as well.

A statistician would strongly urge one to use a much larger sample. My own practice is to retain items with good or promising E_{1-3} and FV but never to trust any item unless it shows good values twice, i.e. on two different samples, and to reject or rewrite items with poor E_{1-3} values, if on inspection I can see what is wrong with the item. If I cannot see what is wrong, I often run the item again, but if it comes out poor a second time, I throw it out.

In other words, one needs at least two trial versions of the test. Professional testers tend to do it the other way. They write at least twice as many items as they actually need, and use a huge, carefully drawn sample. In this way one trial version may be enough.

One of the most frequent reasons why an item fails to discriminate is that the distractors fail to distract. If an item has three alternatives and if one of the distractors does not tempt anybody, there is a 50 per cent chance of passing that item, instead of the intended 33 per cent chance.

Further, a distractor may be so cunning that only the good people fall for it. So the individuals in the upper third choose it and not those in the lower third. This is often the explanation for negative E_{1-3} values.

The item analysis discussed so far has distinguished pass/fail only. But it can easily be extended to distinguish among the fails as well. For distractor analysis, the ranking and grouping are carried out in the same way. The tally sheets are best drawn up to deal with only one-third at a time, since they have to carry boxes for each alternative. Fig. 5 shows what a tallysheet for items which have four alternatives might look like, with the correct alternative indicated.

ITEM ANALYSIS

Test: *English, Grammar*   School: *St. George's*   Date: *6 June 1968*

Draft *1*   Standard: *V* N: 210; $\dfrac{N}{3}$: 70: 70 : 70

Item	Upper				Sum			
	a	b	c	d	a	b	c	d
1	□							
2		□						
3				□				

FIG. 5

The choices of all individuals in each third for all items are marked in the appropriate boxes, and the sub-totals are obtained not only for the successes but for each distractor. Then the E_{1-3} and FV values are obtained for the successes, and for the distractors.

This is not worth doing unless the sample is quite large.

References

Abercrombie, D. (1956) *Problems and Principles* (London: Longmans, Green).

Britton, J. L. (1963) 'Experimental Marking of English Compositions Written by Fifteen-year-olds' *Educational Review*, 16, 2.

Brown, J. I., and Carlsen, G. R. (1953) *Brown-Carlsen Listening Comprehension Test* (New York: World Book Co.).

Brown, Roger, and McNeill, David (1966) 'The "tip of the tongue" phenomenon' *Journal of Verbal Learning and Verbal Behavior*, 5, 325–37.

Buros, Oscar Krisen (Ed.) (1949) *The Third Mental Measurements Yearbook* (Highland Park, New Jersey: The Gryphon Press).

Buros, Oscar Krisen (Ed.) (1965) *The Sixth Mental Measurements Yearbook* (Highland Park, New Jersey: The Gryphon Press).

Carrol, B. J. (1963) Speech Intelligibility (Unpublished dissertation for Diploma in Applied Linguistics, University of Edinburgh).

Carroll, John B. (1941) 'A factor analysis of verbal abilities' *Psychometrika*, 6, 279–307.

Carroll, John B., and Sapon, S. M. (1959) *Modern Language Aptitude Test* (New York: The Psychological Corporation).

Carroll, John B. (1961) 'Fundamental considerations in testing for English language proficiency of foreign students' *Testing the English Proficiency of Foreign Students* (Washington D.C.: Center for Applied Linguistics).

Carroll, John B. (1962) 'Factors in verbal achievement' pp. 11–18 in Dressel, Paul L. (Ed.) *Proceedings of the Invitational Conference on Testing Problems, 1961* (Princeton, N.J.: Educational Testing Service). Also pp. 406–13 in Anastasi, Anne (Ed.) *Testing Problems in Perspective* (Washington, D.C.: American Council on Education, 1966).

Carroll, John B. (1963) 'Research on teaching foreign languages' in Gage, N. L. (Ed.) *Handbook of Research on Teaching* (New York: Rand McNally).

Cast, B. M. D. (1939) 'The efficiency of different methods of marking English composition' *Brit. J. Ed. Psych.* 9, 257–69.

Catford, J. C. (1950) 'Intelligibility' *English Language Teaching* 5, 1.

Chomsky, N. (1965) *Aspects of the Theory of Syntax* (Cambridge, Mass.: The M.I.T. Press).

Chomsky, N. (1966) 'Linguistic Theory' *The North East Conference on the Teaching of Foreign Languages* (New York: Reports of the Working Committee).

Corder, S. Pit (1966) *The Visual Element in Language Teaching* (London: Longmans, Green).

Cox, R. (1966) 'Examinations and Higher Education: A Survey of the Literature' (Society for Research into Higher Education, Ltd.).

Davies, Alan (1965a) Proficiency in English as a Second Language (Unpublished Ph.D. thesis, University of Birmingham).

Davies, Alan (1965b) *Report on Oral English Testing in West Africa* (Lagos: West African Examinations Council, mimeographed).

Davies, Alan *English Proficiency Test Battery* (forthcoming).

de Saussure, F. (1915) *Course in General Linguistics* (Geneva, 1915); translated by W. Baskin (London: Peter Owen, 1960).

Dodson, C. J. (1963) *Oral Examinations* (Faculty of Education, University College of Wales, Aberystwyth, Pamphlet No. 12).

Finlayson, D. S. (1951) 'The Reliability of Marking Essays' *Brit. J. Ed. Psych.* 21, 126–34.

Firth, J. R. (1957) 'The Semantics of Linguistic Science' *Papers in Linguistics* (London: Oxford University Press).

French, John W. (1951) *The Description of Aptitude and Achievement Tests in Terms of Rotated Factors* Psychometric Monographs, No. 5 (Chicago: University of Chicago Press).

French, John W., Ekstrom, Ruth B., and Price, Leighton A. (1963) *Manual for Kit of Reference Tests for Cognitive Factors* (Princeton, N.J.: Educational Testing Service).

George, H. V. (1962) 'Testing—another point of view' *English Language Teaching*, 16/2, 72–8.

Grieve, D. W. Report of an Inquiry into English Language Examining (Lagos: West African Examinations Council, mimeographed, 1963). (Lagos: African Universities Press, P.O. Box 1287, 1964).

Guilford, J. P. (1956) *Fundamental statistics in Psychology and Education*, Third Ed. (New York: McGraw-Hill Book Co.).

Haas, W. (1959) 'Relevance in phonetic analysis' *Word*, 15/1.

Halliday, M. A. K. (1961) 'Categories of the theory of grammar' *Word*, 17/3.

Halliday, M. A. K., McIntosh, A., and Strevens, P. D. (1964) *The Linguistic Sciences and Language Teaching* (London: Longmans, Green).

Harris, Z. (1951) *Structural Linguistics* (Chicago: University of Chicago Press).

Hartog, P., and Rhodes, E. C. (1936) *An Examination of Examinations* (London: Macmillan).

Hitchman, P. J. (1966) *Examining Oral English in Schools* (London: Methuen).

H.M.S.O. (1964) *The Examining of English Language* Eighth Report of the Secondary School Examinations Council (London: Her Majesty's Stationery Office).

Household, H. L. M. (1963) 'Examining Oral English' *Times Educational Supplement* (13 September 1963).

Lado, Robert (1950) 'Language learning—Survey of tests in English as a foreign language' *Language Learning*, 3/1–2, 51–66.

Lado, Robert (1951–60) *English Language Test for Foreign Students* (Ann Arbor: G. Wahr Pub. Co.).

Lado, Robert (1960) 'English language testing—problems of validity and administration' *English Language Teaching*, 14/4, 153–61.

Lado, Robert (1961) *Language Testing—the construction and use of foreign language tests* (London: Longmans, Green).

Lado, Robert (1965) 'Memory span as a factor in language learning' *IRAL*, 3/2.

Lambert, Wallace E., Havelka, J., and Crosby, C. (1958) 'The influence of language-acquisition contexts on bilingualism' *Journal of Abnormal and Social Psychology*, 56, 239–44.

Lenneberg, Eric H., Nichols, I. A., and Rosenberger, E. F. (1964) 'Primitive stages of language development in mongolism' pp. 119–37 in *Disorders of Communication*, 42 (Research Publications, Archives of Research in Nervous and Mental Diseases).

Lieberman, P. (1963) 'Some effects of semantic and grammatical context on the production and perception of speech' *Language and Speech*, 6, 172–87.

Lorge, Irving, and Chall, Jeanne (1963) 'Estimating the size of vocabularies of children and adults: an analysis of methodological issues' *Journal of Experimental Education*, 32, 147–57.

Lyons, John, and Wales, Roger (Eds.) (1966) *Psycholinguistic Papers: the Proceedings of the 1966 Edinburgh Conference* (Edinburgh: University of Edinburgh).

McCallien, C. (1958) *Examination Tests in Oral English. Nos. 1 and 2* (London: Longmans, Green).

Mackenzie, N. (1961) 'English proficiency testing in the British Commonwealth' *Testing* (Washington D.C.: Center for Applied Linguistics).

Mackey, W. F. (1965) *Language Teaching Analysis* (London: Longmans, Green).

Mafeni, B. (1965) Some Aspects of the Phonetics and Phonology of Nigerian Pidgin (unpublished M.Litt. thesis, University of Edinburgh).

Manchester University School of Education (1966) CSE Research Project: English Panel Interim Report.

Mialaret, G., and Malandain, C. (1962) *Test C.G.M. 62* (Paris: Didier).

Miller, George A. (1962) 'Some psychological studies of grammar' *American Psychologist*, 17, 748–62.

Moulton, William G. (1961) 'Linguistics and language teaching in the United States, 1940–1960' in Mohrman, Christine, Sommerfelt, Alf., and Whatmough, Joshua (Eds.) *Trends in European and American Linguistics, 1930–1960* (Utrecht: Spectrum Publishers).

Perren, G. E. (1967) 'Testing ability in English as a second language: 1. Problems' *English Language Teaching*, 21/2, 99–106.

Pilliner, A. E. G. (1952) 'The application of analysis of variance to problems of correlation' *Brit. J. Stat. Psych.* 5, 31, 38.

Pimsleur, P., Sundland, D. M., and McIntyre, R. D. (1963) 'Under achievement in foreign language learning' Final Report (U.S. Office of Education and Ohio State University).

Pimsleur, Paul (1966a) *Language Aptitude Battery* (New York: Harcourt, Brace and World).

Pimsleur, Paul (1966b) 'Testing foreign language learning' in Valdman, Albert (Ed.) *Trends in Language Teaching* (New York: McGraw-Hill).

Rivers, Wilga M. (1966) 'Listening comprehension' *Modern Language Journal* (April) 1–4.

Robins, R. H. (1964) *General Linguistics: An Introductory Survey* (London: Longmans, Green).

Rulon, P. J. (1944) Report on Contract Test for the Army Specialized Training Division, Army Service Forces (mimeo).

Schachter, Paul (1962) *Teaching English Pronunciation to the Twi Speaking Student* (University of Ghana and Oxford University Press).

Schools Council (1966) *The CSE: Trial Examinations—Oral English* Examinations Bulletin, No. 11 (London: Her Majesty's Stationery Office).

Spearman, C. (1936) 'Note on the reliability and validity of measurements' *Essays on Examinations* (London: Macmillan).

Spearritt, D. (1962) *Listening Comprehension—A Factorial Analysis* Australian Council for Educational Research, Research series, No. 76 (Melbourne).

Strevens, P. D. (1954) 'Spoken English in the Gold Coast' *English Language Teaching*, 8/3.

Strevens, P. D. (1956) *Spoken Language* (London: Longmans, Green).

Strevens, P. D. (1965) *Objective Testing* Working Paper at Makerere for Commonwealth Conference (unpublished mimeo, 1961). Also in *Papers in Language and Language Teaching* (London: Oxford University Press).

Thorne, J. P. (1966) 'On hearing sentences' in Lyons, J. and Wales, R. (Eds.) *Psycholinguistic Papers: the Proceedings of the 1966 Edinburgh Conference* (Edinburgh: University of Edinburgh).

Upshur, J. A. (1962) 'Language proficiency testing and the contrastive analysis dilemma' *Language Learning*, 12/2, 123–7.

Vernon, Philip E. (1950) *The Structure of Human Abilities* (London: Methuen; New York: Wiley).

Vernon, Philip E. (1954) 'A further study of the reliability of English essays' *Brit. J. Stat. Psych.* 7, 65–74.

Wilkinson, A. M. (1965) *Spoken English* with contributions by A. Davies and D. Atkinson, University of Birmingham (1965); second revised edition, 1966.

Wilkinson, A. M., and Atkinson, D. (1966) 'A test of listening comprehension' *Educational Review*, 18/3.

Williams, Moyra (1961) 'A test for residual mental ability in senile dementia' *J. Ment. Sci.*, 104, 783–91.

Wise, A. (1963) 'Report on Durham Test in Oral English' *The Guardian*, 22 January 1963, p. 6.

Wiseman, S. (1949) 'The marking of English composition in grammar school selection' *Brit. J. Ed. Psych.* 19, 200–9.

Wiseman, S. (Ed.) (1961) *Examination and English Education* (Manchester University Press).

Language Tests

This list does not attempt to be comprehensive. What it does do is to list those tests which are referred to in the text. In effect this means that most of the most recent well-known tests in print are included.

The list is arranged by country of origin and use of test. Since Achievement tests generally have local applicability it follows that most published language tests cannot be Achievement tests. Of necessity most widely-used language tests are Proficiency tests. As Ingram points out, very little work has been done on Diagnostic tests and there are only two well-known Aptitude tests.

In this list, therefore, most entries are Proficiency tests. No. 3b is the only Diagnostic test; and Nos. 15 and 16 are Aptitude tests.

AMERICAN *English*

1. University of Michigan

   (a) R. Lado: English Language Test for Foreign Students. Ann Arbor, Michigan, G. Wahr and Co., 1951–60.
   (b) Michigan Test of English Language Proficiency, Form A. English Language Institute, University of Michigan, Ann Arbor, 1961.

2. American University Language Center

   (a) English Usage Test. AULC, Washington Publications, 1955–57.
   (b) Listening Test. American Language Test, Georgetown University, Washington, D.C., 1961.
   (c) A Vocabulary and Reading Test for Students of English as a Second Language, 1960.

3. Educational Testing Service, Box 999, Princeton, New Jersey, U.S.A.

   (a) CEEB. English Exam for Foreign Students for College Entrance Exam Board. ETS, 1947, 1956.
   (b) A. L. Davis: Diagnostic Test for Students of English as a Second Language. 1953.
   (c) D. P. Harris: Test of English as a Foreign Language (TOEFL). 1964. (*Closed* and obtainable only for bona fide testing purposes.)

   Other Languages

4. Educational Testing Service

   (a) Modern Language Association Cooperative Foreign Language Tests (French, German, Italian, Russian, Spanish). Two forms.

(b) Modern Language Association Foreign Language Proficiency Tests for Teachers and Advanced Students. (Same five languages above.)

5. Pimsleur Modern Foreign Language Proficiency Tests

P. Pimsleur: Listening, Speaking, Reading and Writing Tests, Forms A and C (French, Spanish and German). Harcourt, Brace and World, Inc., 1967.

AUSTRALIAN *English*

6. Commonwealth Office of Education

English Tests, Form A. Sydney, 1960. (*Unpublished* and *closed* test.)

W. AFRICAN *English*

7. West African Examinations Council

C. McCallien: Examination Tests in Oral English. Nos. 1 and 2. Longmans, London, 1958.

BRITISH   *English*

8. ELBA

Elisabeth Ingram: English Language Battery (ELBA). Oxford University Press (forthcoming).

9. EPTB

A. Davies: English Proficiency Test Battery, Forms A and B (closed to British Council use overseas; *forthcoming* from National Foundation for Educational Research for use in this country).

10. Cambridge

Cambridge Proficiency Examinations in English. (N.B. These are exams and not tests; their use is widespread but they are not standardized.)

Other Languages

11. Nuffield

Modern Language Association, Examinations Project. 1966. (Report available and changes in exams likely.)

12. S.E.D.

Scottish Education Department: French Alternative Oral Exam (Experimental). (Report and specimen available from SED, St. Andrew's House, Edinburgh 2.)

13. London

T. S. Percival:
(a) Standardized French Grammar Test.
(b) Standardized French Vocabulary Test. University of London Press (no date).

FRENCH

14. CREDIF

Test CGM 62 (pour apprécier le niveau des connaissances linguistiques). Ministère de l'Education Nationale, Centre de Recherches et d'Etudes, St. Cloud, 1962.

APTITUDE TESTS (AMERICAN)
   15. Modern Language   Carroll, J. B., and Sapon, S. New York,
       Aptitude Test   Psychological Corporation, 1959.
   16. Language Aptitude   Pimsleur, P., Harcourt, Brace and
       Battery   World, Inc., 1966.

Index of Names

Index of Subjects